✂ W9-AMP-941

Advance Praise for *Tightrope*:

"Steve Villano paints a complex, intimate portrait, intertwined through the two worlds of himself and his brother: Steve, a staffer for Governor Mario M. Cuomo of New York State, and his brother, a reputed bagman for mob boss John Gotti. The story is both brave and jarring. Can one love a person but hate his choices? Describing his relationship with his brother, Steve argues powerfully that one can. The result is a narrative rich both in emotional detail and in historical nuances…"

—Sasha Abramsky, author of *The House of Twenty Thousand Books, The American Way of Poverty: How the Other Half Still Lives, Inside Obama's Brain*

"Steve Villano's book is a frank and unvarnished account of the long struggle in his New York Italian-American family… Steve took an upward path in his career, becoming an impeccable civil servant, working for one of America's most distinguished Italian-American governors, Mario Cuomo. His brother took an opposite path, associating with the most feared Italian-American mobster of his generation, John Gotti. How Villano dealt with these opposing forces of light and darkness, abhorring his brother's choice but still feeling love for him, hiding the truth from friends, and teetering on a tightrope between two diametrically different worlds, is a gripping tale—like a Hollywood story, but it is all true."

—Stephen C. Schlesinger, co-author of *Bitter Fruit: The Story of the American Coup in Guatamala* (with Stephen Kinzer), *Act of Creation: The Founding of the United Nations, The Letters of Arthur Schlesinger, Jr.,* Edited by Stephen C. and Andrew Schlesinger

"Steve Villano is a passionate and compassionate man with whom I've worked over the years—following the political trials and tribulations of his then-boss, Governor Mario Cuomo. Steve's loyalty to Cuomo and his deep understanding of Cuomo's character and leadership skills gives this book special meaning. His depiction of this period in history is spot on, and especially powerful for me is his careful recounting of the moment I informed Steve of a death threat on Mario Cuomo's life. He handled that high tension with grace, while also balancing the knowledge of his brother's association with Gambino Family crime boss John Gotti. *Tightrope*...unveils the fascinating story of how Steve managed the love he had for his brother, with the love and devotion he had for Mario Cuomo."

—Gabe Pressman, Senior Correspondent for WNBC-TV News, New York City, winner of eight Emmys, the Edward R. Murrow Award and the Peabody Award

"Steve Villano's *Tightrope* is a richly insightful, deeply moving account of love, loyalty and family lived out in the complex intersection of organized crime and big-league politics. A true story told with all the narrative power of gripping fiction, there's not a false word in these pages. Villano writes like an angel as he wrestles with the devil. *Tightrope* is a triumph."

—Peter Quinn, author of *Banished Children of Eve: A Novel of Civil War New York, Hour of the Cat* (1st Installment of the Fintan Dunne Trilogy), *Looking for Jimmy: A Search for Irish Americans, The Man Who Never Returned* (2nd Installment of the Fintan Dunne Trilogy), *Dry Bones* (3rd Installment of the Fintan Dunne Trilogy)

TIGHTROPE

TIGHTROPE:
Balancing a Life Between Mario Cuomo and My Brother

STEVE VILLANO

 Heliotrope Books

New York

Cover design by Christopher Bartoloni

Typeset by Naomi Rosenblatt

To my brother, Michael, who lost his way;

To Mario Matthew Cuomo,
who pointed the way to a better world;

To my partner in life, Carol Villano,
who, over the thirty-year journey of this story,
never gave up on me, nor allowed me to give up on myself;

To my son, Matt Villano,
whose existence, persistence and devotion
to the truth kept pushing me forward,
without his even knowing;

And to my three granddaughters,
whose bright eyes convince me, daily,
that all good things are possible.

"You would never have my brother. He lives in a world above you! What he was...what he is...is rare. You are...nothing."

—*Stanley Tucci, as Secondo, to Ian Holm, playing a rival businessman in* Big Night

1 □ Towers

Federal District Court, Uniondale, summer 1988. I sat shoulder-to-shoulder with my 22-year-old nephew, Michael Jr., struck by his resemblance to JFK, Jr., and also to my brother when he was the same age: jet black hair, large dark eyes, and a dazzling, kind smile. Michael and I listened to federal prosecutors lay out their case against his father and my brother.

Earlier that morning Governor Mario Cuomo had called me at home. After three years of working nearly round-the-clock with Cuomo at the Governor's office at Two World Trade Center—even sleeping over in my office during snowstorms—I was now his "man" at the Long Island Power Authority, laboring long hours to shut down the Shoreham Nuclear Power Plant for health and safety reasons.

"You do good work, Steve," the governor said. "You have great, great ability and a great future. It's a pleasure working with you."

"You have a pretty good future yourself, Governor," I said.

"Oh, no. I have no future, Steve," Cuomo joked. "But you," he said in a serious, almost fatherly tone, "you have a wonderful future."

Ninety minutes later, that bright future collided with my brother's present. I was sitting in a federal courtroom, hearing government prosecutors ask an FBI agent if it was true that my brother was a bagman for John Gotti, collecting money from union officials to "buy labor peace." Gotti and Villano: both names spoken in the same sentence by a federal law enforcement official.

My brother, linked to Gotti; I, linked to Cuomo. These were only allegations, I kept telling myself. My brother was not guilty of anything; he could not be; he was my mother's son. Mario Cuomo detested the "bums" in organized crime as much as I did. He was incensed by Mob innuendos about him or anyone in his family. Even the expectation that he had to answer any questions about it outraged him, since he believed that his whole life "has been a statement against that crap."

What if my family name became "the issue?" Would he keep me on staff? Would I have the courage to leave the public service work I loved? I felt naked; nothing left to protect me: not my carefully calibrated career, not my conservative clothing, not my law degree. Nothing. That was my brother up there. We shared the same blood, the same last name. For years, with different dreams, we shared the same bedroom at the top of the stairs in my parents' house: Michael, my brother Vinnie, and me, our lives intertwined.

My brother's attorney, Mike Rosen, a dapper, energetic man in his late forties with long grey hair flipped over his shirt collar at the back of the neck, addressed the judge.

"Your honor," Rosen said. "We have already conceded that my client was a social acquaintance of John Gotti's."

What? Had I heard correctly? Did my brother tell a federal judge he was Gotti's friend? I imagined Gotti calling my brother that morning, telling his "friend" of their "great future," together. I closed my eyes and shook my head slowly. Who was this brother that I loved?

The federal prosecutor's call for a new witness snapped me to attention. John Gurnee, an organized crime investigator with the U.S. Attorney's Office, and a former NYC detective who monitored the Gambino Crime Organization, took the stand.

"Do you recall what happened on December 16, 1985, Investigator?" the prosecutor asked Gurnee.

"Yes, sir," Gurnee replied. "That was the day Paul Castellano was murdered."

"And what about on December 24, 1985, Investigator?" the prosecutor asked.

"That was when many members of organized crime came to the Ravenite Social Club on Mulberry Street to recognize John Gotti as the new boss of the Gambino Crime Organization," Gurnee said.

"Would you identify those pictures you have with you, Investigator?" the prosecutor asked.

"Yes, sir. I have two photos of Michael Villano entering the Ravenite Social Club on December 24, 1985," Gurnee said.

My brother's lawyer interrupted.

"Objection, your honor. We already acknowledged that Mr. Villano had a social relationship with Mr. Gotti," defense attorney Rosen said.

The judge, Jacob Mishler—whose opinions I had admired when I studied at Hofstra Law School, just up the block from the Federal Courthouse, shook his head. "I permit the photos to be admitted," he said.

Rosen got up to look at the new photographs. He smiled as he looked at one and stared over at my nephew.

"Your honor, if I may," my brother's lawyer said, carrying the photo over to my nephew. "Recognize who this is in this photo?" Rosen said, smiling at my brother's son.

"That's me," my nephew said.

Triumphantly, Rosen strutted over to Gurnee in the witness box and pointed to my nephew. "Investigator," Rosen said, "doesn't this person in this picture look like that young man over there?" Rosen waved his hand toward my nephew.

"Stand up, Michael, and tell the Court who you are," Rosen commanded.

My brother's son stood straight up. "I am Michael Villano," my nephew said.

Rosen pounced. "I repeat, Inspector," Rosen said, "Doesn't that young man in the photo look a lot like Michael Junior?"

Gurnee hesitated. "I-I would say it does."

Rosen acted as if he had won the case. "In fact, your Honor, it is Michael Villano, Jr. in that picture," Rosen said, "because for years the father would take his son to pay social calls to friends on Christmas Eve, and that's what they were doing that Christmas Eve, 1985."

A solid wooden railing separated spectators from participants in Judge Mishler's courtroom. I wanted to leap over it, grab my brother by the lapels of his black, double-breasted jacket, and shake him hard until pieces of his brain fell from his head—the pieces that made him think of himself as a hood. How could he drag his precious son down to such a rathole like the Ravenite? I fought the urge to put my arm around my nephew's shoulder, to pull him closer to me, and away from his father. I wanted to rescue him before it was too late, to pick him up as if he were little again and carry him out of the courtroom, far away from my brother, from the mob, far from this nightmare.

But it was already too late. I could not give him the approval and love he wanted from my brother; the same primal pull all men have toward our fathers, not comprehending its complicated power over us. I would return to my professional life once I left the courtroom, barely able to keep my balance, fighting furiously against the force of gravity that threatened to pull me down if my small, safe steps faltered for one moment, or if I took on any more weight, like my nephew. I hated myself for being such a self-centered coward.

I looked around Judge Mishler's courtroom, and winced as I heard our name echo around the room, bouncing off a bench, a chair, the judge's desk. If only I had a sponge, I would scrub the walls, the seats, and make our name vanish from every surface it touched. I wanted everything to disappear, but could not keep myself away from the courtroom. I had to find out what I suspected, but had denied for years. Yet, there was something more, much more. I thought of my mother sitting in the living room of her small apartment in California, watching her afternoon stories, *As the World Turns* or *Search for Tomorrow,* somehow seeing everything taking place in that courtroom. I saw her big round glasses, eyes open wide as her heart, watching in disbelief what awaited her first-born child. I imagined her, fingering her rosary beads, quietly praying, conducting her own trial, prosecuting herself and defending, forever defending, her son. I was my mother's eyes and ears and heart in the courtroom, and I could not leave.

Real mobsters and friends of mobsters fluttered around our family as long as I could remember. Unlike the characters played in the movies or on television by DeNiro, Pesci, Pacino, Liotta and Gandolfini, there was nothing funny or romantic about them. They used everyone around as props, they mocked "working stiffs" like my father, who, for decades, toiled in a beaten-down boiler room in the bowels of the building at 100 East 42nd Street, to heat or cool the offices of the wealthy accountants and lawyers on the floors above. On Sundays, my father swallowed his anger and shame with a chaser of whiskey or beer after learning that his oldest son, Michael, spent Sunday afternoons with Gambino family's Capo, Carmine "Charlie Wagons" Fatico, who married into our family and would serve as John Gotti's real-life godfather in the mob as well as my brother's.

Carmine Fatico, or "Uncle Charlie" as we called him, was not the romanticized picture of a suave "Godfather" as popularized in Francis Ford Coppola's films. That caricature was modeled after another mobster-by-marriage family member, Pat Eboli, who's brother-in-law, Alfred Letteiri—my mother's first cousin—starred in Coppola's first *Godfather* film as the villainous Sollozzo the Turk.

In stark contrast to the debonair Eboli, a rising star in the Genovese Crime Family and a favorite of Lucky Luciano's, Carmine Fatico was short and squat—a local gang member who grew up in the East New York section of Brooklyn. Although always meticulously dressed, Fatico fit the street tough image of the Gambino Crime Family members.

"Uncle Charlie" rose to the post of Capo in 1957, when Albert Anastasia was executed and Carlo Gambino became the new leader of the organization. Fatico earned his nickname "Charlie Wagons" by hijacking trucks loaded with goods that could be easily fenced. Gotti, a 17-year-old high-school dropout and local hood from Brooklyn, became a member of Fatico's crew that same year.

In their book, *Goombata: The Improbable Rise and Fall of John Gotti and His Gang*, (Avon Books, New York, 1990), authors John Cummings and Ernest Volkman detailed Gotti's first meeting with

"Uncle Charlie":

John Gotti, clad in one of his more outrageous purple outfits, stood before a desk in the back room of an East New York social club. Seated behind the desk, Carmine Fatico, attired in his usual conservative business suit, stared at Gotti... 'You look like a fucking guinea," Fatico finaly said. But,...Fatico a shrewd judge of men, had looked deeper than the garish purple outfit. And he liked what he saw.

My brother Michael, nine years older than I, was of a different world than the one Fatico and Gotti were fashioning. Growing up, I idolized Michael for his gentleness and his exalted spot as my mother's first and favorite child. He was calm with me in ways my father frequently was not, with endless patience for all types of people, but particularly for his little brother whose wide eyes revealed every emotion. I stared at the back of my brother's head in court, and recalled how he had looked at the back of mine, when he and his high-school sweetheart Cathy took me to a drive-in movie with them, and let me sit behind the steering wheel while they sat in the back seat.

Our father, a son of South Brooklyn, didn't learn to drive until he turned 40, hated cars and anything associated with them. Alphonse Villano was a poor city guy, who never needed a car until my mother insisted we move to the suburbs, for a "better life for the kids." He would have been comfortable living out his days within a subway ride of everything he needed—work, family, the corner bar, and Yankee Stadium. Unlike Michael, he hated taking the car out, and rarely associated it with pleasure of any kind. My father's first car was a 1950 black Plymouth sedan, a big hulk of a car which took most of his strength to steer, all of his dexterity to park, and a full-tank of expletives to operate. Our once-a-year, family day-trip was from North Babylon, an Italian enclave on the South Shore of Long Island to Cutchogue on the North Shore, a quaint, quiet little town that could be mistaken for being in New England, rather than less than 90 miles east of NYC. We claimed as our own a secluded, rocky, pre-historic looking beach at the end of Depot Lane, surf-casted for Porgies all day from the shore, pulling mussels off the barnacles of boulders submerged in the cold waters of Long Island Sound.

When he was old enough, my brother Michael gave my father a break and drove the pug-nosed Plymouth, stopping at an old white, clapboard restaurant that advertised "Chicken-in-the-Basket: $1.49." It was the one-and-only road trip all year my father enjoyed. If the road represented life to Kerouac, to my father it was nothing but one long detour; a pain-in-the-ass to be endured.

Michael's skill and ease with driving always made car rides an adventure. He knew I was shameless when it came to my unrequited love for drive-ins, once bribing a girl down the block with chocolate bars to get her to invite me to join her family to see *The Ten Commandments* on the big, outdoor screen.

I watched my brother, sitting stiffly in the front of the courtroom, and remembered when he sat, relaxed, in our 1958 Ford Fairlane in the Rt. 110 Drive-In Theater in Huntington, less than an hour from the Federal Courthouse where Michael's life was now playing out in front of me. I was stuck in time, and saw his unlined face chuckling at me while I counted the speaker-boxes in the sprawling parking lot; each speaker and its twin mounted—back-to-back—on cylindrical metal poles. Cars parked on both sides of the pole, and either a passenger, or the driver, would remove the speaker from its cradle, clip it to the closest car window, and roll the window up as high as it would go to secure the speaker. When the pre-movie commercials came on, all it took was a slight turning of a small, black knob, to hear big screen "surround sound." It was all so magical, and to me, my brother made it possible.

Michael was my first glimpse of a Renaissance man, and for years I denied his drift away from the person I thought he was toward a darker, unrecognizable version of someone I once worshipped. To face his fallibilities was to peer into an abyss, just waiting for me to slip down.

Between 1985 and 1988, as Gotti rose in celebrity and power, law enforcement officials looked for anything or anyone to leverage against the new king of New York's crime families. My brother's "friendship" with Gotti was a tempting target to squeeze, and federal court was the perfect place to apply pressure. I studied the smooth, sweet lines of my nephew's face as he sat next to me in court, to see if the turmoil and years of tension took a physical toll on him. He listened as intently as I to prosecutors talking about a prison term for his father; linking our last name tightly to Gotti's.

An old man with a dark, plaid shirt sat in the row in front of me, taking detailed notes. A reporter? My heart beat faster. Each time our last name was mentioned, the old man wrote it down. Suppose someone outside the courtroom, political people I know or other reporters who cover Cuomo, read about my brother in the newspaper? A Villano connected to John Gotti and a Villano on Mario Cuomo's staff. Our family name was "the link" some were salivating to find between Cuomo and the mob. I would not allow it to be used as a weapon against Mario Cuomo.

Two years earlier, during his 1986 re-election campaign, I was prepared to block a bullet to save Mario Cuomo's life. WNBC's dean of political reporters Gabe Pressman called to inform me there was a death threat against the governor. Cuomo and Corretta Scott King were scheduled to speak at Town Hall, NYC, before a gathering of Local 1199 members, a union being torn apart by internal strife. Understandably, King cancelled. Cuomo ignored the advice from staff and state police and went ahead. A few minutes before we arrived at Town Hall, Cuomo, seated in the front passenger seat of the unmarked State Police car, turned to me in the back.

"Steve," he asked, "Do you believe in heaven and hell?"

I panicked. Good God, he was genuinely worried about the death threat. I was silent for a moment. I had to answer Mario Cuomo, who thought deeply about such matters.

"Well, Governor," I said, buying a few more seconds to think, "I'm not sure I'm smart enough to know whether heaven and hell exist."

I paused. "But, I believe in acting as if they do." As we pulled up in front of Town Hall, Cuomo turned to face me, and smiled.

"That's a very good answer, Steve; a very good answer," he said. The student had pleased the mentor. I was gratified by his praise, and terrified at the same time.

We got out of the car and were surrounded by a phalanx of undercover NYC cops who escorted us in through the Hall's small kitchen. My mind instantly replayed the scene of Robert F. Kennedy, life bleeding out of him, on the kitchen floor of Los Angeles' Ambassador Hotel. Cuomo greeted all of the kitchen workers and my eyes darted around the pots and pans, anticipating a pistol pointed our way. I was ready to throw my body in the way of an assassin's bullet, determined not to have another RFK taken away.

This time, in the courtroom, I decided to use myself to shield the governor again. I would not let the reporter's notes out of my sight. If he put his notepad down on the bench next to him, I would lean over and slip it into my jacket pocket. If he went to the bathroom, I would follow him in and scoop up the notepad the moment he dropped his pants. I knew how rumor and innuendo caught fire. I had to get those notes. I stopped myself only moments before I grabbed the notebook. Was I nuts? I didn't even know if he was a reporter or a courtroom groupie, writing his daughter.

Court adjourned that hot, Indian summer day, and I ran to my car, desperate to flee from everything. I headed east on Southern State Parkway and over the Robert Moses Causeway, to a quiet stretch of beach where I had sought solitude as a teen. I changed into my swimsuit in a bathroom, and headed for a private spot. I spread out my towel among the dunes and dashed down to the ocean, diving headlong into the churning water. The waves pushed me down, relentlessly slamming my face into the sand. The roaring surf surrounded me, silencing my thoughts and washing away my tears. Exhausted, I knew I needed to be home for my own son, and back in court the next morning for my brother's hearing.

I arrived at the courthouse a few minutes late in the morning, expecting to find everyone in the courtroom. Instead, I found my brother and two of his attorneys in a small witness room preparing their final arguments. I looked around as we entered the courtroom. I was the only family member present.

My brother's attorney pointed to the old guy taking notes. "That's Tom Renner, *Newsday*'s organized crime specialist," said Rosen.

I closed my eyes and held my forehead. My brother's links to Gotti would be written about in a newspaper story. People who knew I worked for Cuomo would read the name "Villano" in large type, admitting a connection with John Gotti. That's what would stick: "Villano & Gotti."

I remembered December 19, 1985, three days after the killing of Paul Castellano. I was working in the governor's press office that day, when Senator Ted Kennedy announced he would not run for president in 1988. Immediately, a media frenzy began over Mario Cuomo and the presidency. The governor tried to tamp down the wild speculation.

We issued a prepared statement, frantically faxing it out to reporters all day: "I regret that Senator Kennedy chooses not to run for President in 1988. I've said on many occasions that I thought he would be a strong candidate, but on the other hand, no one has a right to tell a member of the Kennedy family he has a duty to the party or the nation." Despite the statement, Cuomo was seen as the Democratic front-runner almost three full years before the election.

Incongruously, Cuomo and Gotti were elevated to national figures within three days of each other, by diametrically different means. Aside from their ethnic heritage, and vowels at the end of their names, they now had only one thing in common: they each were associated with someone named Villano.

Judge Mishler began to speak: "I don't think Mr. Villano is of any significance or importance in the organized crime structure. My impression is that he is just a bagman for John Gotti."

A bagman? Renner wrote everything down in his tiny script, and I could not take my eyes off his pen and his notepad. Then, I noticed the courtroom door open. I recognized the person who walked in, and quietly closed the door behind him. It was Irv Long, a *Newsday* political reporter I knew since I started working for the governor. Irv looked around and spotted his colleague Tom Renner. He noticed me sitting in the row behind Renner, slipped into the row in front of me and took a seat next to his fellow reporter.

"What's going on here?" Long leaned back and whispered to me in his soft, southern drawl.

I shrugged, feigning ignorance, unable to speak. The Cuomo-Gotti connection was the name Villano, and now, the world would know. Judge Mishler asked my brother to approach the bench. Silently, I pleaded with Irv Long to leave the room. Wasn't I always good and decent to you? Please, Irv. Or, at least, don't listen. Whatever you do, don't look at me. Don't let me know that you know I'm still here, watching my brother get sent to jail. Irv stayed as he had to stay; as I had to stay.

Just as my brother was being sentenced, Irv looked at me. Out of the corner of my eye I saw him turn his head ever-so-slightly, to catch my reaction. I stared past Irv, straight ahead at my brother's bald spot, then became fixated on his chunky fingers hanging straight at his sides, and how much they resembled our mother's. To control my shaking, I took careful notes of what Judge Mishler said about my brother, Case #88-00084.

"Some cases are impossible," Judge Mischler said. "We have here what looks like the split personality of Mr. Villano. On the one hand, according to testimonials in his file, he's an angel; on the other hand, according to the government, he's a rascal." The judge sentenced my brother to 90 days in prison, and we, with his attorneys, retreated into a private office.

My brother did not want me to leave the courthouse with him, spotting a photographer there to snap his photo for the newspaper. I was grateful for his sensitivity. As I gathered my briefcase and prepared to leave the room, Michael gave me a tougher choice.

"Don't tell Mommy about this," he asked. "She's got high blood pressure, and this will drive it through the roof. I'm afraid she'll have a stroke."

I was uncomfortable participating in any of my brother's cover-ups. Yet, I could see my mother making herself sick over this, sitting up each night he was in jail, one arm paralyzed by polio, licking the thumb on her "good hand" as she turned the pages of the newspaper. I agreed to keep his secret, walked out of the courthouse, got into my Plymouth Horizon and drove the short distance to my office. Slowly, I climbed the steps, and unlocked the office door, relieved to find no one else there. Putting my briefcase down, I slipped behind my desk, and stared at the phone.

How do I tell Mario Cuomo that a story would appear in *Newsday* the next day linking my brother, our name, to John Gotti? How do I talk about organized crime in my family with the one Italian-American elected official who personified the complete opposite? I pictured myself in our 57th floor press conference room at the World Trade Center, Tower 2, telling reporters that any notion of Mario Cuomo having "mob connections" was bullshit—because the mob was in my family, and the inside word about Cuomo was that he was "unreachable." In my imaginary press conference, I resigned and, as an eyewitness, condemned the mob rumors.

Instead, I condemned myself for not protecting Mario Cuomo from my family, and for being unable to resist the pull to work for him in the first place, looking at my work for Cuomo as penance for the sins of my brother and the mobsters who marred our lives. I would do good through public service. I would clean up the family name. I got up and paced around my office. Finally, I sat back down and wrote out a script to read to the governor:

Governor, I have some very unpleasant news which I feel obligated to share with you. My brother was sentenced to three months in prison for tax evasion today, in Judge Mishler's Federal Court in Uniondale. Judge Mishler, in his decision, also expressed the belief that my brother had some association with organized crime. Two Newsday *reporters were present, one of whom—Irv Long—I knew. I anticipate there will be a story in tomorrow's paper, so I don't want you to learn of this second-hand.*

I read over my little speech, hands trembling. There was no escaping now, no neat rationalizations. I could not pretend everything could be as it was.

I pressed the right buttons on the phone and reached the governor's Albany office. He was busy, but would call me back, his secretary said. "Please make it soon," I said to no one in particular. I looked at the photo of Mario Cuomo and me on my wall. In it, we're smiling, and I'm shaking his hand with both of mine.

The phone rang. It was the governor. I placed the script in front of me, clinging to it like a life preserver.

"Hello, Governor," I said, shaking.

"What's going on, Steve?" Mario Cuomo said, as he usually did.

I read my script, word for word. The governor was silent as I read. I finished, closed my eyes, and waited for Mario Cuomo's response, my heart pounding.

"I don't see how it should affect you," he said, without hesitation. "I certainly feel for you, but I don't see how it affects you. You are a superb public official, and I don't think it should have any effect on you."

Stunned, I thanked Mario Cuomo. We both hung up. I looked, again, at the photo of the two of us. Next to it, on my office wall, hung a large, framed color photograph of the World Trade Center a self-contained world, where I escaped each day, 12 to 14 hours a day for three years; a world of public service and doing good with a brilliant Italian-American of the highest integrity; a world of my own, sealed off from my family, which no one could take from me. I got up and focused closely on the Twin Towers, tracing my finger across the void between the north tower and the south, where more than a decade earlier, the funambulist Philippe Petit walked back and forth eight times across a cable strung between them. He made it look easy and graceful, but spent months practicing and preparing for his quarter-mile high balancing act. Visiting the World Trade Center 200 times, Petit precisely planned every detail, accounting for factors—like the wind—he could not control.

I stepped back a bit, taking in the entire landscape, my mind jumping from tower to tower. My eyes stopped, and noticed the shaft of light between the towers, taller than both, beckoning me forward. My high-wire ballet was just beginning.

2 ▫ Bittersweet Blood

Michael was my first hero, a calming presence in a chaotic life. He was the opposite of our father, whose temper could explode as quickly as the steam boilers he worked. My vision of my brother was always through our mother's large, circular eyeglasses, and that view was rose-colored. To my mother and me, Michael was always there, ever present, ever perfect. He could make or fix anything—the car, a bicycle, or a steaming plate of spaghetti *alglia 'olio* at 11 o'clock at night.

I once stood by his side and watched him cook a meal from scratch for two dozen people, each ingredient carefully chosen, each choice delicately considered, each course better than the one before. My brother's short, stubby fingers mesmerized me. The more I stared at them, and listened to his calming voice describing what he was do-ing, the more I thought of my mother's fat little fingers pushing the dough back and forth, confident that she could mold it into some simple and delicious culinary treat.

It was what she did so effortlessly, Margaret Julia DeSimone Villa-no, with her "one good arm,"—the other being paralyzed from her shoulder all the way down to her wrist. My brother Michael, the oldest of four children, often stood next to her "dead" right arm, quietly watching, getting things my mother could not reach, listen-ing to her carefully explain what she added to the dough, that she sprinkled flour on the wooden macaroni board to prevent sticking, and how long each kind of pasta needed to be cooked. Standing next to my brother, watching him cook, I could feel my mother's lessons, her love, and I was immobilized by memory.

But my mother gave something more. Her family introduced us

to the Mob, well before any of us were born. It happened so matter-of-factly: an act of geography, circumstance and desperation. All three were common ingredients in the lives of many of the immigrant families who clustered in the heavily Italian Greenwich Village neighborhood of Manhattan in the early 1900's. The DeSimone/ Lettieri families were no different. My mother was born on 6th Avenue in a tenement next door to the old Waverly Theatre, which later became the IFC (Independent Film Channel) Center. Her older sister Josephine and several of her cousins also lived in the building which housed 16 families, and her mother, Elvira Lettieri DeSimone, worked as the janitor in exchange for rent. Other Lettieris, my mother's Uncle Pietro and Aunt Antoinetta , lived around the corner on Thompson Street, in the heart of what was then NYC's Little Italy.

There was an elegance and lightness about the Lettieris, my maternal grandmother's family, which the DeSimones and many others in the neighborhood did not have. The Lettieris—people of "letters" as their name bespoke—descended from a line of schoolteachers, artists and municipal officials in Italy and were steeped in literature, the arts and politics. Two of my grandmother's siblings were named Romeo and Juliet, and each died tragically from disease at the age of 17.

In contrast, the DeSimones were coarse, *mezzogiorno* pragmatists. My mother's father, Vincenzo, was a crude, violent blacksmith, who physically abused my grandmother Elvira, and forced her to work scrubbing floors. He beat her so badly on one occasion during the eight month of a pregnancy that he broke her ribs, causing the baby to be stillborn. When he brought the family to New York in 1908, he found an apartment building in the heavily Italian section of Manhattan where my grandmother could be janitor.

My mother, the youngest of four surviving children, and her oldest brother Salvatore were romantic dreamers like the Lettieris. Their oldest sister Josephine married at the age of 14 to escape their violent father, and Brother Angelo reflected the more pragmatic, worldly and defiant DeSimones. Vincenzo favored Angelo, his youngest son, a dashing, sweet talking man, who thought he resembled film star Rudolph Valentino, and acted like "The Shiek" around women. My grandfather feared his oldest daughter Josephine, who constantly challenged him, once throwing a mistress of his down a flight of stairs. He was a classic bully, picking on people he perceived to be weaker, belittling my mother because of her "limp," paralyzed arm. When she asked for eyeglasses so she could see the chalkboard in school, Vincenzo refused.

"You don't need an education; no one is going to hire a cripple," he told her.

He saved his full wrath for sweet, sensitive Salvatore, Grandmother Elvira's favorite and oldest son, who only wanted to be like Damon Runyon, the great baseball and boxing writer. Vincenzo viciously challenged his son's virility for loving language, shaming him into getting one of the toughest, most dangerous jobs available: as a "sandhog," working on the Holland Tunnel construction project.

Sandhogs—the men who dug the underwater pilings for bridges and the holes under the ground for railroad, subway, water and automobile tunnels—did the most hazardous work in New York City at that time. Each new wave of immigrants, first led by the Irish and Germans, sacrificed their strongest men to build the caissons of the Brooklyn Bridge in the 1870s, the train tunnels of the late 1890s, and the Hudson and East River tunnels of the early 1900s. By the turn of the century most of the new, less experienced tunnel workers were Italian immigrants, primarily from southern Italy or Blacks—and all were considered expendable to get the job done.

Against that backdrop, Salvatore DeSimone, a gentle giant of a man, with massive hands and Popeye-sized forearms, became a sandhog on the great Holland Tunnel project of the 1920s. He was 16 years old and determined to prove his toughness to his tyrannical father. But the deadening drudgery of digging deep below the Hudson River day after day fueled Salvatore's dreams of becoming a sports writer, or a boxer like many of those Runyon wrote about for the Hearst-owned *New York American*. Salvatore quit his job as a sandhog, and decided to pursue his dream that would punctuate his manhood— becoming a professional boxer. To do that, in a boxing business largely controlled by the Irish, he changed his name to Jimmy "The Kid" Roberts.

To his father's disgust and relentless derision, he hung around gyms and boxing clubs in Brooklyn and Manhattan. He lived on Runyon's writing, following the journalist's jaunts around town with Al Capone, Arnold Rothstein, and Jack Dempsey. "Jimmy the Kid" Roberts grabbed any paying fight he could get, determined to demonstrate he could make a decent living in the ring. Nearly broke as he entered his 30s and with a young family to feed, "Jimmy the Kid" became enamored with the meteoric rise of a boxer his own age, from New York's Hell's Kitchen, named James J. Braddock. Throughout the late 1920s and early 1930s Braddock fought back from injuries and a string of defeats to win the World Heavyweight Boxing Championship in 1935 by beating the seemingly invincible Max Baer. Salvatore (Jimmy) inhaled Runyon's recounting of Braddock's "Cinderella" story, of a busted immigrant kid rising out of poverty and pain to the top of the boxing world. If Braddock could do it, so could he.

With fewer fights coming his way, Salvatore took a bartending job in The Jolly Friar's, a West Village nightclub, controlled by Vito Genovese, the head of Lucky Luciano's "Greenwich Village Crew," Most of the bars and nightclubs in the Village throughout the early to mid 1930s operated with the permission of the Genovese gang. To get work in any of the clubs during the Great Depression, when any kind of job was hard to come by, was to owe a favor to the guys who ran it. One of Genovese's bodyguards, at the club each night with his boss, was Tomasso Eboli, or "Tommy Ryan" as he liked to call himself, a dapper-looking guy in his early twenties.

He took a quick liking to Salvatore because of their mutual love of boxing and their shared birthplace of southern Italy, just a few years and a few miles apart from each other. Eboli also wanted to make money as a fight promoter, with the added challenge of an Italian beating the Irish at their own game. When "Tommy Ryan" took one look at "Jimmy the Kid's" large, meaty hands, and saw him spar, he began to throw some fights Salvatore's way. But my uncle was no Braddock. His boxing career stalled. His gentle nature betrayed him in the ring, and he took a terrible pounding in a big fight Tommy Ryan set up, healing at home for several weeks. Big time boxing gamblers didn't like to back a loser. He finished out his boxing career as a sparring partner for a rising, young Black fighter named Joe Louis.

Changes in the New York crime family moved as quickly as the flurry of punches that floored my uncle. Following the 1931 murders of "Joe the Boss" Masseria and Salvatore Marazano, Lucky Luciano rose to head, what became known as the Luciano Crime Family, and Vito Genevese was promoted to underboss. The Greenwich Village Crew was coming into the center of the ring, and Genovese's bodyguard, Tommy "Ryan" Eboli's star was rising. Luciano consolidated his power for several years, ostensibly living the life of a wealthy, conservatively dressed businessman in Manhattan's Waldorf Towers. That ended in 1936, when he was convicted on 62 counts of extortion and promoting prostitution by then US Attorney Thomas E. Dewey, and sent first to Sing Sing and then to Dannemora Prison in Upstate New York for 10 years. Luciano continued to play a central role in running his crew, even after the US Government—in exchange for the Mob leader's assistance in World War II to help keep the waterfront free from enemy infilitration—exiled him to Naples, Italy in 1947, where he died in 1962.

Vito Genovese became Acting Boss of the Luciano Crime Family in 1936, but his initial tenure at the top was short-lived. Fearing prosecution for a murder he was alleged to have committed in 1934, Genovese fled to Italy, a full decade before Luciano. While there, for the next eight years, Genovese formed strategic alliances with two mobs: the Sicilian organized crime syndicate, and the Fascists supporting Benito Mussolino, Italy's Dictator. He became both rich and powerful in Italy and his underlings in New York, like "Tommy Ryan" Eboli, prospered as well. With Luciano in prison, and Genovese in Italy, Frank Costello became acting boss of the Luciano Crime Family.

World War II changed life dramatically for men of my Uncle Jim's ("Jimmy the Kid") generation, who, along with Tommy Eboli's younger brother Pasquale, enlisted in the fight against Facism in Europe. Vito Genovese took a different tack. Living in Italy at the outbreak of the war, Genovese befriended Mussolini, providing a steady flow of cocaine to Il Duce's nephew. When Mussolini wanted to eliminate an especially irritating opponent of his, the radical anti-Fascist Italian journalist and organizer Carlo Tresca of New York, he asked Genovese for assistance. On January 11, 1943, Tresca was assassinated on NYC's Fifth Avenue, with evidence pointing to a Mob associate of Vito Genovese's as the killer.

When the Allied Forces invaded Sicily six months later, and Mussolini was arrested by order of Italy's King Victor Emmanuel III, Genovese wasted little time in jumping to the other side. Following the Allied Armistice with Italy on September 3, 1943, Genovese jockeyed himself into a position of Interpreter/Liaison at the US Army Headquarters in Naples. His switch-in-time to assist the United States earned him important friends in the US Government. Despite being arrested by American MP's in 1944 for running a black market of US military provisions in Italy, Genovese was allowed back into the United States at the end of the War. A pending murder charge against him was dropped in 1946 following the suspicious deaths of two potential witnesses.

Vito Genovese was back in business in New York as the boss of his former Greenwich Village Crew, with Tommy Eboli right by his side. Eboli's younger brother, Pasquale, or "Patsy Ryan," just back from the war, joined his brother in the family business. Five years later, in 1951, with Lucky Luciano exiled in Naples, Vito Genovese was named the new underboss of the Luciano Crime Family, with only

Frank Costello outranking him.

My brother Michael was six years old when Vito Genovese came back to New York to run his Greenwich Village crew. My father had just completed a post-War Police Action in the Philippines and returned to my mother, my brothers Michael and Vincent, and a new baby daughter named Vera. Before I was born in 1949, and for several years thereafter, our family struggled to survive in the Crown Heights section of Brooklyn. During and after the war, we shared a three-family house purchased by Grandpa DeSimone. My father, with nothing higher than a ninth-grade education, found work as a porter in a Manhattan office building. Uncle Jim—arms and body tired of shadow boxing—ran through a series of menial jobs, before moving out to New Jersey. Not counting Uncle Jim's brief boxing arrangement with Tommy Eboli, the closest contact our family had to the mob was when the local bookie took my father's bets on the horses or the "numbers." For "working stiffs" like my father, the drama of New York's mob families was restricted to the pages of the *New York Daily News*, the *New York Daily Mirror*, and the *New York American*.

Events took a different turn for the Lettieri family. After the war, my mother's first cousin, Eugenia—who bore a striking resemblance to Sophia Loren—met and married tall, dashing, dark haired Pasquale "Patsy Ryan" Eboli. "Patsy's" visibility in the Greenwich Village neighborhood grew as the stature of his brother Tommy "Ryan" Eboli's did, as one of Vito Genovese's closest associates. Over a ten-year period culminating in the May, 1957 shooting of Frank Costello, and the assassination five months later of Albert Anastasia, Genovese gradually ascended from his old position as head of the Greenwich Village Crew, to the boss of what would become the Genovese Crime Family.

In his rise to power, Genovese took the Eboli brothers with him. One shrewd beneficiary of the Lettieri's newly elevated economic status, was my mother's oldest sister, Josephine, who always maintained a close relationship with the cousins on her mother's side of the family. Eugenia (Jean) Lettieri was the oldest one, born in 1926. Her brother, Alfred Lettieri, born in 1928, would later go on to play "Sollozzo the Turk" in Frances Ford Coppola's movie *The Godfather*. Aunt Josephine was a brilliant, scheming and homely peasant woman, born in Italy in 1899, who survived on the strength of her iron will and extraordinary wits. Married at 14 to a man 11 years her senior to escape her violent father Vincenzo, she spoke every dialect of Italian fluently, and learned to cook foods from every region of Italy. When she moved from the DeSimone's three-family house to her own apartment on Stone Avenue and McDougal Streets in East New York in the early 1950s, her culinary skills caught the attention of the newest "extended" family members of the Lettieri's, Tommy and Patsy Eboli. On several occasions, the Eboli brothers brought Vito Genovese to taste Aunt Josephine's incomparable cooking. In addition to having a taste for using all the freshest ingredients and seasonings, Aunt Josephine had a keen nose for money. She charmed Genovese while preparing delicacies he hadn't tasted since he left Italy, and even entertained some of his mistresses.

One of Don Vito's "girlfriends" came on to me two years before the mob boss died in prison. My mother, father, and I were spending Palm Sunday, 1967, with Aunt Jo and Uncle Mike at the Woodside, Queens apartment to which they moved when East New York became heavily Black and most of the Italians left. Upon arriving, we discovered that Cousin Jean Eboli was visiting, along with one of Vito Genovese's, favorite mistresses, named Charlotte. To a sexually inexperienced 18-year old, Charlotte's thick, sensual French accent was mesmerizing. She used her accent to flirt overtly, despite my mother's presence. After her cousin Jean and Charlotte left, my mother—a devout Catholic—expressed her fury with her older sister for welcoming a "puttana" into her home on Palm Sunday.

From time to time, Aunt Josephine and her husband Mike Bavoso further ingratiated themselves with Vito Genovese by dog-sitting for his high-strung dachshund named "Lucky," while Genovese took frequent trips to Naples to visit his mentor, and the dog's namesake, Lucky Luciano. Tommy and Patsy Eboli often accompanied Genovese on those business trips. The Eboli brothers were different personalities. Tommy, 13 years older than his brother and born in Italy, was rougher around the edges and far more phlegmatic. As a long-time bodyguard for Genovese, and a boxing aficionado, he had a reputation for being hot-headed. In 1952, he was supporting boxer Rocky Castellani in a major a fight at Madison Square Garden. When the referee, Ray Miller, rendered a decision against Castellani, Eboli jumped into the ring and began pummeling Miller with his fists. Tommy "Ryan" Eboli was arrested for assault, served a 60-day jail sentence—his only jail time ever—and was banned from boxing for the rest of his life. While Tommy's aggression may have impressed Genovese, and other mob guys who worked with him, it did not sit well with Luciano. He considered Tommy unable to control his emotions, and was suspicious of his unyielding loyalty to Genovese. Luciano began to favor the younger Eboli brother, Patsy, who was calmer, quieter, and much more business-like—a reminder to Luciano of the low-profile demeanor he himself carefully cultivated when he lived at the Waldorf.

That impression of Patsy Eboli being the model of a cool and calm capo was not only held by Luciano. During filming of Francis Ford Coppola's first part of *The Godfather* trilogy, when Tommy Eboli's power was at its peak as the head of the Genovese Crime Family, it was Pat Eboli, not his more powerful brother, who impressed some big names in the film business. His brother-in-law, actor Al Lettieri, introduced members of the cast—including Marlon Brando, Al Pacino, James Caan and Robert Duvall—to his sister Jean and her husband Pat at their home in Fort Lee, New Jersey, where Jean prepared a sumptious Italian meal.

A *Vanity Fair* article by Mark Seal on February 4, 2009, entitled "The Godfather Wars" explains how Brando got his inspiration for the role of Don Corleone:

"… for his brooding character he turned to Al Lettieri, who was cast as Sollozzo, the drug-dealing, double-crossing upstart. Lettieri hadn't had to study the Mob to get into his part; one of his relatives was a member. Brando had met Lettieri while preparing for his Oscar-winning role as Terry Malloy in *On the Waterfront*. According to Peter Manso in his biography of Brando, it was through Lettieri that he had gotten a lot of what he put into the 'I could have been a contender' scene. 'It was sort of based on Al's [relative], a Mafioso who once put a gun to Al's head, saying, *You've gotta get off smack. When you're on dope you talk too much, and we're going to have to kill you*. For Marlon the story was like street literature, something to absorb." In preparation for *The Godfather*, Lettieri took Brando to his relative's house in New Jersey for a family dinner, "to get the flavor," says Lettieri's ex-wife, Jan....Soon Brando had the voice of Don Corleone. 'Powerful people don't need to shout,' he later explained."

A subsequent *Vanity Fair* piece by Seal ("Meadow Soprano on Line One!", February 26, 2009, March Edition) confirmed, in an interview with Pat and Jean Eboli's daughter, who helped her mother serve the full cast dinner that evening, that Pat "Patsy Ryan" Eboli was the "relative who once put a gun to Al's head."

Pat Eboli's strong, controlled manner and movie-star good looks not only seduced Marlon Brando, but our entire family. Pat and our cousin Jean Lettieri popped up intermittently in our lives over a period of about ten years, from 1962 through 1972. Each time they did, my mother was worshipful of how wonderfully he treated her cousin, and how kind he was to all of us. No one spoke of what "Pat"—his name always uttered in reverent hushes—did for a living. What could possibly be bad about a man who was so good? It was a model of behavior that would not be lost on my brother Michael, years later.

Swift changes were occurring within the Luciano/Genovese crime family. Vito Genovese was finally sent to prison in 1959, convicted on a narcotics charge at the peak of his power. Three years later, Lucky Luciano died of a massive heart attack in Naples airport, putting Genovese, still serving jail time, in complete control of what was now officially a crime family that bore his name. With Vito unable to handle day-to-day operations, Tommy "Ryan" Eboli was named Acting Boss of the organization. The change sweeping the country of the "New Frontier" in 1960, with John F. Kennedy's election as President of the United States, was also being felt within New York's organized crime families. The new generation, Tommy Eboli and his brother Pat, stepped forward.

I was fourteen years old when I first met Pat Eboli in October, 1963 at his family's summer home in Canaan Lake, Long Island, just outside of Patchogue. It happened out of an act of extraordinary generosity on the part of Pat and his wife, Jean. Aunt Josephine and her husband Mike were celebrating their fiftieth wedding anniversary, and Cousin Jean phoned my mother a few days before asking if we were planning on having a celebration for "Josie and Mike."

"We can't afford much," my mother said, explaining that she was having a quiet family dinner with an anniversary cake.

Jean, always fond of her cousins, told my mother not to worry about the cost.

"Pat will supply the wine, beer, and liquor and we'll pay for everything," Jean told my mother. She asked her to invite Pat Eboli's sisters as well.

The Saturday of the party, my father and I drove our used Ford Fairlane out to the Eboli's, Patchogue, home to pick up the beverages. We pulled our plain white sedan around to the side of the stylish ranch house that had a commanding lakefront view. Pat warmly welcomed us into his home, asking if we wanted something to eat. My father thanked him for the offer, but said that we had a few more stops to make before the party, and declined. I looked around, taking careful mental notes.

We followed Pat into his den, paneled in light-colored knotty pine, and saw the sweeping bar, which held several boxes of liquor and wine. In front of the bar was a large circular wooden table, surrounded by big carved-out wine barrel chairs that could spin around when you sat in them. The walls were covered with photographs of race horses wearing garlands of flowers around their necks. In each photo, Pat Eboli stood smiling among a group of people standing next to the winning horse. So, he's a horse owner, I thought. He owns and races horses; *that's how he makes his money*. It was a perfectly rational rationalization for a 14-year-old boy. My father loved horse-racing, placed two-dollar bets on the ponies each week with his bookie (in the days before Off-TrackBetting), and memorized all of the statistics about each professional horse and jockey the way I could recite baseball box scores. Of course he would admire Pat. He owned and raced horses that won.

My father and I loaded up the trunk of our car with boxes of beer, wine and liquor. Pat thanked us for hosting the party and for driving out to pick up the refreshments, and told us he'd see us later that evening. We thanked him and drove off. All the way home from Patchogue to Babylon along the Sunrise Highway, my father kept looking into his rear view mirror.

"I think someone is following us, Rock," my father said, using the nickname he called me

"Why would someone be following us?" I asked my father.

"I don't know," he said, abruptly ending the conversation. Years later I learned that when my father and I arrived back at our house, he told my mother he thought the FBI had followed us home. It wouldn't be the last time our entire family was under FBI surveillance. If the FBI stayed in front of our house all day, they would have observed the first face-to-face meeting between representatives of the Genovese and Gambino crime families since the infamous Commission meeting up in Apalachin, New York, convened by Vito Genovese six years earlier.

Fittingly, the meeting at our house occurred at a celebration for Aunt Josephine who adroitly played each side off against the other, getting the most she could out of her friends and relatives in both crime families. Aunt Jo was mobster neutral, and exquisitely skilled at parlaying her loyalty, gracious hospitality, and extraordinary Italian cuisine into winning the favor of both major New York crime families. Genovese or Gambino affiliation didn't matter—what mattered most was money. Both Pat Eboli and Carmine Fatico had plenty of it and were always generous with her.

She was best friends with her younger brother Angelo's first wife, Rose Coletti, who divorced Angelo in the early 1950s, and married East New York mobster Carmine "Charlie Wagons" Fatico. Aunt Josephine chose her friendship with Rose over her relationship with her brother, with whom she never "saw eye to eye," she'd say. She was delighted that my mother invited Aunt Rose and "Uncle Charlie" to the party. They just moved to neighboring West Islip a few years earlier, and Aunt Josephine made sure to see them on every visit to Long Island. Carmine "Charlie Wagons" Fatico was as dramatic a contrast to Pat Eboli. A local gang member who grew up in Brooklyn, Fatico was short and squat. Always meticulously dressed, Fatico could never achieve the elegance of Eboli. He fit the street tough image of the Gambino Crime family members and rose to the post of Capo in 1957, when Albert Anastasia was executed and Carlo Gambino became the new leader of the organization.

The killing of Anastasia, and the serious wounding of Frank Costello coming within six months of each other, elevated Gambino and Genovese to the head of their enterprises, and promoted the Eboli and Fatico brothers—Carmine and Danny—along with them. John Gotti, then seventeen years old and a Franklin K. Lane High School drop-out, and also from East New York, became a Fatico protégé that year.

My brother Michael lived in an entirely different world. Never a tough guy, but a shy, gentle, respectful person, he attended St. Francis of Assisi Parochial School in Crown Heights, before our move to Long Island in 1953 where he graduated from Babylon High School. My brother joined the Navy in 1959 and served his country overseas, while Gotti served his local Capo, Carmine Fatico, in Brooklyn. Michael was a model citizen; Gotti, a model street hood in training.

Jerry Capeci and Gene Mustain in *Mob Star*, (Franklin Watts, NY/Toronto, 1988) recounted Gotti's hero worship of the Fatico Brothers:

The Fatico Brothers (Carmine and Danny) operated out of a storefront they called 'The Club' and were active in hijacking, extortion, gambling and loan-sharking...they were always looking for a few good men. When John Gotti thought of successful men, he thought of Carmine and Daniel Fatico. They wore fine clothes and drove big cars. At the track, they could lose with cheer, as opposed to despair. They were respected, maybe not by the wider world, but by the young men of John's world.

In *Goombata*, Cummings and Volkman catalogue Carmine "Uncle Charlie" Fatico's accomplishments:

Fatico was one of the most powerful capi in the entire Gambino organization...a prodigious money-earner, grossing about $30 million a year, mostly from hijacking, illegal gambling and loansharking..."

I met "Uncle Charlie" Fatico before I met Pat Eboli, and worked for him years before my brother Michael did. "Uncle Charlie" and Aunt Rose were living in West Islip for about a year, in 1960, when Aunt Josephine came out from Brooklyn to stay with us for a few days. The Fatico's new Long Island home on Higbie Lane was only a few miles from where we lived in North Babylon. Aunt Josephine was eager to visit Rose and Charlie, since she knew it would be worth her while financially. My father agreed to drive my mother and her older sister over to the Fatico's home, and he took me along for company. Aunt Rose's three grandchildren, all a few years younger than I, lived right next door, and we usually had a wild time running around in their large backyard when we got together. Their mother, my first-cousin Sissy, was very close to my mother, who had helped raise her. On a muggy, summer day when we arrived, Aunt Rose was pulling weeds out of their front garden and perspiring heavily.

She gave us her usual, over-the-top greeting when she saw us. When I offered to finish her weeding for her, she was delighted.

After a few hours of toiling in the fertile soil of the Fatico's garden, I went around to the back of the house, cleaned myself off, and started to drink from the garden hose to cool down. Aunt Rose saw me and came running out.

"Stephen, don't do that; here—come inside and have some fresh lemonade," she said. She opened the sliding door to their downstairs study and let me in, serving me a tall, chilled glass of lemonade.

As I drank, I watched my father on the far side of the room, sitting next to "Uncle Charlie," still in his bathrobe, each with an empty whiskey glass in front of them discussing horse racing.

"You know, I went to college, Al," I heard Charlie tell my father.

"Ya did? Where, Charlie?" my father said, playing along.

Charlie got up and poured more scotch into their glasses.

"Wait. I'll show you." He shuffled over to a bookcase and pulled out a photo from an album. "Uncle Charlie" walked back over to my father, and standing over him, put the picture in my father's hands and pointed to it.

"That's where I went to college," Carmine Fatico said to my father, smiling slightly. "Leavenworth. Leavenworth Federal College. That's where I got my degree."

A tightly, controlled laugh come out through "Uncle Charlie's" crafty smile. He had served jail time on and off since the 1930s for grand larceny, bookmaking, and felonious assault. My father laughed along with Carmine Fatico, feeling good from the expensive scotch and having few other choices. "Leavenworth" quickly became a part of family folklore, when my father recounted the story of "Uncle Charlie's" college days" in his thick Brooklyn accent, especially after he had too much to drink and too much time to think about the lure Charlie's money later held for my brother.

Aunt Rose, who had walked around the front of the house to see my handiwork, shouted inside to "Uncle Charlie."

"Charlie, pay Stephen something for this beautiful job he did in the garden. Just be-yoo-ti-ful. Pay him something," she said. My mother and Aunt Josephine had come downstairs and were ready to leave.

"No, that's okay, Aunt Rose, I can't take money from you. You're family," I said, knowing that was what my mother wanted me to say. My going rate for weeding was fifty cents per hour.

Suddenly, Aunt Josephine came over to me, smiling, forcefully whispering in my ear as she pulled on it with her right thumb and forefinger.

"Stephen. Don't be so stupid," she said. "Charlie's got plenty of money. He can afford to pay you for this. Don't be a stupido!"

She turned toward everyone in the room, flashing a Cheshire cat grin. I stood there and smiled the dumb, awkward smile of a clueless 11-year-old boy. "Uncle Charlie" walked over and placed a ten-dollar bill in my hand, and patted me on the head.

"Nice job, Stephen," he said. "If Rosie's happy, I'm happy."

Ten dollars was a fortune to me in 1960. I thanked "Uncle Charlie" profusely as we were leaving, without an inkling of just how plentiful was Carmine "Charlie Wagons" Fatico's money. "Uncle Charlie" and Aunt Rose came to our house the day of Aunt Josephine's anniversary party, and the meeting between the Gambino and Genovese crime families was brief, cordial and formal. Pat Eboli shook Charlie Fatico's hand, their wives exchanged hugs and kisses, and each couple went their separate ways. They were there for "Josie"—nothing else—and, as usual, she managed to make peace between two powerful men, and tap into their deep pockets. Unfortunately for Tommy Eboli, the next time both crime families cooperated the outcome was not so friendly.

In 1970, the year after Genovese died and Tommy "Ryan" Eboli was the new boss of the Genovese organization, Eboli decided to diversify his business in a big way. He borrowed $4 million from Carlo Gambino to back a start-up idea: a drug trafficking operation. The crew Tommy Eboli assembled to carry out his operation was quickly caught by Federal Law Enforcement officials and arrested. While the Boss himself avoided jail, the failure of his start-up left Tommy Ryan with a very big problem: he didn't have the $4 million to pay back his principal investor, Carlo Gambino, when Gambino and his top assistant Paul Castellano came in person to claim their money. Two years later, on July 16, 1972, Tommy "Ryan" Eboli was shot dead at 1:00am in the Crown Heights section of Brooklyn, as he left his girlfriend's apartment. I was on my honeymoon in Las Vegas when I learned of Tommy Eboli's murder.

Walking out of the Frontier Casino in downtown Vegas, a big, bold newspaper headline stopped me cold: "TOMMY EBOLI SHOT DEAD."

"Holy shit," I said to Carol, fumbling for coins to buy the paper.

I read the story aloud to see whether there was any mention of Pat Eboli or my mother's cousin Jean being harmed, or—even worse— any mention at all of my brother Michael who was just starting to work with Pat Eboli. Just a few months earlier, Michael had traveled up to Albany to drum up business for a medical screening company for which he worked. He came to the state capital to schmooze with AFL-CIO union leaders holding their annual statewide meeting.

I was living in Albany and running as a progressive Democrat for New York State Assembly in a Democratic primary election against the Albany county political "machine" of Dan O'Connell and Mayor Erastus Corning. My anti-Vietnam War activism, and work on health and education issues as a State Legislative Aide, propelled me to run for public office one year after I graduated from SUNY Albany with a degree in Political Science. My brother and I arranged to have breakfast at the Thruway Hyatt House, just across the street from the uptown campus of the State University, where I had graduated the year before. He told me he was there to pitch the labor unions for sales contracts for his company, and that he would also be working on a "few things," for Pat Eboli.

I stopped chewing my food. I looked at my brother carefully, studying his kind, clean, eager face.

"Pat's gonna help me out," Michael repeated to me, his deep, dark eyes glowing.

My brother, then 32 years old but appearing much younger, had a look of optimism he had lost over the past few years, following several failed business ventures, and a move back to New York from Phoenix, Arizona, which he regretted. He had moved there with all the promise in the world; moved to a bright, unsettled place, in the shadow of Camelback Mountain, with his wife and young, beautiful daughter; moved as a respected technician in a new electronics business that was destined to bloom in the desert. The sweeping life change did not work out, and both his confidence and his career suffered. He came back and lived in the basement of his in-laws' home, while his new, narrow, high-ranch house was being built on a postage-stamp lot in North Babylon, just a few doors down from his wife's parents. He was hopeful that now, with Pat Eboli's help and connections, this was, at last, the break he needed.

My brother had come to seek my approval, and it made me uncomfortable. I was his kid brother; he was my hero. I admired him for precisely the things that worked against his making it in business: he lacked the instinct to take advantage of people, or to use them. I was working as an editor for the teachers union and running for political office at 23 years old, and he looked at me as a success with the world opening up for me, as it did for him when he went to Arizona. I felt like crying for him.

"Michael," I said, looking straight into his eyes, "be careful. You have a gentle and good nature and you're liable to get hurt playing with those guys."

I didn't know what else to say. This was my older brother, and I was not accustomed to giving him advice. There was an awkward silence. He looked down at his food, picked up his fork and started playing with it. Then, he looked up at me, and I could see he was already gone, with the kind of look we all get when nothing anyone can say will change our mind because they can't possibly understand everything pulling at us; they can't possibly be in our shoes.

"Don't worry, I'll be careful," he said. "Everything is above board.

I'll be fine."

"I hope so, Michael; I hope so for your sake," I said, searching his face for some sign of deception either of himself or of me. I could find none.

I wanted to reach out and embrace my brother, but the men in our family didn't have that kind of intimacy, even when we wanted it. We pretended to be tough, strong, stoic. We changed the subject.

"Did you see *The Godfather* yet?" Michael asked me, noting that it was playing at the movie theatre right next to the hotel. "Did you see Alfred?"

The Godfather had just opened around the country during the last week of March, 1972, breaking all box office records. In its first six months of release *The Godfather* did a bigger box office business than *Gone With The Wind* achieved in thirty years. The first film in the Coppola trilogy was all anyone talked about.

In our family, it was a matter of obsession and great pride since my mother's cousin Alfred Lettieri, starred as the sinister villain of the film, Sollozzo "The Turk." Sollozzo was shot in the head in a memorable scene with Al Pacino. He was killed for attempting to murder Don Corleone, the character played by Marlon Brando, because the Godfather would not agree to move his business into narcotics. Sollozzo's death on the big screen foreshadowed what was to come in real life for the Ebolis. Less than four full months after the film burst into the American consciousness, a botched attempt to move into the narcotics trade by Tommy Eboli resulted in his being gunned down just the way Sollozzo was, and for the same reason.

"Yeah, I saw it when it first opened," I said, looking away. "I'm not crazy about how it portrayed Italians."

"It's just a movie, Stephen," he said. "Just a story. And it's a big break for Alfred."

I shook my head. "It sends such a bad message about us."

My brother side-stepped my disapproval. He was not looking for confrontation; it simply wasn't in his nature. Al Lettieri, a dead-ringer for my mother's brother Salvatore "Jimmy the Kid" Roberts, was rapidly becoming a deity in our family. Within weeks of the movie opening he brought his then-girlfriend and actress Sally Struthers to have dinner with my mother and Aunt Josephine at our house in North Babylon. My brother figured he was on safe ground by keeping the conversation focused on cousin Alfred.

"Alfred introduced Jean and Pat and their whole family to Pacino, Brando, Coppola—the whole cast," he said.

I did not give my brother a chance to change the subject, nor did I even pretend to be impressed. "Just be careful, Michael," I said. "Please, be careful."

He assured me that he would, wished me luck in my primary campaign, paid the bill, and we went our separate ways. I searched for my brother's name in the story about Tommy Eboli's assassination and when I did not find it, I was relieved. Pat Eboli was still alive, but the head of the Genovese crime family was dead, and with it my brother's prospects of getting some help from family mob connections, at least for now.

3 ▫ Prisons

I had not reached, nor could I understand, the darkness of desperation and doubt that drove my brother to seek financial help from the only members of the family capable of providing it.

I knew I was different from the rest of my family, an outsider determined to find my own way; that the chaos in our lives was so constant I wanted nothing to do with anyone I associated with such disorder. I believed I did not need anyone's help, since my father told me throughout childhood I was special, capable of doing anything.

"You are the third son of a third son," he said, especially when he was feeling good after a few glasses of beer and whiskey. "You are destined for great things. One day, you will sail to Italy and clean up the family name. You won't want to go; but you must."

I stared at my father's full, fat face, his jowels jiggling, eyes bulging out, and his bulbous nose glowing soft red from all the booze he consumed. My mind recorded every word, every nuance of his voice. I was afraid to ask him *when* I had to make the trip. Each time he saw how intently I hung on every word, and how my brow would wrinkle with worry about leaving home, my father winked at me. It was a big, dramatic wink, easing my fears, and it became part of the game we played each time he told the "third son" story. It was the same big, generous wink he flashed the day of my high school graduation, when, standing at the end of a long row of folding chairs, he caught my eye. I watched him, dressed in his worn grey suit, grey felt fedora cocked perfectly on his head, standing at the end of my row, grinning a wide, unselfconscious grin. I was the third son of a third son and destined for great things, his look told me. But was I up for it? And when would I know it was time to go? I felt imprisoned by my family, but feared leaving the comfort of the cozy cell I helped create. I was my mother's son, and like my brother Michael, never wanted to disappoint her. As long as I did what she told me to do, I was "never any trouble," as she was fond of saying about Michael and me. I became enamored with the familiar: the sight of my mother rotating fresh bell peppers over an open flame, the hand on her paralyzed arm guided by her "good" hand; a slathering of gravy on hot, crusty Italian bread each Sunday when my father and I returned from church; and the smell of fresh made tomato sauce that took our reason away.

In summers, I'd play baseball with some neighborhood friends, until darkness forced us inside. I'd clean up for dinner, and then sit, with my father, watching the Yankee game on WPIX Channel 11. Back and forth, as if watching a tennis game, my eyes focused first on my father, snoring loudly in his worn-out chair, then on the small screen of our black-and-white television, where finger-sized figures of baseball players scurried across the field. The voices of Mel Allen, or Red Barber or Phil Rizzuto punctuated the rhythm of my father's snoring, but the only alarm that could jolt him upright was the high-pitched music of the Mr. Softee Ice Cream truck. As if on cue, my father would jump up, reach into his pocket for a few dollars, and call out my nickname.

"Hey Rock," he said. "Softee! Go get us some!"

My father's affectionate name for me, "Rock," had a double meaning. I was as solid as a rock to him; always there, always dependable, by his side, unshakeable in my loyalty and love. I was also his, and my mother's, thumb in the eye to the old world Italians, the "stupid guineas" as my father referred to the mustache Pete's, who pressed their thumb against their other four fingers, hands shaped like an upward cup, held the "ayyyyy" in "Hey" far too long, a smug look fixed on their faces, and thought that on limited intelligence they knew all the answers to everything. He'd change "Rock" to "Rocco" on those occasions when he wanted to push me right smack in their "puss," as he'd call their self-satisfied faces, holding the last syllable like the final notes of a song. Each time he did that it had the dual, conflicting purposes of reminding me where I came from, and how different I was from everyone else.

He would thrust the dollars into my hand, and I would open the front screen door, stick my head out, and whistle loudly to stop the ice cream truck. I would run down the front stoop, money clutched in hand like a tribute to the God that kept me locked away—night after summer night—loving the sweetness, hating the sameness, and despising myself for not being able to resist either. Dependable routine was paired with despair; Yankee announcer Red Barber's sweet sounds of calmness, punctured by a constant, cacophony of chaos. Living a life like my father's frightened me: gone before dawn until after sunset, commuting into New York back and forth each day on the Long Island Railroad, six days a week, fifty weeks a year. Work and chaos, work and chaos; never enough money, never enough time to think or to catch your breath, until the next crisis hit; take the punch, absorb the blow, never flinch, get up off the ground, ready for the next blow.

My way of making peace with constant crises, to survive, was to become preternaturally calm, almost catatonic, in the teeth of the snarling chaos. It was precisely how I reacted one night in high school, when I was rummaging through the storage closet over my parents' bed. The closet, built where wealthier families hung artwork, was set deep into the wall, with two sliding doors big enough for a teenager to climb through. I was looking for some old books my mother stored there to use in a report I was doing for school. I heard a car door slam on the street out front. Suddenly, I could make out my sister's voice downstairs, arguing with my father. I heard my father raise his voice. My sister ran back outside, slamming the front door of the house behind her.

Within minutes, my father raced up the one flight of stairs to his bedroom, and began furiously searching for something in the floor-to-ceiling closet in the corner of the room. He didn't notice me sitting up in the storage closet across the room from him. His face red with rage, my father emerged from the closet with a shotgun he had stashed far in the back, behind hanging clothes. I froze.

With the shotgun in one hand, my father began tossing underwear out of his dresser drawers, looking for the rifle's cartridges. I watched all of this, my legs dangling over the edge of the storage closet, in disbelief, as my father screamed that he was going to "kill the son-of-a-bitch who did this to his daughter." My sister, not yet married, had informed my father that she was pregnant. Before my father could find the bullets he wanted, my mother burst into the room.

"Al, Al! What are you doing? What are you, crazy?" she hollered.

She slammed shut the bedroom door, throwing her body in front of it, her huge breasts heaving up and down in terror and courage and instinct, like a female lion protecting her cubs.

"You'll have to shoot me first," she cried out, blocking the door.

They stood there for what seemed like minutes, staring each other down, my mother sobbing, chest pounding. She did not budge from her position in front of the door, knowing that my father would never harm her. I watched in silence from the storage closet, holding a book in my lap, thinking that what I was witnessing was not real. Decades later, when my brother-in-law became as close to my parents as another son, and he and my sister lovingly cared for my mother when she needed a wheelchair, I thought back to the moment where my mother's courage saved his life. Never knowing that, he repaid my mother with kindness and love many times over.

My mother stood my father down. He lowered his head, then the shotgun. He slowly walked over to the bedroom closet where he had found it, and placed it back behind the hanging clothes. I sat there, still motionless and silent in the storage closet, observing my father embrace my mother when he walked over toward the bedroom door where she stood like a sentry. I watched them walk out of the room together, without saying a word to me, and wondered how I had stumbled into the middle of all of this. I was an observer, not a participant in this chaotic life. The following day, my brother Michael came over to my parents' house from where he was living on the other side of town; he went up to their bedroom and found the shotgun in the back of the hanging clothes closet. He gave me a slight smile as he carried the shotgun down the stairs into the living room.

"He'll never see this again," Michael said calmly, as he walked out of the house with the shotgun wrapped in a bed sheet, and drove off back to his own life.

But something had seized me as well, and carried me away just as my brother made sure the shotgun was gone. Numb to what I had witnessed, I removed myself from my family, wanting no part of it. I became obsessed with getting out, living a new and different life. I was terrified of staying stuck in my father's world, with no time to think or calm down, or breathe. His rage and violence frightened me. I feared falling into the same deadening pattern, of just getting through each day, getting up, getting out to work; to earn, back home to eat, to rest, to sleep, to brace himself for more of the same the next day and for days and weeks and months after, until something makes you snap. I had no idea of where I would go, or what I would do, but one thing was certain: I had to get out.

College was never an "option"; it was a necessity for survival, an acceptable path for escaping my family; not getting locked in the prison of their lives, but not abandoning them either. I was drawn to learning, like the Lettieris, from an early age. My mother, forced to leave school after the sixth grade, was determined that, unlike her, I would not be denied a formal education.

Obsessed with writing, reading and public speaking, I excelled in academics, pleasing my mother with my grades and school awards. My heroes, in addition to the Yankees' second-baseman Bobby Richardson, were writers like Pearl Buck and John Steinbeck; storytellers like Edgar Allen Poe and Arthur Miller, and newspaper or sports reporters Jimmy Breslin, Pete Hamill, Phil Pepe of the *Daily News* and Jimmy Cannon, who was, to me, what Damon Runyon was to my Uncle Jim.

When John F. Kennedy ran for President in 1960, the same year I was elected Student Council President by one-vote, our fates were linked, and I was captivated by his promise. If an Irish–Catholic could become President of the United States, why not an Italian–American? Although we were practicing "Cat-licks," as my father proclaimed our faith in his Brooklyn dialect, only my mother and sister shared my love and adulation of JFK. To my father, and my brothers, he was Irish and liberal—two huge strikes against him—and led a gilded life far different from ours.

President Kennedy's assassination set me further apart from the men in my family and on a path unfamiliar to them. I was 14 years old, and consumed with television and newspaper coverage of every detail of JFK's life and death. They were busy working long hours each day, earning money to make ends meet. They didn't have time to mourn for someone they neither liked, nor were related to. The more I learned about the Kennedys, and the working class Irish politicians who supported them, the more I learned that I could lead a different, better life than the one I knew. I wouldn't have to be one of the "Corner Boys", like my brothers were for a time, hanging out in front of Anna Jeans' Bar in North Babylon. They may have looked cool and fast, laughing too hard at one another's jokes, but I saw a sadness there, buried deep inside. Too macho to admit their fears, they were scared of staying stuck on the corner forever, never hearing the laughter aimed at them behind their backs nor paying attention to the names which mocked them, —"guidos" or "greasers"—genteel, acceptable slurs meant to demean and to keep them down, at the bottom of society's pile.

"You don't belong in this family," my brother Vinnie's wife Edie said to me at dinner one Sunday, shaking her head and laughing at how different I was from my father and my brothers. "Are you sure you weren't adopted?" Meant as a compliment, her comment both stung and spurred me on.

Education was my escape hatch, and in my mind public service and politics, as represented by the Kennedys, were inextricably linked. You couldn't have one without the other, and I wanted both. I kept speaking and writing, and like Lin Manuel Miranda's *Hamilton*, I "wrote my way out" of my circumstances and into a full four-year journalism scholarship at New York University. As the first in my family to attend college, NYU was my ticket to escape, I thought; a ticket to any place I wanted to go beyond the front storm door with the large aluminum "V" in the center; an all-expenses-paid ride to new and unfamiliar places and far different experiences. Those experiences came quickly, during my first and only semester at NYU.

Sitting on a bench in Washington Square Park, just a few blocks from where my mother was born, I took out my copy of Plato's *Republic* to read for my first-year Politics course. Washington Square Park in the late 1960s was not a gentrified place. Drug dealing and Bocce were the two most popular sports. Each time I tried to read a page I was badgered by some disheveled looking guy asking for money or cigarettes, or whether I wanted a blow-job, or a prick up the ass.

"You want a nickel bag?" asked the raggedy guy, sitting next to me on the bench.

I edged away toward the end of the bench.

"No, no thanks," I said, pretending to go back to reading my book. I didn't know what a nickel bag was, assuming it was some kind of cheap condom since his offer came on the heels of a few offers for quick sex.

I got up from the bench and went back to my dorm room at the old Brittany Hotel on East 10th Street, extra housing NYU purchased for its growing student population. I shared a room on the tenth floor with four other roommates, all wealthier, worldlier guys from far away places like Scarsdale, Shaker Heights, and Santa Monica. Embarrassed to reveal my ignorance about sex or drugs, I kept my "nickel bag" story to myself, climbed up on my bunk-bed and tried to continue reading my book. If I couldn't compete with them in life experiences or spending money, I'd push myself even harder to keep pace academically. I read quietly, curled up in a corner of my bed for about an hour.

One of my roommates, a handsome, broad-shouldered athlete

from Scarsdale, came striding into the room. He came over to the side of my bed and flashed a dazzling smile.

"You mind disappearing for about an hour, Steve? I've got this girl coming over for a quick fuck, and I need a little privacy," he said.

"Oh–uh–s–s–ure, sure," I stammered. Of course I'd leave. Here was a cool, confident college man about to have actual sex, a subject about which I knew nothing. I'd want someone to offer the same courtesy to me, if ever I could even imagine what a quick fuck entailed, or any fuck, for that matter.

I left the dorm and headed to the Loeb Student Center to try to study some more. I watched sophisticated, self-confident couples embrace and kiss and laugh with each other. Their intimacy underlined my loneliness. I felt like an outsider within my own family; a misfit in Washington Square Park; and an outcast from college roommates, who saw me as the token poor boy, taking up their time and a place in an overcrowded classroom. I walked slowly back to the Brittany, a few hours later, and found the room empty. All of the beds, except mine, were unmade. I looked out the window to East 10th Street to see if I could find my roommates coming or going up the block to grab some dinner. No sign of them.

I stared down at the sidewalk and imagined what it would feel like if I jumped; what it would look like to passers-by, my head smashing on concrete, arms and legs splayed in every direction, like the scarecrow in the Wizard of Oz when the Flying Monkeys attack, and toss his straw stuffing asunder. The thought of strangers leering at my crumpled body parts, tsk-tsking in sympathy, and of my roommates giving each other the smug "we-knew-he-wouldn't-make-it" look, repelled me. I stepped back from the open window, knowing it would be impossible to grab onto a passing ledge, if, somewhere along my journey down to East 10th Street, I changed my mind. I wanted to hedge my bets. Instead, I took the elevator down from the 10th floor of the Brittany, stepped out into the crisp, fall night air of New York City, and walked past the spot where my body would have landed.

Without jumping out of any windows, I was tumbling out of control, unable to catch my breath. At night, I was too frightened to leave my dorm; in class, I was intimidated by how self-confident everyone appeared to be. I was awed by the Orthodox Jewish students, dressed alike, traveling in groups, always gesturing at each other, arguing, sounding so certain. I studied them carefully: their dress, their manners, their long, unkempt, curly sideburns running down the sides of their faces. They knew who they were, where they belonged.

Overwhelmed by my surroundings and the people in them, I cut classes, and spent days wandering around the City. I fell behind in my readings and class assignments. I isolated myself from my roommates, wandering the streets for some solace, and stumbling into St. Anthony's Roman Catholic Church on Sullivan Street, just below Washington Square Park. I needed a quiet place to get away from the sounds of the street, and the even louder noises of my mind. I knelt in a pew at the back of the church and looked up at the ceiling.

"Sanctuary, sanctuary," I said quietly, remembering the scene in the *The Hunchback of Notre Dame* when Charles Laughton, playing Quasimodo, defiantly rang the church bells. Like the Hunchback, I felt deformed, out of place; someone being stared at because I was so different from my classmates at NYU in the late 1960s. Unrecognizable, even to myself.

I sat inside St. Anthony's and thought of my father, sitting next to me in church on Sunday mornings. I had grown to despise the Catholic Church, for the hold it had on me, the fears it fueled about sex, its support of the war in Vietnam, its predictable regimentation binding me closer to everything that was familiar. All that the Church still held for me was a quiet place where I could be with my father, alone. I looked around the sanctuary and remembered a few years back, just after the shotgun incident, when I dialed the rectory of my home church to speak to the pastor.

"Father," I said, hesitation in my voice, "I'd like to talk to you about becoming a priest." I heard the priest on the other end of the phone suck in air.

"Uh, well," he stammered, "this is a very serious question; a very serious decision. We'll have to set up an appointment to talk in person..."

I listened carefully to his heavy breathing on the other end of the phone. The priest, a portly, red-faced man, was breathing just as my father did when he had too much to drink. He was slurring his words.

"This is very serious, very serious," he said. "These decisions are not made casually. We have to talk about this in person. It's too serious to discuss over the phone; too serious. Call my office in the morning."

The pastor hung up, and I held onto the phone's receiver for a few moments, and laughed. The pastor was drunk; a prisoner in pretty vestments, and his repetitive mutterings reminded me of a character in *Alice in Wonderland*: very serious; too serious, very serious. I looked around the church and closed my eyes. I never wanted to see the inside of a church again, to feel its tether to a life I wanted to leave. I looked to my right, and caught myself wishing my father was there to tell me that I could make it at NYU; that everything would be fine. I wanted the church, or better still, my father, to offer protection from the callous city which shrugged me off each time I tried to look it in the face. I stared at the flickering memorial candles behind the altar rail. My eyes fixated on the flames dancing wildly, side by side, catching each current of air as someone walked by; licking up, over the edges of the shot-glass sized candleholders, with wax filling their red-tinted bottoms. I stayed in the church pew through the late fall afternoon, watching the flames burn down to the pool of wax at the base of each candleholder, until finally, the candles quietly closed their eyes, ending their short, bright existence. In the soft, darting light, and the twists of wispy black smoke that followed the candles' disappearance, the outline of a simple plan emerged: I would quietly snuff out my own flickering little light. I would know when the time was right.

Less than a week later, my brothers and sister and their families came over on a Sunday to celebrate our parents 28th wedding anniversary. As my mother cooked and we all made small talk around the dining room table, my father turned to my brothers and brother-in-law asking if they wanted to go out to grab a drink at a local bar before dinner. I sat there, as invisible as I was the day of the shotgun incident. All the other men, the macho, tough "real" Italian men in the family, jumped up and followed my father out the door. I was stung, an observer again, not a participant, even in the midst of my own. I wanted to be invited, not excluded. My sister, noticing the look on my face, asked me if I was okay. I lied, assuring her that I was, pretending that I would rather be home anyway. It was that final, small slight, the last gasp of my own quivering light, that convinced me there was no other way out than the one I had chosen.

There is a clarity that comes when you decide to end your own life. All chatter stops—in your mind, from others, from any other sources. A shroud of silence envelops you, which nothing and no one can penetrate. Everything moves in slow motion, and the tiniest action, the movement of a finger, the parsing of lips, the fluttering of an eyelash, is magnified. I was dumbfounded how I had not seen the simplicity of this solution before. The way out for an outsider is to leave; one way or another, just leave. During dinner, I watched my brothers' lips moving, my father's eyes glistening from a few drinks too many, but I heard nothing. Nothing anyone said mattered anymore. My decision was made; the scar tissue had, at last, hardened. I was immune to any more slights or pain.

That night, after everyone left and my parents were asleep, I slipped quietly to the bathroom. Carefully, I opened the medicine cabinet and picked an everyday poison as easily as I picked a pair of socks to wear that morning. The poison was a common household ointment collecting dust—a small tube of salve with a tiny skull and crossbones on the back of it, warning against swallowing the white stuff that could be mistaken for toothpaste. I squeezed a small section of the contents of the tube onto my left forefinger, rubbed it onto my tongue, and ran back into my bedroom to wait for it to work. I climbed into bed, the poison on my tongue, and pulled my covers up tightly against my chin. I expected that my body would go cold once I swallowed the little dab of mercuric oxide which, as fast as Mercury could fly, would deliver me from my demons, amen. My death would be painless and quick—no muss, no fuss, unlike jumping out a 10-story window at NYU, or like those suicides you read about in the *New York Post* where some poor soul blows his brains out by sticking a loaded gun into his mouth. Too messy; I wanted clean and quiet, like the wick of a candle, whispering itself out in its own wax.

I lay in bed, every sense on alert, my heart knocking hard on the inside of my chest as if it wanted to get out and have no part in what was going on. I stared at the shadows which moved across my ceiling, sometimes gliding slowly, sometimes fast, as cars passed up and down the block, headlights piercing the darkness of my room like giant searchlights slicing through the night sky, looking for anyone trying to escape. I slid down under the covers to get free of their glare, all the time hoping the lights would find me and make me part of whatever it was they were doing. I closed my eyes tightly to make visions of my parents disappear; of my mother standing down my father with a shotgun in his hand; of my father telling me for the thousandth time that I was the "third son of a third son, destined for great things." I touched the soft lump of poison on my tongue to make sure it was still there. I watched the walls, which appeared to be moving closer to my bed, to me; almost touching my feet, now my arms, pushing in on the headboard, driving me under the covers into a tight curl; giving me a few more seconds of life, a few more quick breaths, before I suffocated.

"This is crazy," I said aloud. "I don't want to die. I just want a different life. Live, you asshole!" I commanded myself.

I threw the covers off my head, gulping for air, desperate for some saliva for my dry mouth, forgetting for a moment about the blot of poison on my tongue.

"Shit," I said. "Shit. Shit. Shit." The poison slid down my throat.

I jumped out of bed and, wearing only my underpants, ran downstairs through the darkened house into the kitchen. Swinging open the refrigerator door, I fumbled among the beer and soda bottles and orange juice containers until I found a nearly full half-gallon of milk.

"Induce vomiting," I babbled, "induce vomiting," remembering the instructions on the side of the tube of salve in case it was accidentally swallowed. Milk, milk; drink lots of milk.

I ran back upstairs, clutching the cold milk container to my chest, careful not to trip or make too much noise that would wake my parents. I ducked into the bathroom, locking the door behind me. My heart was pounding against my chest. I tore open the milk container and started swigging huge mouthfuls from it, one after another, with milk dribbling down the sides of my mouth, dripping from my chin and neck and chest and onto the tiny, square white-and-black tiles covering the bathroom floor.

I watched the reflection of my mouth and throat and the milk carton in the medicine cabinet mirror. I swallowed and swallowed again, not coming up for air until I felt my stomach swell. I placed the milk container down on the floor next to the sink, grabbed onto the side of the toilet with one hand, and thrust the fingers of my other hand down my throat, frantic to reach past my tonsils and pull out the poison by hand. The milk, pushing up from my stomach, and my fingers, reaching down from my mouth, helped the heaves begin. They did not stop until there was nothing left to bring up.

"There. There it is," I said softly in a weak declaration of triumph. I watched the white lump float to the surface of the milky water in the toilet bowl. I stared at the poison for a few seconds; just long enough to be certain of what it was, and then, I flushed it away. The white, cloudy toilet water was replaced with a small, clear, clean whirlpool of water; a fresh start; a rare chance to begin again.

Reprieved from death, I set about to rebuild my life.

NYU was a mistake—far from my family philosophically, but close to them physically, it was too easy for me to retreat into myself and my old safe world when I felt overwhelmed or uncertain in the new one, which was all the time. For a kid from a family with scarcely enough money for essentials like food, shelter, or heath care, the brightness of the scholarship money blinded me to the bind I created for myself. I escaped, but not far enough on one hand, and too far on the other. I jumped from one circumstance in which I didn't fit—my family—into another where I felt like even more of an outsider. I needed to regain my footing, and knew one way for me to achieve that was to attend college far enough from home where I would not be tempted run back to the familiar. I withdrew from NYU, giving up my full scholarship, and wrote to the State University of New York at Albany to activate an earlier acceptance for the following semester. But a possible barrier was the war in Vietnam—a potent, pressing political reason which weighed heavily on every *personal* decision made by many male college students in the late 1960s.

While a full-time student at NYU, I had a 1-S student deferment protecting me from being drafted into a war I opposed. The Selective Service Law required that once a student's status changed, the local draft board must be notified. My local draft board on Long Island, a bastion of support for the war, was funneling too many young men from working class families like mine to the jungles of Southeast Asia. I knew that if I notified the pro-war local board, the chances of my being sent to Vietnam would be high. I wanted to comply with the law, but slow the process down long enough to allow SUNY Albany to activate my acceptance, thus resuming my student deferment status.

So, I devised a plan to gum up the bureaucracy. I mailed my NYU student ID card to the Selective Service System in Washington, DC, accompanied by a letter informing them of my change in student status. The out-of-the-ordinary move had the desired effect. The day *after* I received my acceptance letter from SUNY Albany, I received another letter: this one was from the Selective Service System: I was being reclassified from I-S, or student status, to I-A, or draft eligibility status. I quickly hand-carried my SUNY Albany acceptance letter to the local draft board on Long Island, where they reissued my student deferment. Less than one month later, after beginning my studies at Albany, I learned that Henry York, a friend of mine from elementary school, was killed during the Tet offensive in Vietnam. Given another reprieve from death, twice over a few brief months, I began to believe that I had to do more with my life than simply escape it.

Albany made sense for several reasons. As the State Capitol, it was a natural environment for my love of politics and my growing activism. I won a full New York State Regents Scholarship to the University, so costs would be minimal, and I could afford to pay for college on my own. And, there were large numbers of other students from middle- and working-class families who were also first-generation college students.

I plunged headlong into campus and national politics in the spring of 1968, when President Lyndon B. Johnson announced he would not seek a second term in office, and Senators Eugene McCarthy of Minnesota and Robert F. Kennedy of New York campaigned for the Democratic presidential nomination. National events overshadowed everything swirling around my family. Away from home for the first time, nothing seemed more important than being a participant in and not just an observer of the anti-war politics and human rights issues of the time. It was a complete reversal of my role in the family, and I thrived.

Nothing stayed the same that Spring. I watched LBJ's announcement on an old television set in our dorm lounge on the night of March 31, 1968. Two days later, his name still on the Wisconsin Democratic primary ballot, Johnson was crushed by Eugene McCarthy who rolled up 56% of the vote on his anti-Vietnam War platform. The following night in Memphis, Tennessee, Dr. Martin Luther King, Jr. told a packed church at the Mason Temple "something is happening in our world." King, speaking at a rally supporting Memphis' striking sanitation workers, told the crowd, "The issue is injustice. The issue is the refusal of Memphis to be fair and honest in its dealings with its public servants….Let us develop a kind of dangerous unselfishness….And when we have our march, you need to be there." I was 19, eager for my own personal revolution, and ready to commit my life to the kind of "dangerous unselfishness" Dr. King required. Less than 24 hours later, Martin Luther King, Jr. was assassinated.

I was on my way home for spring break—my first trip back since starting college at SUNY Albany—when I learned of his murder. Mired in my own selfish little world, I was worrying about how my family would react to me, and how I would feel about them, when a college classmate came running onto the bus, breathless, with the news that Dr. King was dead. Instantly, my family's chaos seemed calm in comparison to what was going on in the world. After Dr. King's murder, universities around the country, including ours, were in turmoil, with parts of major American cities on fire. It was no longer enough for me to escape my family and the life we lived, but to "be there," as Dr. King urged, and to be "dangerously unselfish" in fighting for a better world.

Education and politics were pathways pointing a way out of my personal prison, and I seized them. Home for the summer break, I succumbed to the steady rhythm of suburban, working-class life, like the constant background noise of cicadas emerging after 17 years underground. Each morning, every day except Sundays, my father caught an early morning train to his job in midtown Manhattan. If I wanted to use the family car for work, or to go to the beach at Robert Moses State Park, or to campaign for Robert Kennedy for President, I had to rise a little after 5am and drive my father to the Long Island Railroad Station in Deer Park or Babylon.

Wednesday, June 5, 1968, looked and sounded like every other day my father and I went through these morning motions.

"Hey Rock," my father yelled to me. "Time to get up."

"I'm up," I mumbled, jerking my body out of bed and pulling on the clothes I left draped over my desk chair the night before.

Each morning I wanted to use the car, I followed the same pattern of rituals and relationships: I kissed my mother good-bye and followed my father out the front door. We got into the car early that Wednesday morning and turned the radio on WCBS, the all-news radio station, as we did every morning to find out the late night baseball scores from the West Coast. This morning, there was no sports report.

"Senator Kennedy has been shot," the announcer said. "It happened just a few hours ago, California time. It appears the he has been shot in the head as he was leaving the Embassy Room of Los Angeles' Ambassador Hotel, just minutes after he delivered a victory speech to hundreds of supporters following the defeat of Senator Eugene McCarthy in the California presidential primary."

I doubled over, putting my head right up against the car radio.

"Just like his brother," my father said. "They got him, just like his brother."

"No, no," I insisted. "They didn't say he was dead. Listen…"

I turned up the volume. The announcer was in mid-sentence, repeating what he said: "…he was taken to Central Receiving Hospital in Los Angeles. Early reports that we have are that Senator Robert F. Kennedy of New York has been shot in the head, just a little after midnight, California-time, after delivering his victory speech in the Embassy Room of the Ambassador Hotel in Los Angeles. We understand that several other people were also wounded and that the Senator is still alive and has been rushed to Central Receiving Hospital in Los Angeles…"

I stared at the radio, dazed. The morning before, I had handed out "Kennedy for President" flyers at the Babylon Train Station after I dropped my father off, urging commuters to "Vote for Bobby Kennedy in the June 18 New York State residential Primary," only two weeks away.

"Hey Rock, are you okay?" my father asked as we pulled up in front of the train station. "Will you be alright to drive home?"

"Yeah, yeah, I'm okay, Dad, don't worry," I said quickly, wanting him to be quiet so I could hear the radio. "I'll see you tonight. Six-thirty?"

"Six-thirty," my father said.

He got out of the 1968 Green Plymouth Fury and I slid over behind the steering wheel from the passenger's side. I watched him walk off to the waiting Manhattan-bound train, a copy of the *New York Daily News* tucked under his left arm and his trademark grey fedora on his head. The radio report kept repeating the same information: "Kennedy shot; Ambassador Hotel; California primary victory." It was a few minutes after 5:30 am when I stopped at a traffic light at the intersection of Deer Park Avenue and Woods Road, and glanced at the darkened stores in the Sunset City Shopping Center, to the spot where, four years earlier, I met Bobby Kennedy campaigning for U.S. Senator from New York. I looked over and saw RFK standing there, smiling, admiring the banner I made out of an old, white bed sheet my mother gave me, on which I painted in deep blue, all caps, the words, "HELLO, BOBBY!"

On the day of his visit, I drove to the rally with our local Democratic Committeeman Chet Clarke, who lived right behind us and was thrilled to have a committed young campaign worker in the heavily Republican town of Babylon. He knew how hard the murder of my first political hero John F. Kennedy had hit me the year before, and how I worked long hours handing out leaflets to help Bobby Kennedy get elected. Chet moved me right behind the rope line where I'd be able to meet RFK and my huge, blue and white, "Hello, Bobby!" banner would be seen by everyone. A small group of young, female, campaign cheerleaders, dressed in short felt skirts and shaking white pom-poms like the cheerleaders for our high school football team, belted out the campaign song to the tune of "When You're Down and Out:" "Bobby Kennedy, Vote on November three, There's gonna be a great day."

The crowd in our largely Irish and Italian community gave Kennedy polite applause when he followed the cheerleaders to the stage. He gave a short speech and began to make his way around the rope, shaking hands. He started directly across from me, but my eyes were riveted on the bird-thin legs of Dorothy Kilgallen, the talk show host and journalist walking beside RFK. Her legs were so skinny that her stockings flapped in the wind, as did Bobby's wild, wispy hair, which he kept pushing out of his face. Working his way around the rope to where I stood, Bobby Kennedy put his hand on my shoulder, and said: "That's quite a sign you've got there! Thank you!" He continued around the rope to shake every hand. As he was leaving, there was a scuffle a few feet behind me. An obnoxious, anti-Kennedy kid from my high school class was pulled down from a light pole by Suffolk County police for pointing a plastic water pistol at RFK. The kid laughed, but no one else in the Sunset City parking lot found it funny. It was the same obnoxious classmate I once punched in the nose for tormenting me and calling me a "guinea."

Four years later, on the morning Robert F. Kennedy took a bullet in his brain—"just like his brother"—I pulled over into the parking lot where RFK touched me. I turned the car off, and cried until I could cry no more. My eyes cleared of tears, and I could see the sun coming up in the distance. The next day, Robert Kennedy died. His body was flown back to New York to St. Patrick's Cathedral; intuitively, I knew I had to go, to be there, to feel this loss as deeply as I could and never permit anything to turn me back toward my family's life of quiet desperation.

On the first day Kennedy's body was laid out at St. Patrick's, I rose early with my father, slipped on a pair of black dress slacks, a short-sleeve white dress shirt, a dark grey tie, and my black double-breasted sports jacket that I bought in the same shopping center where I met RFK.

My father and I stopped at the newspaper kiosk at the Babylon train station's lower level, picked up a copy of the *New York Daily News* for him, and the *New York Times* for me. We boarded his regular early morning train that was already waiting at the station. Both newspapers predicted huge crowds of mourners would jam

Manhattan that day. I pored over every word of every story about RFK's death, devouring each detail in the *Times*. Leaning over my father's arm, I looked at the pictures in the *Daily News* and read the giant headlines, until he flipped the paper over to the sports section to check the horseracing handle from the day before. The last three digits of that total would tell him if he "hit" the number with his bookie.

The contrast of our lives struck me. My father was doing the same thing he had done for 15 years of life on Long Island: catching an early morning train, looking at the horseracing results in the same section of the same newspaper each day, hoping that maybe, this time, this day "our ship would come in," as he chanted each time he looked. Each day he got up before everyone else and went to the same job, taking care of tempermental steam boilers that belched hot water and hot air through the pipes running like elevated roadways in the basement of the office building where he worked in Manhattan. He barely made enough money to support our family, and only because he worked on Saturdays, too, earning overtime pay.

I watched the train conductor punch my ticket and thought of how my father must have watched countless conductors perform the same ritual, ticket after ticket, trip after trip, until he no longer knew it was happening. I sat and stared out the train window and watched Woodside whiz by, hearing my mother's refrain repeating itself to the cadence of the train car's wheels whispering over the tracks: "We live in hopes and die in despair; live in hopes, die in despair; live in hopes, live in hopes…" I looked over at my father, asleep, the *Daily News* folded in his lap.

No, I insisted to myself, I am the third son of a third son, and I must live a life like no one in my family has ever dreamed. I would learn about the mysterious "they" that my family fussed about whenever something happened out of their control, which was frequently. What I had to guard against, was *becoming* one of "them," an unspoken fear between my family and me. We knew I would be different, but *how different?* Would I become unrecognizable to my mother and father? Go on, take, take, take; but don't take too much...don't change too much.

I looked at my father again, his dapper grey fedora resting gently on his head. I could not imagine him going to a politician's funeral, to pay his respects to one of "them." To Al Villano, it was all distant, part of another "woild," as he would say. He had all he could do to survive and feed his family in his world.

"Will you have to give *la busta?*" he kidded me, when I told him I was going to RFK's funeral, referring to the Italian custom of putting a little money in an envelope and giving it to the family of the deceased to help pay funeral expenses. His humor got me to smile.

"I don't think the Kennedys need it, Dad," I said, winking back.

We got off the train at Grand Central Station.

"Be careful and watch your wallet, Rock," he said to me. He headed down to the basement of the building where he worked, putting on his brown maintenance man's uniform as soon as he got there. He wore it all day, the way the wealthy lawyers and accountants on the floors above wore their designer-label suits and ties, while he made certain they were comfortable all day long.

I started walking uptown to St. Patrick's Cathedral, where the body of Senator Robert F. Kennedy lay in state. Blocks before I reached the church, I noticed the lines, stretching in all directions. It was still early, 6:45 in the morning, and the closest point I could join the line was at 45th Street and 5th Avenue, some five blocks from the main entrance to St. Patrick's. People were dressed in all kinds of clothing; tourists in shorts and tee-shirts and bold summer colors; New Yorkers, mourning the death of their U.S. Senator in somber business suits and dark ties; a small group of older Black women were dressed up as if it were Easter Sunday, wearing pastel-colored suits and pillbox hats with fine lacey black veils pinned over the front part of their hats, ready to be draped over their eyes when they entered the sanctuary. I studied these elderly, elegant Black women carefully, picturing them praying together two months earlier when they learned Martin Luther King, Jr. was killed. I saw them standing in their church somewhere uptown in Harlem, or in Brooklyn, or out on the Island in Roosevelt, in the same bright pastel-colored suits and pillbox hats, with their fine lacey black veils pulled down over their eyes, unable to hold back their tears. We moved agonizingly slowly, a few people talking quietly to each other. I waited on line for nearly three hours and began perspiring heavily under my sport jacket as the warm June sun began to get higher and hotter. When we finally reached the front steps of St. Patrick's Cathedral, I shuffled up the flat steps, through the castle-sized wooden doors and into the merciful coolness of the church's foyer. I marveled at how the older Black ladies looked as cool and calm as the moment they joined the line hours ago.

Entering the Cathedral, I reached two fingers into the massive bird-bath shaped font of holy water in the rear alcove, dabbed water on my forehead and made the sign of the cross. My eyes were immediately drawn to a life-like statue, dressed in red and white vestments, in a large glass case off to the right side of the sanctuary, behind the last pew.

"Don't tell me," I muttered to myself, disgusted at the thought of a statue to Francis Cardinal Spellman, the Catholic Church's biggest cheerleader for the war in Vietnam, overseeing Robert Kennedy's wake. Edging closer to the glass case, I was relieved to see it was not Cardinal Spellman's likeness, but a wax figure of Pope Pius XII.

"Just as bad, in so many other ways," I said quietly.

The line of people in front of me abruptly turned the corner, and we began to move slowly up the center aisle of the Cathedral. I stood on my toes and craned my neck to get a glimpse of RFK's coffin, at the foot of the grey stone altar rail. I strained to see more up front, past the last row of four large pillars where the coffin was placed. I looked off to one side and then the other and saw huge wooden doors, three times the height of the guards standing by each one. The doors were topped by circles of stained glass, and each was surrounded by eight Saints, four sitting and four standing on pedestals, with names like St. Basil and St. Christopher, St. Gregory Nazianzen and St. Athanasius. On the pillars in front of the main altar, I noticed a large statue of St. Patrick, carved carefully in the stone, with a long flowing beard and rows of hair running down to his chest, wearing a cap that covered his head, garments tumbling down to his feet, and a glowering look aimed at any communicant who would dare to sin before the eyes of an angry God.

The line shifted just a bit and I could clearly see Robert Kennedy's coffin, surrounded by six-foot high silver candle holders, each with a flame flickering inside. Directly behind the coffin, standing erect, hands falling stiffly by his side, eyes staring straight ahead, was Jack Paar, the television talk show host, a close friend of the Kennedy family. Flash bulbs went off, and I shot an angry look at a few idiots with instamatic cameras who saw this as simply the latest tourist attraction in New York. I wanted the statue of St. Patrick to strike them down, or at least turn them to stone. I took a few steps forward and stopped. In front of the coffin, less than 10 feet away from me, stood a young boy not more than 14 years old. His facial muscles quivering, fighting back tears, his hands were clasped tightly in front of his body. It was Robert F. Kennedy, Jr., and the sight of RFK's son, so fragile and alone, overwhelmed me with grief. I wanted to jump out of line and hug this frail child and apologize for what had been done to his father.

I genuflected on one knee, under the stony glare of St. Patrick and the mournful eyes of St. Basil and St. Christopher and all the other saints looking down from the walls of the Cathedral, in the bright morning light filtering through the stained glass. Before the tomb of the man who inspired me to do good and the young son who was robbed of his father's warm smile and comforting embrace, I vowed to do what no one in my family had contemplated nor understood—to become, as Dr. King suggested, "dangerously unselfish" and dedicate my life to public service.

4 ▫ Breakout

"Forget about trying to get to Mario Cuomo," I overheard one of my brother's associates say to him. "He's unreachable."

That was precisely why I could not forget about Mario Cuomo. I was drawn by the power of Cuomo's intellect, integrity, compassion and persona as a bold contradiction to the stereotype of Italian-Americans as uneducated buffoons, coarse corner boys, or members of neighborhood gangs. Cuomo's vision and values were compelling to me, offering a clear pathway from my past; a chance to contribute to the greater world out there, and still retain my family's love. If Mario Cuomo could do it, faced with a set of different challenges—like not speaking English until he was eight years old—then so could I.

Years later, even John A. Gotti, Jr., writing with great emotion in a few passages of his book, *Shadow of My Father* (self-published, 2014, p. 232), understood the terror of being trapped by family history:

Death and jail had consumed many fellows. We were really selfish. Wives with no husbands present. They were the innocent sufferers for our guilt. With the increased media attention to mobsters, the children of men in The Life would be teased, ostracized.

Still more revealing was a conversation between Gotti, Jr, and his best friend John Ruggiero, recorded in the Federal Correctional Institution at Ray Brook, near Lake Placid, on October 5, 2003, (*Shadow of My Father*, pps. 358-359):

GOTTI: *We used to go with our fathers—our fathers never really spent time with us. When they did, they drove us by the Club (the Bergin Hunt & Fish Club), dropped us off at the Club and that was it. We were 10, 11, 12 years old in a club full of men. . . You're*

almost forced to emulate these people. OK, you're almost forced to em-
ulate them....there were some guys I genuinely loved; Danny, Danny
Wagons, Carmine Fatico, I loved these guys....but it just seems that
most of the people out there today, John, are real garbage pails.

RUGGIERO: *Yup.*

GOTTI: *John, if we are stupid enough to raise our children near*
this, then we deserve to die in jail. I'm sorry, but we do. My sugges-
tion, John, to salvage our children, you gotta move away. You gotta
move away, John. You gotta stay away from these people. You gotta
stay away from these people.

RUGGIERO: *I don't see how to get out of here. How to get*
away...You're smart.

GOTTI: *Yeah, I'm real smart...Smart? Smart would have been*
running away a long time ago. Smart...I got trapped. All my father
had in this world was me, and I was the only one who could go see
him, and he had me for the lawyers, running around for the lawyers,
and so on and so forth. I got trapped. I couldn't tell him, "Listen,
Dad, I don't want to live in New York. I want to leave. I want to
move to Carolina...I couldn't disappoint the guy. I had to stay....

I did not care who I disappointed. I knew I had to flee, to build a
new life and reject the easy seduction of accepting the old one. My
driving desire to get out overrode any concern about whether or not
my family's mob-related connections would be bad for Mario Cuomo's future, if I ever had the opportunity to work with him. They *were*
not me, I kept telling myself; Carmine Fatico, no matter how much
my brother and John Gotti, Jr. loved him, was not me; Pat Eboli, no
matter how debonair my mother and brother found him, was not me.
Even my brother Michael, as much as I worshipped him as a child and
still wanted to believe the best about him as an adult despite mounting
evidence to the contrary, was not me. I was the third son of a third son;
destined for special things. *I was my father's hope, his ambition, and the*
small slice of himself that he allowed to dream.

Mario Cuomo's rise and his passionate erudition pointed in another direction; I wanted to be just like him; no, I wanted to *be* Cuomo. Once I saw the escape route Cuomo clearly marked out, *I would not let anything*—mob-relatives through marriage, suspicions about my brother, risk of becoming estranged from my family, not even Mario Cuomo's political future—block my path.

In May, 1984, seven months before Andrew Cuomo hired me to work in his father's administration, I brushed past John Gotti, Sr. at my brother Michael's wedding to his second wife. In the year before Gotti rose to notoriety, I didn't know who he was, nor why he was fluttering around our "Uncle Charlie" Carmine Fatico and his brother Danny Fatico. The Fatico brothers were treated by my brother as guests of honor at the posh Huntington Country Club on Long Island. "Uncle Charlie" God-fathered Gotti into the Gambino crime family, and gave my brother a benevolent lift as well. They rushed to pull out Carmine Fatico's chair every time he squatted to sit, an honor not even accorded to my parents.

Less than a decade earlier, Michael ran up sizeable gambling debts and it was "Uncle Charlie" who picked my brother up and gave him some props, with payback parceled out over decades. My father was a penny-ante gambler for years, with his two-dollar wagers on the horses, and his two-bit bets on the "numbers." But playing for big money with big-time gamblers was always out of his league. It was out of Michael's league, too, and he needed Carmine Fatico's help—with long, layered strings attached—to haul him back onto his feet, and hustle him into a whole new world.

Without considering the consequences, Michael had already ventured into the Mob's vestibule four years earlier, asking the sainted Pat Eboli for help, and telling me about it with wide-eyed excitement. It was easy to be seduced by the elegant, quiet and strong manner of Pat Eboli; even Marlon Brando and Frances Ford Coppola were when making the first *Godfather* movie in 1971, enjoying dinner at the Eboli home in Fort Lee, New Jersey, with Pat, his wife Jean Lettieri, and brother-in-law Alfred Lettieri (Solozzo the

Turk), my mother's first cousins. It was another thing entirely to become enamored by a stumpy street-hood like Carmine Fatico. "Uncle Charlie" was the founder of the Bergin Hunt and Fish Club, in Ozone Park, Queens, the epicenter of "The Life," of the Gambino crime family as described by John Gotti, Jr., in his book *Shadow of my Father:*

> *I hung out more and more by the Club (Bergin Hunt & Fish Club). The camaraderie, the activity, all were very attractive. Maybe some 60 guys hanging out, cooking, drinking, playing cards, watching sports on television, breaking balls. It gave one a real sense of belonging.* (p. 71)

The gang was all there, but unlike "Uncle Charlie" or John Gotti, Sr., my brother was not born into it. He didn't join a local gang at 16 years old like Gotti, didn't drop out of high school, or pick on people for fun and profit. He was never a street punk, and he didn't like watching sports on television or "breaking balls." It was a way of life we knew about, but were consciously steered away from for fear of becoming "bums."

My mother's insistence on sending my brothers to St. Francis of Assisi parochial school and then fleeing Brooklyn for bucolic Babylon, was designed to move from a changing neighborhood, keep her children out of "The Life," and give us a better one. But after Michael stumbled in business a few times, and could not find his footing, he realized that, as the oldest son in a family without money, he had no safety net. He grew to resent our father, an uncomplicated man whose meager maintenance worker's salary barely supported us. If we faltered, there was moral support but not much else.

My brother grew to see Fatico's crew as shelter in a storm where he would not be judged for his failures, nor be faced with his own father's lack of ambition. He could pretend to be *somebody* here. Few guys in "The Life" had served in the military as my brother did, had a high-school diploma, or spent any time working in a legitimate, modern occupation like electronics. He was more accomplished and polished than all the others who worked with Carmine and Danny Fatico, much kinder, and far more debonair. With his small, gracefully shaped nose, his thick, dark hair and large, intense eyes, Michael bore a physical resemblance to Pat Eboli at the peak of the Genovese crime family's power, and my brother carried himself that way, even though "Uncle Charlie" clearly instructed him never to mention the Ebolis. This was, afterall, the *Gambino*'s crew, and only a few years earlier, Tommy Eboli was murdered by them because he failed to repay $4 million he had borrowed from Carlo Gambino to faciliate a move into the narcotics business.

My brother did not have to mention Pat Eboli; he channeled him with his understated manner, and was cautious to straddle the edge between our family's past and his own present, seeing this new chance provided by "Uncle Charlie" as his shot at redemption and riches. He convinced himself he was tough, even though he wasn't, and persuaded a few others along the way, who did not know him as well as we did. "The Life" to my brother Michael held the promise of restoring him to the respected role of oldest son, as the favored first born, and as the real head of our family capable of providing for everyone, and building the safety net none of us ever had. To my brother, what "Uncle Charlie" offered him was a lifeline; a path to break out of his losing streak by virtue of the longstanding family relationship. With no other opportunities in sight, and nothing to cushion his fall, my brother grabbed the rope, and used it to hold up the pants to a new personality which, like an out-of-date suit, was ill-fitting.

Michael's new relationship with Carmine Fatico mugged me during a visit with my brother on Long Island shortly after my son was born. He asked me to go for a ride with him. In a childhood filled with crises, Michael was always a steady anchor, able to calm roiling seas that threatened to swallow us. Growing up, his presence always made it seemed as if nothing could ever go wrong; he would know just what to do. He could fix anything, and always made me feel safe. I figured he was inviting me for a noon-time Sunday drive just to be back together and tell me something he didn't feel comfortable saying in front of our wives.

With my guard down, and feeling good to have a few minutes alone with my brother, Michael told me he had to make a "quick stop" at "Uncle Charlie's" home in West Islip, just a few miles from where my parents lived. He was using my affection for him to give him cover, and I was stunned into silence. We were greeted by the wild barking of two large German shepherd dogs the moment Michael knocked on the front door. Aunt Rose opened the inside door and smiled at us, while screaming at the dogs to be quiet.

"Michael! Stephen!" she shreiked. "Wait until I quiet these dogs down."

We heard a voice shout down from upstairs.

"Who is it, Rosie?" It was "Uncle Charlie".

"It's Margaret's boys, Michael and Stephen, Charlie." .

"Well keep those goddamn dogs quiet, and send them up," he hollered down the stairs to her.

Aunt Rose rolled her eyes at us and whispered: "What the hell does he think I'm trying to do?"

We walked upstairs into the Fatico's raised ranch house on Higbie Lane. "Uncle Charlie" was still in his bathrobe.

"Come on up, come on up," he waved to both of us. "I just got up a little while ago."

We walked upstairs and "Uncle Charlie" shook our hands.

"I had a big night last night," he said to my brother, placing his hand on Michael's shoulder and giving him wink.

Michael shot a sly grin at "Uncle Charlie," and his behavior changed abruptly. He was deferential, bordering on obsequious, reminding me of my father walking backwards out of the Douglas mansion in Belle Terre, holding his hat in his hand. He had slipped into the role of supplicant. Aunt Rose pulled me aside into the kitchen and asked to see pictures of my three-month-old son. Michael and "Uncle Charlie" settled around the massive Italian provincial dining room table.

"Rosie, where's the espresso?" "Uncle Charlie" barked, sounding like one of the German shepherds.

"Fuckin' pain in the ass," Rose whispered to me.

She got up from looking at the photos, picked up the silver *M'edaglia D'oro* pot of espresso from the stove, and poured it into fine, flowered demitasse cups for my brother and "Uncle Charlie." I helped her carry the small cups into the dining room and carefully observed my brother. He was sitting serenely, nodding his head "yes" at everything Carmine Fatico was saying. This was a ritual, with carefully rehearsed roles, with each actor reciting familiar lines. I was uncomfortable watching my big brother act like this, uncomfortable in Charlie Fatico's presence, uncomfortable with the sound of the German shepherds barking from behind a locked door downstairs. Dogs, especially big dogs, can smell fear, and I sensed that they wanted to get to me and tear me to shreds. I chatted with my aunt for a little while longer, and then asked to excuse myself to go next door and visit with her daughter, my cousin Sissy.

Later that afternoon, at my parents' house for dinner without my brother, I told my father of the odd scene I had witnessed between "Uncle Charlie" and Michael. I described the setting, barking dogs and all, hoping his sharply honed sense of humor and his dry disdain for "Uncle Charlie" would sanitize my suspicions. Instead, my father's festering anger exploded.

"He spends his Sundays visiting that bum and he doesn't have any time for me?" my father said, his fat face turning bright red.

I looked at my father, and he averted making eye contact. He was simultaneously furious with my brother and disgusted with his own failures, and did not want his youngest son to see how deeply he was wounded. Instantly, I regretted scratching open the scab, wanting to pull the words back from where they hung in the air, swallowing them. My father forcefully pushed himself away from the table, walked to the refrigerator and pulled out another bottle of beer. He opened it without saying another word, swilling it down to chase away the bitter taste in his mouth. Carmine Fatico's position of power gave my father few other options, and it pained me to watch him when he realized his own impotence and of how little consequence he was to his own children. His love for my mother was clear, and despite intermittent fits of rage when he would put his fist through a door, overturn a table, or scramble for a shotgun to defend his daughter's honor, he would eventually calm down, beaten, and do whatever my mother asked. He knew he was all bluster, and did not know how to make money, legally or otherwise. He was without ambition, content to be with his family, have a beer or whiskey, and play the ponies for a few bucks a week. His children were all the ambition he ever had.

"He's a good man who likes his beer," my Aunt Josephine said of my father in one of her more charitable moments. Of course, her unsweetened assessment was correct.

A big gamble for Al Villano was an exacta boxed: that was his style—a little money that might win him a lot. After he moved to California the year after my son was born, my father would ask me to bet the big races for him—the Derby, the Belmont, the Preakness. I'd go over to the local Off-Track-Betting parlor, sometimes by car, sometimes by bike, and bet for him, penciling in the little boxes on the OTB racing cards, feeling a connection to my father even though he was 3,000 miles away. I would wait on the bettor's line, looking around the room, searching for an old, familiar face—my father's full face, with his oversized glasses perched on his cheeks as he stared at the charts on the wall or scoured the racing form he carried, folded under his arm.

Each time I walked into OTB, I was sure I smelled my father, smelled his Old Spice shaving lotion through all the burnt hopes hanging in the air, like paying customers. I was sure I'd see him there, standing at the round, hi-top tables, staring at his racing form, still trying to make his ship come in. I didn't know how to bet a horse without my father telling me; how to play the right combinations for win and place or how to link a favorite with a long-shot to win a little something extra. Going to place a bet without him, I felt like a lost child, separated from my father by the crowd. Yet the longer I stayed in the seedy OTB parlors, standing next to guys in need of a shave and worn-out looking women with peroxide hair and raspy voices singing the sounds of too many cigarettes, the closer I felt to him, so I lingered as long as I could.

My brother Michael's "Sundays with 'Uncle Charlie'" seared my father like a hot poker on raw skin, and may have been the final push he needed to pick up his life of 62 years in New York, and move to California, taking my brother Vinnie up on an offer to leave the dreaded New York winters behind. If it was Carmine Fatico's money or power that attracted my brother's attention, my father knew he could never compete. So he simply poured himself another drink, swallowing his bitterness, until it exploded and he planned his own escape.

My father didn't share another drink with Carmine Fatico until my brother Michael's May, 1984, wedding where Gotti was also a guest. He and my mother had moved to Southern California seven years earlier, leaving me and Michael as the last members of our family living in New York. We were an odd couple, well aware that our lives were quickly moving in different directions, with dramatically opposite networks of colleagues, associates and friends. In an emergency, we were all we had. My love for my brother was primal, part of me, but I saw a seismic shift taking place in the plates of his personality, especially around "Uncle Charlie." I was no longer sure of what to say to him, or how close I wanted to get to his fault lines.

Yet, the earth moved on its own accord. With the rest of the family in Southern California, Michael surprised me with a phone call the night before my son's second birthday, telling me he was flying up to Albany with my niece and nephew for the birthday party the next day. I struggled not to show my surprise.

"Sure, Michael," I said. "We'd love to have you. I'll pick you up at the airport."

I hung up the phone and was overcome with curiosity. If he had such a big gambling debt a short time ago that he had to be bailed out by "Uncle Charlie," how did he now have the money to fly a family of three back and forth from Long Island to Albany for one day? Why was he coming? Did he miss our family in California as much as I did? Did the absence of his wife signal marital problems? Did he want to be immersed, at least for a day, in my normal life, a quiet, steady life which, in contrast to his, was not spinning out of control? When my brother arrived with his children, I was overwhelmed by his kindness and his desire to connect my son with his two cousins. He treated the 200-mile flight as matter-of-factly as if it were a two mile drive around the corner. He was my brother; this was a celebration of my son's birth, and he conveyed the warmth of how natural it was for them to be there. I doted on Michael's children for years, and he was giving them a chance to fuss over mine. The thought, the effort, their presence, all meant a great deal to me, and visibly moved my brother as well.

Two years later, my brother's father-in-law died of a heart attack in the driveway of his North Babylon home, and I flew down to attend the wake. Michael picked me up at the airport, bringing me to his home. After dinner, he asked my nephew to show me a book he bought him about the life of Lucky Luciano. The book itself did not necessarily mean anything, but read in the context of what was to come at the funeral parlor the next day, it spoke volumes. At the wake, my brother sat in the back of the chapel, while his wife was up front in the mourner's first row of seats.

One after another, a parade of Michael's friends and associates filed in to pay their respects. Many were dressed alike in expensive cashmere coats, dark designer suits and dark ties. I caught snippets of their conversations—tough guy talk, punctuated by four-letter words. A few times, I heard them drop the names of men the FBI alleged were mobsters on Long Island.

I was appalled by my brother's behavior, showing more concern for greeting his cronies in the back of the room than for his grieving wife who required comforting. That role, that tenderness, fell to my 13-year old nephew, forced to act like an adult well beyond his years. I wanted to grab my nephew and take him back to Albany with me to give him back his childhood. Even if I offered him a new life, he would not take it, I thought, watching this sweet kid gracefully move between his mother and father. He was as much in need of my brother's approval and love—and much more so since it was his father—than I was when I was thirteen.

Just then, there was a commotion out in the funeral home's foyer. Carmine Fatico arrived, and one of my brother's friends came running into the main room to tell him. Michael rushed up to "Uncle Charlie," took his coat, and welcomed him. His pals peeked at "Uncle Charlie" from around the edges, in awe that the Gambino family Capo came to pay his respects for a death in our family. My brother had turned an emotional moment for his wife and children into a show of force and power, and it made me ill. I greeted Carmine Fatico with a terse "Hello, 'Uncle Charlie,'" excused myself, and went to the restroom. When I emerged, I reminded my brother I had to catch a plane back to Albany. He summoned one of his friends, who told me he was happy to give me a lift to LaGuardia Airport. I kissed my sister-in-law and my niece and nephew goodbye, embraced my brother, and walked out of the funeral parlor.

Parked directly in front was a long, black limousine with my brother's friend sitting behind the steering wheel. I hesitated to get in, until his friend got out, greeted me, opening the back door. I thanked him, and we drove away.

All the way to LaGuardia, I chatted with the limo driver about the cold weather, and how I missed Long Island. I wanted to ask who he worked for, but was fearful of getting an answer I did not want to hear. When we arrived at the airport, I offered to pay, but the driver wouldn't hear of it, nor would he accept a generous tip.

"This is a favor to your brother," he said. "I'm honored to be able to do it."

On the flight back upstate, I wondered who my brother was to command such favors? Why was he chatting up those wise guys at his father-in-law's funeral? Why did they fawn all over him? Why was "Uncle Charlie's" arrival such a big production? I stared out of the small, round airplane window and shook my head. My brother

Michael and I; randomly thrown together by births and deaths; 200 miles between us, and too many differences to count. Yet, despite my nagging concerns about my brother's strange new life, my longing to return home grew stronger each time I went back to Long Island and drove by the waters of Babylon. I wanted to give our only child the opportunity to grow up knowing his cousins on both sides of the family, and to experience a big slice of my life.

Within a year's time, I began studies at Hofstra University School of Law, moving closer to a public life and the law, while my brother was moving further from it. Our lives, bending toward the same sources of emotional nourishment, became intertwined like roots from neighboring trees. Law school was a financial hemorrhage for me and my small family. Living on Carol's teacher's salary, we rented a run-down house with an attic room as tiny as Raskolnikov's where I read case law at night. The last Christmas of my studies approached, and I descended into a depression over our lack of money, dearth of job prospects as an older law student, and our inability to afford a trip to California to spend the holiday with my parents. We were preparing for a modest Christmas Eve celebration at home when there was a knock on the kitchen door. My brother Michael appeared, carrying two big brown supermarket bags, with the tops of each folded closed.

"Michael…what…?" I said, surprised to see him, having avoided calling him for months.

"I thought you might like these," he said, pulling two large, live lobsters out of each bag. "I got them from a friend of mine who owns a restaurant."

I looked at the lobsters and wondered which friend he was talking about; if these lobsters had "fallen off a truck," and had, somehow, gotten up and climbed into those brown paper bags. I looked at my brother's face, then at the lobsters again, and suddenly, didn't care how he got them. He had tapped into my loneliness, and his smile told me I could not refuse this thoughtful gift he carried to us on Christmas Eve, a holiday with deep meaning and memories for both of us. He stayed a short while, showed us how to cook the crustaceans, and was off to keep his other appointments. My brother's act of kindness lifted me out of my melancholy, foreshadowing more such actions to come. I wanted to separate his act of giving from the gift; his instinct for generosity,from his need for gaining acceptance. I loved my brother for who he was, for the gentility in his eyes, not for whether or not he would pick up the check for dinner, which he did often, or deliver lobsters to our door. Somewhere along the way, something got lost, and he translated love as loot, and money and material goods as the admission price for admiration. Yet, his desire to take care of everyone he loved was genuine.

Graduating from law school that summer at 34 years old, deeply in debt, with an eight-year old son and the Bar Exam six months away, prospects for my immediate employment were dim. Well-educated, well-meaning, and well-connected friends wished me luck, and sent me on my way, certain I would land something.

I masked my desperation to everyone but my brother, who, having experienced it daily, could smell it a mile away. He knew I studied Communications Law and had an article published in the *Federal Communications Law Journal*. He told me about a friend of his who ran a small cable company, interested in exploring the budding technology of cellular telephones. He thought they might have an opening for someone who knew about FCC regulations. I kept away from my brother for weeks, afraid to respond to his offer and convinced that if I kept looking for even entry-level legal work, something would develop. Nothing did.

Michael followed up with his offer, and I agreed to meet him and several principals of the company for dinner at Guilio Cesare, a posh, dimly-lit Nassau County Italian restaurant. I was welcomed by meticulously-dressed waiters speaking broken English and Italian, and wanted to turn around and run, but had no place to run to. Michael introduced me to everyone around the table, and his gentle manner and quiet voice calmed me, as they usually did. Sensitive to my discomfort, he watched me scrutinize the waiters scurrying around to serve us, looking for the tiniest hint that they were treating us with any more deference than the other customers.

After dinner, we drove a short distance in the company president's Cadillac to the parking lot where my Plymouth Horizon was parked. There, in the darkened back seat of a late model Caddy, my brother and one his friend's offered me my first paying job out of law school. There was a long silence. My head pounding, a voice inside me was screaming to jump out of the Cadillac's back seat and run as fast and as far away from my brother as I could.

Politely, I told my brother that I wanted to think about the offer, and would come in to get a tour of the business during the week. For days, I agonized over whether to get involved with anything my brother touched. Law school had been a way out for me, a chance to completely break away from my past and pursue my dream of public service. The last thing I wanted to be was a lawyer who worked for a Mobbed-up company, if that's what this was. I decided I would thank my brother for his generosity and then leave; this was much more than four lobsters on Christmas Eve.

Entering the company's offices, I was surprised by its professionalism and the rows of high-tech equipment. I was led down a long hallway to an office with finely polished wood parquet floors where my brother sat at the desk. He embraced me, asking me to sit on a grey velour couch, and began calmly explaining the company's work and mission. I listened carefully, eyes wide open, nodding my head, hesitating. Get out, a voice inside my head was saying; get out.

"Can I see the company's books, Michael?" I asked.

Surprised at my own directness, I wondered if I was that blunt because I wanted him to get insulted and defensive and call me an ingrate. Maybe, I wanted him to throw me out of the office so I wouldn't have to get up and leave on my own, or to save me from myself. Without hesitation, my brother got up and went into the bookkeeper's office, bringing back the latest information about the company's financial status, which I inspected carefully. Michael again sought to quell my fears.

"Everything is legit, Stephen," he said, reassuring me that the part-ners were all experts in the fields of computers, transmission, cable and telephone installations. He kept talking to me in even, measured tones, telling me that I would be only doing FCC research, traveling to Washington, DC, and handling the company's applications for cel-lular telephone licenses. He was, once again, the older brother I idol-ized, not the stranger who stoked my suspicions. His mild, fatherly manner mesmerized me, put me at ease. How could I insult him? I told him I would take the job.

The office with the oak parquet floors became mine and Michael's. My brother would stop by occasionally to make some phone calls while I read through volumes of FCC cellular regulations. I liked the closeness to him, feeling a cautious reconnection to my family that I had consciously pushed away for years for fear of getting suffocated. Around me, my brother was elegant and kind, a patient instructor on technical engineering issues, his area of expertise. There was nothing about him that reminded me of the wise-guy way he behaved at his father-in-law's funeral, or in front of Carmine Fatico. But, over the next few months, I noticed that Michael was becoming increasingly nervous. During one of those less laid-back visits he kept trying to reach his attorney, Mike Rosen, by phone.

"I have a tax problem," he said, covering the receiver with one hand to speak with me. "I've got to reach my attorney to get his advice."

I nodded and immersed myself in the FCC regulations I was read-ing, making it clear to my brother that I did not want to know any-thing more about his tax problems.

A few days later, I got to the office before 9:00 am, unlocked the door, and found Michael seated behind the desk. Spread out in front of him, where I frequently ate my lunch while pouring through piles of legal regulations and documents, were stacks of cash in different sized piles and denominations. He looked up at me in a frenzy, frantic and startled; his eyes narrowed, possessed by counting out the money, again and again. I had interrupted the intensity of his cash tally.

"Could you excuse me for a few minutes, Stephen?" he asked, looking back down at the money.

"Sure, Michael," I said, backing out of the office.

I walked downstairs to the coffee shop in the basement of the building, wondering what my brother was doing with all that cash, and how he had gotten it. How much of it was his? Why was he counting it so carefully, over and over again? What could explain his frenzied nervousness? I ordered a cup of coffee, sat down at a small table in the back of the café, and thought of all those questions. I knew I could never ask him for answers.

Michael's calm, reassuring manner was gone, and I was angry at myself for being so desperate to accept his generosity of a job. Within weeks, rumors were rampant that the cable company was running out of money. Having just moved into a modest raised ranch in East Northport that we purchased, I panicked when a co-worker said that our next payday might be payless. How would I pay my mortgage? My law school debt? We had nothing in the bank, little to fall back on, and the sound of chaos, so familiar to me in childhood, was once again pounding in my ears. Just before 5:00 pm on payday, the company's vice-president for finance announced we would receive our checks that week, but he could not be sure about the future. Then, he handed out our paychecks.

I took my check and raced to the bank upon which the company checks were drawn. I knew that if there were scarce funds in the company's payroll account, a check from one bank to another would never clear. I would run to the originating bank and ask for my pay in cash. I handed my check to the teller, and watched as she counted out the stack of bills in a neat pile right in front of me, on the other side of the bank window, with only a few metal vertical bars separating us. She was about to hand my cash to me when she looked carefully at the company's name on the check. She told me to wait one moment, and took the company check over to her supervisor at the rear of the bank to get his approval.

She left the money, *my money* that I earned over the past two weeks, just inside the window, within my reach. I stood there, staring at the cash, convinced that the teller would come back and tell me that the company was broke, that the bank could not cash my check. Everything in the bank started spinning; my mind thinking too much, too fast, frenetically, of how I could get money, any money to pay my mortgage and take care of my son. I looked back and forth, first at the money, then at the teller talking to her supervisor in the back of the bank. Back and forth, my head was turning; the money, the teller, the boss, the black metal bars. *My money.* I saw her locked in conversation with her boss, her back turned toward me and measured how far I would have to reach in to get the cash.

"Take it, it's yours, you earned it; you need it; you have bills to pay," I told myself.

I looked at the cash again, so close to me, and barely stopped my hand from taking the money and running out of the bank. The teller had my check with my name and address on it. The police would have an easy time tracking me down. The teller came back to the bank window smiling. She apologized for the delay and handed me my pay, though the black metal vertical bars which came frighteningly close to taking on a whole different meaning for me. I thanked the teller for the cash, and began counting it out in small piles right in front of her.

I watched my fingers stacking the money, *my money*, and saw my brother counting the piles of money, *his money*, in our office, a few short weeks ago; I felt as desperate and frantic as he was that day. I understood why he swallowed any pride he had left and asked "Uncle Charlie" to bail him out, and why he sat and sipped espresso with him, Sunday after Sunday, nodding his head in tune to Carmine Fatico's seductive song, hating himself the whole time, until he became numb to everything and everyone, including the hero he once was.

Just a few months after I came within a razor's edge of slicing my life open by stealing my own pay, Mario Cuomo vaulted to national celebrity status by delivering his electrifying keynote speech at the Democratic National Convention in San Francisco. I was buried in debt the night of Cuomo's speech, with two advanced degrees, a nine-year-old son, and a mortgage. My brother's attempts to help ended badly, leaving me battered and floundering. I kicked around in a few temporary jobs, including working as a process-server for a lawyer friend, where I chased down angry spouses with divorce papers and stood outside tattered screen-doors seeking to serve writs of habeas corpus in tense, child custody battles. That summer, I retreated to the quiet of a community college campus, teaching classes in Business Law. Cuomo's keynote address was a personal wake-up jolt, a call to public service I hadn't felt since RFK's funeral. Only this time, the message was coming from an intelligent Italian-American public official of impeccable integrity who showed we weren't all greaseballs, or guineas, or Mobsters. I listened to Cuomo speak and thought back to a conversation I eavesdropped on between my brother and a few of his cronies discussing which New York politicians they could "get to," and overheard them emphatically rule out Cuomo as "unreachable." It made me like Mario Cuomo even more.

Cuomo was speaking directly to me that night, and his words and emotions overshadowed any concerns I had about whatever Mob connections existed in my family and what they might mean to me, or him. I shut the television off after the speech, sat down at my desk, and wrote Mario Cuomo a letter on a warm summer's night in 1984:

Dear Governor Cuomo:

Having just finished reading your new book (Diaries of Mario M. Cuomo: The Campaign for Governor Random House, 1984) and the complete text of your keynote speech, I felt compelled to write. Your words and deeds have served as a great inspiration during a particularly difficult period in my life. The reference in your speech to young families who can scarcely afford a mortgage is poignant and very real to me.

I believe that my personal testimony to unemployment and how it ravages those with ample professional skills, as well as those without, can serve a useful purpose for the benefit of others. I would very much like to join your adminis-

tration during this period of your reorganization and put my professional skills and personal experience to work on behalf of the "family" of New York State. Having lived that message, I believe I can articulate it well...

This has not been an easy letter to write. Yet, I believe that if the lessons I have learned from this extremely difficult period in my life can be used to benefit others, then good will have come out of adversity.

Sincerely,

Stephen Villano

I mailed the letter the following morning, with no expectation of any response. My correspondence with Mario Cuomo was a longshot, like my father betting an Exacta boxed. I had nothing to lose; all he could say was "no," or nothing at all. If that happened, I would be just where I was, on a bucolic campus as far from my brother and his friends as I could get.

One week later, I received a letter on State of New York Executive Chamber stationary, with one name listed as the inside address: "Mario M. Cuomo, Governor." I rubbed my thumb over the raised seal of the State of New York at the top of the page, to prove to myself that the letter was authentic. My eyes darted down to the bottom of the letter, to a bold black signature by Mario Cuomo. Then, I read it:

Dear Mr. Villano:

Your letter describing how unemployment "ravages those with professional skills as well as those without" is as eloquent as your resume and published work are impressive.

I am sending your application to my Appointments Office. I don't know if there is any position appropriate to your skills right now. I do know that if we don't find something quickly, a man with your talent and credentials will not be available long.

Thank you for the kind words about the "Diaries" and my Keynote Speech. I am glad you established contact.

Sincerely,

Mario M. Cuomo (signature)

I read and re-read one simple sentence:"I do know that if we don't find something quickly, a man with your talent and credentials will not be available long."

I was 35 years old, struggling to find work with a law degree, and my carefully calibrated professional life —so different from the constant chaos of my family—was falling apart. Doubts about my "talent and credentials" drove me toward darkness, peering into the abyss that swallowed my brother Michael. Mario Cuomo's words, like Carmine Fatico's benevolence to my brother during his moment of desperation, were an elixir to me. Here was a different kind of political figure: he read, he wrote; he knew what it was to bleed. My long-shot letter launched the chain of events which landed me in Albany, just outside the Governor's Office, waiting to be called for an interview for a job within the Cuomo administration.

I arrived at the Governor's office ahead of my scheduled interview, and took a seat in the Appointments Office, outside the conference room where the job interviews for State Ombudsman positions were being conducted. Dressed in a ten-year-old, wide-lapelled, three-piece grey pin-striped wool suit, I sat quietly, pretending to read the *New York Times*, while other job applicants arrived. We politely greeted each other, making small talk. They were each so raw and eager—some, fresh out of college. I recognized the ravenous look of my young competitors. They would jump off Albany's Alfred E. Smith Building to get the job. They looked at me—calm, congenial with flecks of grey in my hair—as if I were a wide tie, waiting to come back into style.

At 35 years old, I was the age of the other candidates when I bought the suit I was still wearing. I looked at my perfectly creased costume, tugged at my button-downed vest and sat straight up. I took off my eyeglasses, to appear younger, neatly folded them, and tucked them away into my inside jacket pocket. My game was on, focus intense—even if everything in the distance appeared as a blur.

If the Cuomos were looking for youth, I'd give them more sassiness than all the younger candidates combined. I carried myself with the relaxed liberation of having nothing to lose, coming close to losing everything a few times during the past year.

Now, I sat steps away from Mario Cuomo's office in the State Capitol, marveling at the bustle in and out of the Governor's Office. I was transfixed, watching a film unfold in front of my eyes, only it was someone else's life up on the screen, not mine, and I was enjoying the show. The day was particularly momentous for the young Cuomo administration, and not because it was the 43rd anniversary of Pearl Harbor. New York's Lt. Governor Alfred DelBello had just announced his resignation to take a higher-paying private sector job.

The State Capital was humming with sotto voce speculation that DelBello was leaving his elected office because the former Westchester County Executive, who had supported Cuomo's Democratic Primary opponent New York City Mayor Ed Koch in 1982, was frozen out of all decisions during his first two years as Lt. Governor. I paid scant attention to the political scuttlebutt. What mattered most to me was that DelBello's departure brought Andrew Cuomo, his father's most trusted adviser, up to the Capital to put the best public face on the Lt. Governor's resignation and respond to the administration's latest emergency. Furthest from my mind was any thought I would be hired by Andrew Cuomo that day; I was simply dazed to be there.

Andrew celebrated his 27th birthday the day before, and was working as an Assistant DA in the office of Manhattan District Attorney, Robert Morgenthau. In a little over two years, Andrew Cuomo had proven himself to be a superb political operative and strategist. Not only had he engineered his father's upset victory over heavily-favored Ed Koch in the Democratic State Primary for governor in 1982, but he had managed his father's general election win over wealthy Republican candidate and heir to the Rite-Aid pharmaceutical fortune, Lew Lehrman, who outspent Mario Cuomo by more than two to one. No delicate issue or important decision was handled without Andrew Cuomo's involvement.

Six months earlier, Andrew served his family in a far different, far more personal way. His maternal grandfather, Charles Raffa, then eighty years old, was brutally beaten on May 22, 1984, outside of a vacant commercial property he owned in a run-down neighborhood of East New York, Brooklyn. With Mario Cuomo in Albany, his son sped to the scene to find his grandfather badly bloodied with part of his scalp hanging over his eyes. Charles Raffa had been robbed and left for dead; his crippling injuries contributed to his death four years later.

The younger Cuomo's immediate presence at his grandfather's side at the hospital not only comforted his family during a time of great stress, but was a powerful counterpoint to the cascade of vicious and false rumors surrounding Raffa which began spreading immediately. One lie being circulated, easily disproven, had Mario Cuomo at the scene of the crime trying to cover things up, despite the fact that the Governor was in Albany. The Cuomos spent months, and then years, exposing a series of sinister scenarios, which ranged from an arson attempt gone bad (despite the building being uninsured and full of valuable refrigeration equipment, which would have resulted in a huge, uncompensated loss to the Raffa family) to attempts by the Cuomos to clean the NYPD computers of any references to the crime or to Charlie Raffa.

The most pernicious and persistent rumor of all was that the father of Matilda Raffa Cuomo was somehow mixed up with the Mob, and his beating was the result of a Mob deal gone wrong. Dozens of investigations by police, private investigators, and media outlets, found no truth behind any of the allegations.

Andrew Cuomo handled all of these crises—personal and political—evenly and with an unflappable confidence in the facts. His presence in Albany on the day of my interview was as surprising to me as it would turn out to be serendipitous. I closed my eyes thinking of the improbability of everything that was happening, when a young secretary called out my name.

"Mr. Villano?" she said.

"Yes," I said, coming to attention and nodding my head. She asked me to follow her.

She escorted me into a small office, introducing me to two of the Governor's young aides, John Iaccio and Gary Eisenman. Eisenman, a tall man who resembled a young Ben Affleck, was Andrew Cuomo's law school classmate. He shook my hand and we all sat down and talked. They asked me questions about myself, about politics, about what I thought of Mario Cuomo. We got along well, and the interview ended with Eisenman pumping my hand to assure me that they would "definitely" be in touch.

Thanking them, I left the room, convinced that my chances for being hired by such a young 20-something staff, over younger candidates, were slim. I had several hours to pass until my return flight home, and wandered leisurely around the Capitol's second floor, determined to maximize my trip to the Capitol Building, even if nothing else came of it. I stopped to look at a political cartooning exhibit in an open area no more than a few hundred yards from the office where Governor Mario Cuomo sat, behind closed doors. I was inside Albany's aorta, steps away from Cuomo, and was savoring how odd it all was. Suddenly, I heard hard-soled shoes clicking on the marble floors of the cavernous hallway, looked up, and saw Al Gordon, an aide to the Governor, who had a neatly-trimmed black beard and an undertaker's demeanor, coming towards me.

"Oh, good. We thought you might be here," Gordon said, catching his breath. "We want you to come for a follow-up interview right now—everyone we need is here."

Gordon hurried me back down the long Capitol corridor, past portraits of former Governors Carey, Rockefeller and Harriman, and into the Governor's suite of offices. We entered a huge, ornate conference room, which had, at its' center, a long, thick, wooden conference table. An empty chair was at the end of the table, closest to me. At the opposite end sat 12 people, all men, wearing dark suits and dour looks. Since I had taken my eyeglasses off earlier to appear more youthful, each face at the far end of the table was fuzzy, indistinguishable from the next. Unable to see much, and convinced

I was the oldest person in the room, my natural pre-performance nervousness disappeared. All of the circumstances were preposterous to me, incomprehensible. Minutes before I was looking at political cartoons, preparing to head back to my everyday existence teaching business law at a community college. Compared to the other candidates, I was ancient and blind. They'd never hire me, so I might as well have fun. I tried to break the ice.

"Well, if you'd like to know whether I would accept the opening you now have for Lt. Governor, the answer is 'yes,'" I joked.

No one laughed. This could be a long session, I thought, startled by my own ballsiness at mentioning such a touchy subject that day. A big-boned guy with a large head, and dark, curly hair seated at the center of the group broke the silence.

"We'll keep that in mind," he said, smiling.

I strained to see who the comment came from, but without my eyeglasses everyone's eyes, noses and mouths looked like off-centered etchings, enhancing the feeling that I was inside a Dali painting. The big guy with the dark, curly hair began asking questions, starting with why I wanted to work for Mario Cuomo. When I answered that the Governor's keynote address and his book touched me deeply, and that we shared the same belief of public service as a noble calling, the big guy nodded approvingly. The rest of the room became silent. Everyone waited for the big guy to ask another question. All eyes were riveted on him.

"Suppose you were a Regional Rep," the big guy said, beginning the first of several hypothetical questions. "Suppose the Governor was due to land by helicopter in your region in a few minutes. A big story affecting the Governor has just broken. How are you going to warn him?"

Oh, come on, I thought to myself. This is supposed to be a tough question? This is the big time?

"If I couldn't reach him aboard the helicopter, "I answered, "I'd make damn sure I was the first one to reach him as soon as he landed."

The big guy with the dark, curly hair nodded approvingly. Other heads around the table nodded as if on cue, resembling a collection of bobble-head dolls that sit on the rear window shelves of cars, swaying up and down as the car speeds along. All of the bobble-heads became still. They waited for the big guy to move his lips again.

"Suppose," the big guy said, "the Governor kept getting criticized by a weekly newspaper editor in your region. What would you do?"

Is this guy for *real*? This was Journalism 101; the kind of thing I did during my years of work as a labor journalist for the teachers' unions. I decided that for my own entertainment, I needed to loosen things up a bit.

"I'd schmooze the guy to death," I said, eliciting muffled laughter from a few people around the table. "I'd call him so frequently, take him out to lunch, give him so much information about Mario Cuomo that he'd print good stuff just to have me stop!"

The big guy with the dark, curly hair loved it. He laughed and the rest of the room laughed with him. For the next hour, he asked questions, I answered, and heads around the table bobbed in agreement. I was enjoying myself; enjoying being myself. The big guy paused and lobbed one final question at me.

"Stephen, what do you see yourself doing in 10 years?" he asked.

"Oy, ten years…" I said. "My son will be 18 by then. If I have survived through that I'll consider that an accomplishment."

The big guy with dark, curly hair laughed and so did everyone else around the conference table. I was on a roll, so I added a postscript.

"In 10 years, I'd like to still be in public service, as I'm sure everyone else in this room would," I said with a wry smile. The big guy smiled and nodded.

"Thank you, Stephen," he said. "We'll be in touch with you soon."

I thanked everyone around the table and got up to leave. John Marino, Deputy Secretary of State in charge of the Regional Representative Program, walked over to me. A terse-talking Italian political operative from the Bronx, Marino—who would later become Chairman of the New York State Democratic Party—headed the Governor's "Ombudsman" program. It was a field organizing operation started when Mario Cuomo was NY Secretary of State under his predecessor, Hugh Carey.

"Andrew liked you," he said, shaking my hand.

"Andrew who?" I said, knowing well who the Andrew of the Cuomo administration was, but wanting to appear cool and unimpressed.

"Andrew Cuomo," Marino said, looking at me with a smirk, and quickly sizing up my smart-alec game. "He was the guy asking you all the questions."

"Oh," I said, "I was wondering who that big guy was."

Marino congratulated me again, and told me they'd be in touch. I put on my heavy winter coat, headed down one of the Capitol's large, stone staircases to the main floor, and pulled the thick, fake black fur collar of my coat up around my neck. I braced myself for the freezing Albany air, anticipated that the split second it stung my skin, I'd be snapped out of my dream.

5 □ Sunlight

The sun was at my back when I headed up to Albany on an early morning Amtrak train to attend Governor Mario M. Cuomo's State of the State message in January, 1985. Exhilarated and uneasy by my dramatic change of luck, I stared out the window of the train traveling to Albany, my eyes following the ice chunks on the Hudson River glistening in the morning sun, randomly thrown against each other, reminding me of how my brother Michael and I were tossed together and asunder in under a few years.

As a newly hired Regional Representative, I was joining my colleagues from around the State to hear the governor's speech in person, followed by a reception at the Executive Mansion to meet Mario Cuomo and New York's First Lady, Matilda Cuomo. It was complete immersion in Cuomo culture, getting inspired by the Governor's calls to action on policy initiatives and for the "Cuomo Team" to gear up for the year ahead. Scheduled to start work in New York City the following day, the opportunity to meet the Cuomo family was an unexpected gift.

There was a chill coming in from the cold outside the ice-glazed train windows, as well as from knowing I had come so close to falling into freezing waters of my own more than a few times. I shivered, wrapping my heavy winter coat tightly around my body, trying to nestle down deeper into its soft, plush collar, to hold back the cold. So easy to slip; to slide down into a dark, desperate place with the slightest shift of weight—my brother sharing espresso on Sundays with Carmine Fatico; me, heading to Albany to meet Mario Cuomo. I closed my eyes tightly to shut out the past, expecting the conductor to come up from behind, shake me by the shoulder, and escort me off the train because I didn't have the right fare.

The State Assembly Chamber, where New York governors delivered their annual State of the State messages to the assembled legislators, guests, and the public, was a familiar place to me. Fifteen years earlier, as a college intern working for a Democratic Assembly member from Brooklyn, I carried messages onto the chamber floor. During breaks, I sat in chairs along the back wall, listening to desultory floor debate and observing the show. I marveled at how a suit and tie, and a look about you as if you knew what you were doing, could gain a person access to just about anywhere. Now, as new Cuomo staff members, we were ushered to the same seats along the back wall of the Chamber where I used to daydream. I was safe from my brother in the secure cocoon of the State Capitol, free from my past and my parents in California.

After Cuomo's speech, staff members were escorted out of the Capitol Building to the Executive Mansion a fewv blocks away on Elk Street. The Mansion, the official residence of the incumbent Governor of New York State and family, was an eclectic mix of architecture, built during the mid-19th Century. We approached the front portico where a staff member held a clipboard containing the official guest list. I held my breath and smiled. The State's Bureau of Criminal Investigations (BCI) performed background checks on all new hires. Surely, alarm bells sounded when they looked up the name "Villano." Fortunately, no asterisk appeared near my name on the guest list; there was no notation about either my brother or "Uncle Charlie." We were welcomed inside, out of the cold, past a sweeping staircase, and into a large reception room where the Governor and Mrs. Cuomo were warmly greeting everyone on a receiving line. I waited my turn to shake the governor's hand and when I did, he grabbed it firmly.

"Steve," Mario Cuomo said, "I've heard good things about you. We're glad to have you with us."

I thanked the governor and moved down the receiving line, dazed by what he said, and how convincingly he said it.

"Good things about me? From whom?" I thought.

John Marino spotted me across the room and gave me his trademark tight smile. I shook his hand. Then, it dawned on me. The last time I saw Marino was on the day I was hired when he told me "Andrew liked you." It was Andrew. Of course—the big guy with the dark, curly hair: Andrew Cuomo. *That's* who the Governor heard good things from: *Andrew*. One good word, one nod of the head from Andrew Cuomo, age 27, and my life was changed. Less than a year earlier, I was so desperate I came close to stealing a pile of my own pay. Just six months before, I was reading Mario Cuomo's diaries in a lop-sided luncheonette on Long Island, watching him deliver his keynote address on television and worrying how I was going to pay my mortgage. Now, Mario Cuomo, the most respected Italian-American public official in the nation, was telling me he heard good things about me, and his son, Andrew—*the* Andrew— was my advocate. I stepped back, away from the crowd surrounding the Governor and Mrs. Cuomo. I needed to take a deep breath and settle myself down. I looked around the festively decorated Executive Mansion and closed my eyes. This was the longest running daydream I ever experienced, and I was beginning to believe it would never end.

On my second day of working for Mario Cuomo, my 36th birthday, I was promoted.

"VILLANO!" John Marino shouted from his office at 270 Broadway. "Come in here!"

My heart began beating hard. They found out about my brother. The BCI report finally found my family's connections to both the Genovese *and* Gambino crime families. I had done little more since beginning my tenure as a public servant than fill out health and pension forms, so what else could it possibly be? They dug up my skeletons. My heart, pumping hard, leapt from my chest up to my throat. I walked into Marino's office and sat down, expecting the worst. I could not read his face for any hint of trouble. He was masterful at masking emotions.

"Get your coat and go over to the Governor's Office at the World Trade Center," Marino said in a deadpan voice. "Marty Steadman wants to see you."

"Why?" I asked, perplexed.

Is this how they did it? They brought you over to the Governor's Office to have the State Police give you the bad news?

"He wants to talk to you about a job in the Governor's Press Office," Marino said.

"What?" I said, stunned. Quickly, I hid my incredulity. Better to act pleasantly surprised than shocked that I wasn't being found guilty by family association, and booted from a new job.

"What...what for?" I asked. "I just started here."

"They have an opening they want to fill right away and he wants to talk to you about it," Marino said.

He looked at me as I just sat there, not moving. Numb.

"So what are you waiting for, dummy? Go. Get out of here," Marino said, showing a slight grin.

I raised my eyebrows, shaking my head in disbelief. This was not my life.

"Oh. One more thing," Marino said. He held a long pause. "Happy birthday."

I walked the few blocks downtown to World Trade Center Tower 2, and took two banks of elevators up to the 57th floor, where the Governor's Office was located. Entering through inch-thick glass doors, with the seal of the State of New York emblazoned on them in gold decal, I introduced myself to the State trooper seated at the reception desk, and sat on a long couch waiting for Marty Steadman to finish with a meeting. Steadman, a seasoned reporter who worked for both newspapers and television, was Mario Cuomo's new Press Secretary. Steadman succeeded Tim Russert in late 1984, after Russert went to NBC News to head the network's Washington Bureau. Now in his 50's, Steadman ran for Congress in 1966 in a heavily Republican District in Nassau County, Long Island. He lost the election but campaigned with Robert F. Kennedy, then a U.S.

Senator from New York. The tragic events he lived and reported on over a 16-year career in journalism hadn't dampened his idealism. We instantly hit if off.

"I, eh, I looked over your resume and I, eh, I like what I see," Steadman said. He spoke in a clipped, choppy Bronx Irish accent that also had a Kennedy-esque cadence. "You've, eh, you've got good experience, you can write, and I, eh, think you'd fit in nicely with my team here."

We chatted briefly about my work as a Sports Correspondent for the long-defunct *Suffolk Sun* daily newspaper and his for the *Journal American*, a crusading paper with a superb Sports Section that my father brought home from the city each night.

"Between the two of us," Steadman said, smiling, "we, eh, probably closed down more papers than there are still in business in New York."

He told me to sit tight for a few weeks since a position was opening up he wanted me to fill. I liked everything about Marty Steadman: his sincere, care-worn eyes and forthright open face, and his experience as a street-toughened reporter for a newspaper my father and I loved. We shook hands.

"I'm, eh, looking forward to working together," Steadman said, looking me straight in the eyes.

So was I, once my head stopped spinning. Andrew Cuomo made it clear to Steadman he wanted me to move quickly into the Governor's New York City Press Office. It was Andrew—not any highly-paid media consultant—who conceived of an internal News Bureau concept that would communicate on the administration's behalf directly with hundreds of community-based newspapers and radio stations across New York State. He was gearing up to run his father's re-election campaign in 1986, and I was Andrew's choice to implement his in-house News Bureau idea.

In a 9-page, single-spaced, confidential memo drafted "To: Governor, From: Andrew," the younger Cuomo documented the administration's failures in dealing with the press during its first two years in office. His evaluation of the shortcomings of Tim Russert's tenure as Cuomo's first Press Secretary, without once mentioning Russert's name, was damning and spoke volumes about Andrew's approach: he understood the importance of style and personality in politics, but was consumed with making things work every single day, down to the most granular level. He took nothing for granted, and trusted no one to do what he or she said they would until it was actually done. Andrew was roughest in assessing what he saw as the Administration's deficiencies in the electronic media operation—a powerful irony since Russert had put it together, then left after less than two years to work for one of the nation's major electronic media outlets, NBC News. In all caps, Andrew Cuomo wrote:

If there is one major flaw in our operations over the last two years, it is that we do not give electronic media the attention it deserves…Electronic media is more important than print for the following reasons: a.) it reaches far more people; b.)people remember visuals better than the written word or audio, and we control visuals better than commentary; and, c.) while the tape of a speech or appearance can be cut or edited, the final product is still you talking directly to the people (at least more directly than in a newspaper article.)

What made the 27-year-old Cuomo's media analysis especially notable was his attention to the most microscopic requirements of a good media operation, his analysis of what a "press operation" in government should be, and a vision of how much more it could be. Andrew Cuomo was relentless in his follow-up with every aspect of the State bureaucracy, and so for many who worked in the administration, the most feared words were: "Andrew Cuomo's on the line." His name became synonymous with fierce accountability in all matters pertaining to his father's administration. No one knew Mario Cuomo better, or what his exacting standards were, than Andrew. One good word from the Governor's son could elevate your standing in the eyes of Mario Cuomo; a few critical words could derail a career. Writing years later in his biography *All Things Possible: Setbacks and Success in Politics and Life* (Harper Collins, 2014), Andrew

Cuomo revealed how deep the desires to be with and please his father were:

I *learned early that if I wanted to spend time with my father I had to tag along. Sometimes I'd sit in the library at his law firm in Brooklyn, doing my homework or trying to decode one of the books that lined the walls, unable to resist rubbing my fingers along the embossed leather bindings...* (p. 15)

Intuitively he understood at an early age the importance of the work his father was engaged in:

Today my father talks about how much he regrets the time work took him away from our family. If he could redo those years, he says, he'd strike a better balance. At that time, the absence was hard. Much responsibility fell to me as the "man" of the house, and his absence when other fathers were present at Boy Scouts and little league was palpable. But I saw hard work as a function of his passionate belief in what he was doing, and I was proud of the personal skill and courage he showed... (p. 24/25)

Andrew's vision of how all elements of the government should be integrated in advancing the governor's agenda, and his ideas for creating original content, were years ahead of what was being done by many governments or most politicians at that time at the State Government level—as evidenced in this internal memo from Andrew to his father:

We should have interns reading weeklies/constituency/ethnic papers and preparing responses to them. . . calling local publishers/editors with news, especially news daily papers would not take; informing local publishers/editors about upcoming visits by top administration personnel. So far, we've talked about doing this out of Albany. Why not get interns from NYC and have them work under Steve Villano in the New York City Press office?

So there I was—written into Andrew Cuomo's overarching plan for creative, new media and for implementing the administration's goals. Only I didn't know it yet, and we hadn't even agreed upon a starting salary or starting date. I bargained back and forth on salary with Deputy Press Secretary Gary Fryer, Andrew's designated negotiator for Press Office positions.

"The highest Andrew will go is $35,000," Fryer said.

"It's less than I need, Gary," I said. "I don't know if I can swing it for that amount, with the long commute into the World Trade Center on the Long Island Railroad and by subway. I need more time to think about it before I give you an answer."

A little over a year earlier, I needed more time to think about accepting an offer from my brother to go to work for a small company he was connected to, which was angling to get into the cellular telephone business. They offered me more money than the Cuomo Administration did, plus a car, with the office located less than 30 minutes from my home. I hesitated giving my brother an answer for weeks, fearing the hidden costs of such generosity, and the personal price I'd pay for entering my brother's world.

Now, it was Mario Cuomo's world I was poised to enter, and I knew if I turned down Andrew's final offer it was unlikely I would receive another which carried as much importance to the Cuomos, or to me. Plus, in less than six months time, I was about to move from the balls of my ass to working for Mario Cuomo, with not a single question raised about my family's Mob connections. The only thing that mattered to the Cuomos was whether I was the right person for the job, and if I would be loyal to them. That was extraordinarily persuasive. Their faith in my abilities gave me permission to bury my suspicions about my brother; to convince myself that whatever mob-related work he might be doing was *his* problem, not mine; to pretend that I lived on a separate plane of existence from my family. The closer I could get to Mario Cuomo, the further away I could get from my brother and his life. I telephoned Fryer the following Saturday to accept the offer.

"Tell Andrew I'll accept the $35,000, even though I need more money to support my family," I said, amazed at my statement with nothing at all behind my back.

"You can tell Andrew yourself, tomorrow," Fryer said. "There's a campaign strategy meeting tomorrow afternoon in the Pool House of the Executive Mansion in Albany, and you've been invited to attend; Andrew'll be there."

I took the train up to the Capitol District from New York City that Sunday and grabbed a taxi to the house where the Governor lived. We pulled up to the glass-enclosed guard house at the foot of the Executive Mansion's long driveway. The wrap-around front porch was bathed in floodlights, radiating warmth on a cold February night. The guardhouse intimidated me, resembling the narrow "Checkpoint Charlie" stations depicted in countless movies about East Berliners trying to escape to the West. The spotlights enhanced the effect of being under interrogation.

"May I have your name," the State trooper said, leaning out.

"Villano," I said, watching him look carefully down his list. Uh-oh.

I was certain that, finally, *finally*, I would be found out. Now that I was becoming a member of the Governor's Management/Confidential staff, I was sure the State Police's Bureau of Criminal Investigation uncovered the information they missed the first time around. They've got to know *everything* about everyone who works closely with the Governor. I'll bet they know I was inside Pat Eboli's house and carried away liquor from him, or that Carmine Fatico paid me to weed his garden, or that my brother got me my first job out of law school. If they asked me if I had ever taken contraband from the Mob, what would I say? The State trooper spotted my name on the guest list and smiled. He pressed a button, opening the front gate.

"Go right on up, Mr. Villano. They're expecting you at the Pool House," he said.

Dazed, I thanked the guard, and the taxi took me past the black wrought-iron gates to the top of the parking lot on the grounds of the Executive Mansion. I was in.

The Pool House was a recreation room located on the side of the Executive Mansion. It overlooked an in-ground swimming pool, installed originally in 1929 under Governor Franklin D. Roosevelt. Restored to its original condition during the Cuomo years, the Governor and Matilda Cuomo wanted the public to view the swimming pool as a symbol of strength in the face of hardship, as it had been under FDR. Roosevelt used the pool religiously for physical therapy treatments for his polio which paralyzed both legs. The pool and FDR's iron determination were a powerful metaphor for Mario Cuomo about overcoming adversity. The Governor continually referenced FDR's fortitude and pledge to never give up in many of his speeches, elevating the metaphor to a melody which became his mantra for public service: "FDR lifted himself out of his wheelchair, so he could lift this nation from its knees.".

The Roosevelt references held even deeper meaning for me. They were reminders of my mother's courage in the face of her own disability. She was born during the polio epidemic of 1915, in Greenwich Village, paralyzed on one side of her body by the disease and carted off to a "Crippled Children's Home" (the actual name of the place). There, my mother witnessed children her own age living in an iron-lung, fighting for each breath, and considered herself fortunate that only her right arm was disabled by the disease. Kept out of public swimming pools in NYC because she was a "polio kid," my mother taught herself to swim off the beaches of Coney Island and found her public champion and life-long hero in FDR. She spoke reverentially of Roosevelt when she remembered being driven by bus to a special camp for disabled children, passing towns in the Catskills with huge, nasty signs at their borders which read: "NO POLIO KIDS ALLOWED." For years until the polio vaccine was discovered in 1954, my mother dutifully dealt out her supply of dimes to the March of Dimes, convinced, as a matter of faith, she was helping make it possible for medical researchers to find a cure and spare another child from the same kind of suffering and stigma she endured. Every time Mario Cuomo mentioned FDR's name, visions of my mother, counting out her dimes, marched in front of my eyes, cementing my commitment to Cuomo even more. I looked out at the Roosevelt Pool, illuminated by soft lights, and wished my mother could be there to experience it. For her, FDR's healing pool would be as sacred as a baptismal font.

The Pool House's interior was dominated by a handsome, stone fireplace with pictures of sports figures on the walls. In the center of the room was a large conference table surrounded by chairs put in place for the special pre-campaign meeting. As soon as I entered the room, Andrew Cuomo spotted me. He strode over and gave me a gracious greeting.

"Stephen," he said, shaking my hand, smiling warmly, and pronouncing my name precisely the way my mother did. "Gary told me you accepted the Press Office position, and I want to thank you for biting the bullet for us. We'll make it up to you."

I thanked Andrew and repeated his words to myself to make certain I would never forget them, writing them down when I took my seat.

The Pool House session on February 3, 1985, was a major pre-1986 Gubernatorial campaign meeting. The Cuomos were known for meticulous preparation, and Andrew wanted to make sure nothing was left to chance with his father's re-election campaign still two years away. Every participant was given a huge 170-page white vinyl looseleaf binder, with the words "The Family of New York" emblazoned across the front in royal blue and the compelling logo of two large hands in a solid handshake coming together across an oversized "NY." The binder, produced by the Friends of Mario Cuomo Committee, Inc., was tabbed into sections ranging from polling to thematic strategy, from press operations to scheduling, advance work logistics to research, and fundraising to field organization.

Attendees brought with them specific expertise in many of the areas highlighted within the binder. It was a roster of Cuomo appointees that read like a "Who's Who" of top ranking State government officials: Fabian Palomino, Special Counsel to the Governor and Mario Cuomo's oldest and dearest friend; Tonio Burgos, Director of Executive Services; Ellen Conovitz, Director of Governor's Appointments Office; Al Levine, Executive Director of the NYS Thruway Authority; William Eimecke, Director of Housing & Community Renewal; Eileen Margolin, Assistant Secretary to the Governor for Human Services; John Marino; Gary Fryer; Mark Gordon, Assistant to the Governor's Chief of Staff Michael DelGuidice; Bob Sullivan, Director of Research; Drew Zambelli, staff member for former Lt. Governor Al DelBello; Leslie Stern, Director of Scheduling; Matt Monahan, of the Governor's New York City Press Office; and Al Gordon. I looked around the table, after writing down every name, and struggled to suppress a smile. Nine months earlier I was having dinner with John Gotti and "Uncle Charlie" and a few hundred others at my brother's second wedding on Long Island. Now, I was seated around an oversized conference table in the house where Mario Cuomo lived, munching cold cuts with the political and governmental powerhouses of New York State and was a key component of Andrew Cuomo's media operations plan to make sure his father was re-elected Governor of New York State. It was all so impossible.

Having both Andrew Cuomo and Marty Steadman counting on me to improve the Governor's media coverage at the local level, and electronically, was not without risk. Andrew expected perfection and he was personally invested in the success of the project he entrusted to me. It was his idea, as was putting me in charge of it, and there were people on staff—jealous of my being championed by both Andrew and Steadman, and of the early success of the operation—who wanted to see me fail. Andrew Cuomo called me at near midnight one evening to follow up on rumors that I wasn't working hard enough. Carol and I were in the early stages of sleep and jumped out of bed, worrying that it was the "death call" from either coast, since our aging parents lived in California and Florida.

"Hello, Stephen." It sounded like my brother Vinnie calling from California. My heart began pounding; something had happened to my mother or my father.

"Who is this?" I asked abruptly.

"This is Andrew, Stephen," he said.

He caught me off guard. "Oh, Andrew," I said, relieved. "What's up?"

"I just got chewed out by the governor, Stephen," Andrew Cuomo said. "He said people are telling him the Press Office News Unit is not working out—that it's not doing what I said it would do."

"That's simply not true, Andrew," I said. "I don't know where the governor is getting his information, but wherever it's coming from, it's inaccurate."

"Well," Andrew continued, "the governor's hearing that things are not working out the way they should be, and that you're not working hard enough on putting everything together."

I was furious. Fuck you, you little spoiled punk, I wanted to say. I've missed days of not tucking my son into bed at night to make you and your father look good. Go fuck yourself if you don't believe me. I came right back at Andrew, using other words.

"What?" I said. "The governor is simply mistaken and is receiving bad information. I've been working 14, 15, 16 hour days to get this thing going as quickly and efficiently as possible." I recited the names of specific radio stations and weekly newspapers around New York State already using our material.

"I'd like to have all that down in memo form tomorrow, Stephen," Andrew said.

"I'm glad to set the record straight, Andrew," I responded. "I'll have a brief in your hands tomorrow afternoon, detailing all of the work we've done, all the media contacts we've made, and all the hits we've gotten," I said.

The following day I prepared a detailed 12-page summary for Andrew, cataloguing every story sent to every radio and TV station and local newspaper around the State. I modeled it after the memo Andrew did to his father.

"That put the fire right out," Marty Steadman told me, knowing as well as I did that I passed my first Cuomo toughness test. Andrew Cuomo called me a few hours later.

"Stephen. Andrew here. I saw your memo, and I believe we owe you an apology. Obviously, someone was giving the governor the wrong information."

I had passed through the first ring of the Cuomo Administration's rococo staff rituals. They had pushed hard and discovered, as I did, how hard I could push back and that I was not easily intimidated. Being at the bottom of a long, dark well for so long made me fearless. The only thing that could frighten me now was a threat to the safety of my son. Everything else was simply noise.

My value to the Cuomos rose quickly. In May, 1985, I accompanied the Governor to a presentation he was delivering on "Human and Civic Values" at John Glenn High School in Elwood, Long Island, a few miles from my house. The speech was vintage Mario Cuomo, pointing out to 1,500 students jammed into the gymnasium how his immigrant parents and their example of hard work influenced his life.

"They just showed us by living every day in that grocery store, by working, they taught us what strength was. They taught us what commitment was," Mario Cuomo said. "They came from other parts of the world, and had nothing...It can only happen here."

The students applauded wildly. Then, Cuomo asked for questions from the audience, and got one he did not expect from a young, sandy-haired female student who rose from the crowd, cleared her voice and looked straight at the governor.

"Governor," she asked. "If you were president, would you have gone to Bitburg?"

Cuomo was caught off guard, and he bought some time to construct an answer by explaining to the students about President Reagan's recent visit to the Bitburg Cemetery in Germany, where former Nazi SS Officers were buried. He described the intense feelings on both sides and then, in a long apologia for Reagan, expressed understanding for the president's difficult decision.

"I probably would not have gone to Bitburg," Cuomo said, "but I can respect the president's decision to do so."

In conservative Suffolk County, where Reagan was idolized and won overwhelmingly in 1984, not a murmur was heard from the crowd. I cringed.

As a new convert to Judaism, I was furious with Cuomo for sounding like he was pandering to Long Island Republicans. Where was the thoughtful public official I was attracted to from his writings and his speeches? Was he, like every other American politician of the time, afraid to take on Ronald Reagan? I knew if I swallowed my anger over his answer I would dislike myself, and him, and that sour taste would not easily go away. My presence on his staff was improbable. I had fallen off the edge of the world I grew up in, and now, impossibly, was rising in another, completely different universe. If I was willing to block out my past, and push my family into the background to work in public service, I was determined not to be silent on something which struck me to the core.

The Cuomo Administration was big on memo-style position papers, so I went home and dashed off a three-page memo addressing his Bitburg answer:

In your effort to be fair to President Reagan, you may have unintentionally been unfair to Jews and Gentiles whose deep feelings about the Holocaust I know you share.

Just a few weeks earlier I had accompanied Mario Cuomo when he addressed thousands of Jews, many Holocaust Survivors, and their families at the Warsaw Ghetto Commemoration Service in Madison Square Garden:

Despite the heroism of the Warsaw Ghetto, Cuomo said to those gathered at the Garden that night, *despite the horror of the box cars and the gas chambers and the crematoria, despite the careful records the Nazis kept, there are those who deny the Holocaust ever happened. They still preach the ancient lies, and invent new reasons to vindicate their venom.*

Cuomo went on, his voice resonating throughout the high rafters of the Garden:

For to confront the fact of the Holocaust is to look into the heart of darkness to comprehend the scope of evil in this world, to measure the human capacity to hate and to murder and to destroy. It is to acknowledge the abyss.

His words were still ringing in my ears when I heard his response to the Bitburg question. I could not believe he was sanctioning Reagan's insensitive trip on the heels of bringing Warsaw Ghetto survivors to tears with the depth of his understanding and compassion about the Holocaust. I argued to him that as a new Jew and his staff member, I was deeply offended. I had his attention, and was in a position few others were privileged to occupy to make my outrage known:

I am keenly aware of the sentiment in some segments of the Jewish community of reluctance to criticize the president's Bitburg mistake for fear of an anti-Semitic backlash. As a Jew, and as head of the Social Action Committee at my Temple, I understand the sentiment, but do not agree with it.

I went on to quote the writer and concentration camp survivor Elie Wiesel's condemnation of the Reagan visit:

I believe that the president's mistakes surrounding Bitburg—mistakes he must take ultimate responsibility for—are not deserving of your understanding or your defense. Your public thoughts, public words and public deeds, mean too much to Jews and Gentiles alike to be misconstrued as supportive of the president...

Cuomo called me that same afternoon and we discussed the memo at length. He saw that I was not intimidated by his position, his arguments, or his strong personality. I had faced down my own mother's fierce Catholicism, and latent anti-Semitism, on my decision to become a Jew; by comparison, discussing Bitburg with Mario Cuomo was a breeze. He was fascinated with my decision to convert to Judaism, and perhaps saw a similarity in our journeys to find how to fit our philosophies of life, and a path of social action, into our faiths. The memo transformed my relationship with the governor. He thanked me for sending it, and told me to feel free to write him with my thoughts on how we should approach any issue. Bitburg, and its aftermath, forged a special bond between us: emotional, spiritual and intellectual, to accompany the political and philosophical connection already in existence.

I had been raised on a diet full of passionate argument about all things big and small, with the most heated shouting matches originally related to money, or other family members. Later, politics became the flashpoint, especially if one of my politically conservative uncles was present, or if my brother Vinnie was just looking to get under everyone's skin by saying something outrageous. At times, when debating with Mario Cuomo, I felt right at home. In appearance and intensity, the Governor reminded me of a much more educated, more intelligent version of my Uncle Nunzio Ruisi, a longshoreman from Brooklyn, with hands as large as Cuomo's and opinions just as strong. I grew up debating my Uncle constantly on issues from welfare, to race, to the war in Vietnam, which, to a Navy Submarine veteran from World War II, was the most explosive of all issues between us. Yet, no matter how loud and impassioned our arguments got, I knew that when they were over, all would be forgiven and we could count on each other for anything. Somehow, I felt the same way about Mario Cuomo.

My star continued to rise with Andrew and the governor. The News Unit, which we established within the World Trade Center Office, took off like a high-tech start-up. Staffed by some of the brightest college students from around the nation, our in-house News Bureau pumped out print and electronic stories about Mario Cuomo as quickly as we could create content. In pushing hard for this boiler-room press operation, Andrew Cuomo knew that young college interns would be willing to dedicate long hours at no pay to advance the values his father had articulated at the Democratic National Convention the summer before. Initially, I was skeptical that

Andrew's model could work, especially when we started out manually unscrewing the mouthpiece sections of desk-top telephones and hand wiring the receivers to send recordings of the governor's voice to radio stations. But Andrew pushed hard to obtain the newest recording equipment for our operation, and our experiment in home grown news hummed with efficiency. At a time of rampant materialism, Mario Cuomo captivated the imagination of a new generation of idealists, and I no longer felt like a relic of the 1960s, out of step with the self-centeredness of the Reagan era. These interns tackled their tasks with vigor, viewing unpaid public service not just as a valuable paragraph on their resume, or the chance to be in proximity to the country's newest political celebrity, but as a chance to make the world a bit better.

On my first helicopter ride with Mario Cuomo to attend a public event, he asked me how the Intern Program was working. I informed him about the daily achievements of the News Unit, but he wanted to know more.

"How do they *like* what they are doing, Steve? And why do they do it?" the governor asked, looking straight at me as our knees touched in the State Police helicopter's small passenger area.

"They view you the way my generation viewed Robert Kennedy and Martin Luther King, Jr., Governor," I said. "You give them great hope for the future, during some pretty dark times."

Cuomo emphatically shook his head, "No."

He wrinkled his face, looked out the helicopter window and again shook his head, "No." He could not conceive of himself in the same category as Kennedy and King, and he did not encourage the comparison. Despite Mario Cuomo's protestations, the comparisons were coming not only from me and our group of idealistic college interns. The following summer, during his 1986 re-election campaign, Cuomo met with National Democratic Party Leader Jack English. English, the former Nassau County Democratic Leader, was a close friend and supporter of the Kennedy family for many years, having played key roles in John F. Kennedy's election to the presidency in 1960 and the election of Robert F. Kennedy as Senator of New York State in 1964. English served as Deputy National Director of Jimmy Carter's 1980 presidential campaign, when Mario Cuomo, then NY's Lt. Governor, headed the Carter campaign in New York. Cuomo and English were friends and former colleagues, both having practiced as lawyers, and clerked for judges in New York State. They were both progressive pragmatists, sharing beliefs in many of the same causes, and a similar approach to politics. Mario Cuomo graciously welcomed English into his World Trade Center office, showing him the commanding view of New York Harbor, with the deference a student has for a mentor, although English was only six years his senior. The governor motioned for English to sit in an armchair with a view of the Statue of Liberty while Cuomo sat down behind his desk. I sat on a leather couch, close enough to both to record their conversation.

English minced no words, perhaps an indicator that he had little time left to wait for Mario Cuomo to make up his mind.

"Governor, I think you ought to consider running for president," he said. "I think you are exactly what the Democratic Party needs at the head of the ticket in 1988 to take back the White House."

Cuomo made the same face to Jack English that he made to me on the helicopter, and shook his head, "No."

"I'm very grateful for your confidence, Jack," Cuomo said, and then proceeded to tell his guest how busy he was running the State of New York and how much he loved being governor. Cuomo went on for a while about the challenges of fighting for New York against a national administration hostile to the needs of the Northeast, and intent on pitting region against region, race against race, and rich against poor.

"You need someone like a Bobby Kennedy," Cuomo said, artfully steering the conversation to a discussion of how well English knew the Kennedys, how hard he worked for what they believed in, and what Robert F. Kennedy and the Kennedy family meant to the country.

"It's why no one could second guess Teddy's decision not to run," Cuomo said. "The Kennedy family has given far beyond what could be expected of any family to give to serve their country."

English nodded his head in agreement, looking off in the distance at New York Harbor, glistening in the afternoon sunshine, and let the Governor continue.

"We need someone like Bobby today," Cuomo said. "Someone who can unite black and white, rich and poor, who can speak to the needs of working people, and get people in the suburbs and the cities to see we are all part of the same family."

I held my pen perfectly still and looked carefully at English, waiting for him to speak. Jack English's Irish eyes twinkled, and he leaned forward in his chair.

"Well, I think you're that person, Governor," he said.

Cuomo again, wrinkled his nose up and shook his head, "No." He would not allow himself to be held to a standard that he could not control—not even from as towering a Democratic Party figure as Jack English. The conversation ended on a cordial note, with Cuomo asking English to stay in touch. A little over a year later, Jack English died, at age 61, from liver cancer.

Mario Cuomo could be unshakable on certain things, and the desire on the part of others—with or without political power—for him to seek the Presidency was one of them, regardless of how intense the pressure became or who was making the pitch. Andrew described his father's determination:

...He is a truly grounded individual, at peace with himself and his view of the world...he believes what he believes. It doesn't matter what anyone else thinks—even the public at large...Nothing and no one can shake him. Public affection or disaffection doesn't move him...His sense of right and wrong and his pursuit of principle are paramount. (*All Things Possible*, by Andrew Cuomo, Harper Collins, 2014, p. 79)

In everything he did, if Mario Cuomo believed a certain action was not appropriate to the situation, nothing could move him to act otherwise. One powerful example of this came at the funeral of Leon Klinghoffer, the 69-year-old, wheelchair-bound New Yorker, shot in the head and chest by a member of the Palestinian Liberation Front (PLF), one of the terrorists who hijacked the ocean liner *Achille Lauro*, just outside of Egypt, in October 1985. Klinghoffer was celebrating his 36th wedding anniversary aboard the cruise ship with his wife Marilyn. He was singled out for execution by the terrorists, who then forced two of the ship's crew members to dump his dead body, and his wheelchair, overboard. The nation was outraged by the brutal assassination of Klinghoffer, and the front entrance to Temple Shaaray Tefila, on Manhattan's Upper East Side reflected the magnitude of the story with a large crowd of news reporters and television crews gathered five and six deep on the wide sidewalk, eager to get reactions from public officials attending Klinghoffer's funeral. When we pulled up in the black unmarked State Police car carrying Cuomo, Senator Al D'Amato had already plunged into the sea of reporters, darting like a killifish from one TV interview to the other. He was up for re-election in 1986, and D'Amato was campaigning hard on the corpse of Klinghoffer, to demonstrate how tough he was on terrorism. Cuomo spotted D'Amato and shook his head in disgust.

"I don't want to do that," Cuomo said to the State trooper driving the car, nodding his head toward D'Amato.

"I just want to pay my respects to the family, and leave. Is there a side entrance we can use?"

We pulled around the corner to the Temple's side entrance, where there was no press present, and slipped up a flight of stairs to the Rabbi's study. Cuomo met with Leon Klinghoffer's family in private, expressing his condolences quietly to each family member, while D'Amato was still out on the sidewalk on East 79th Street spouting his outrage through the blowhole in the front of his face into every camera in sight. Mario Cuomo did not care what the press expected from him, nor would he participate in the media circus that was taking place on the sidewalk. He would do what he felt was appropriate and respectful to the circumstances.

I made it my business to meticulously study everything about Mario Cuomo, memorizing each line in his face, each inflection in his voice, each change in his demeanor. The role of observer came naturally to me, having played it throughout my life within my family, where every event was a crisis that I wanted to escape. I could separate Cuomo's everyday frustrations from his fury, his genuine anger, from his petty gripes. I relished his playful moments, and his mental challenges, and loved when he was enjoying himself so purely he'd say, "we're having too much fun." It was the Italian fatalism of my mother saying, "You're laughing too hard today; you'll cry tomorrow." Being around Mario Cuomo was like being around my family, without all of the years of baggage or the state of constant siege.

The week after Klinghoffer's funeral, Cuomo was being honored as the Goldschmidt Fellow at Columbia University. He delivered an inspiring speech to students, some of whom worked for us in our Intern Program. Dinner and far-reaching conversation with a dozen students followed in a professor's apartment after the speech, and we stayed overnight in one of the campus' better dormitories which housed visiting dignitaries. The following day, the Governor met with more students, accompanied by *New York Times* reporter Maurice "Mickey" Carroll, and taught a public policy class. By mid-afternoon, Mario Cuomo was exhausted, but buoyed, from spending an intense period of time in penetrating discussion with bright young students committing themselves to a life of public service.

We arrived back at our World Trade Center office later that afternoon, and all I wanted to do was head home to Long Island, since I hadn't seen my son in two days. A few days before, a freelance article I wrote for *Working Mother Magazine* entitled "A Father's Story," appeared in the magazine's November, 1985 issue (pps. 128 & 130) in their "Guilt Department" section. It detailed my guilt as a working father, being away for long days from my son.

In the piece, one particular paragraph struck a chord with the Cuomos: *I know that millions of fathers work long hours, see little of*

their children and stoically accept a fixed place in the family constella-
tion. But, I tell myself, I am not one of those fathers. Having watched
my son grow each day, I know what I am missing. Other fathers,
born in other times, or unable to escape the expectation that men must
always choose career over family, are not as fortunate. A little less
guilty maybe, but not nearly as lucky.

The article, published nationally, was circulated widely throughout the governor's office. Mario Cuomo phoned me from Albany when the essay reached his desk.

"Congratulations on a beautiful piece of writing, Steve," the governor said. "Maybe we could work it out so you could leave the office by 4:00 pm each day, so you could be home in-time for your son's Little League games."

I thanked the governor for his thoughtfulness, insisting that I didn't expect any special treatment, and it wasn't why I wrote the article.

"I knew what I signed on for when I came to work in the Press Office, Governor," I said. "The busiest hours here are between 4:00 and 6:00 pm everyday when reporters are on deadline and the evening news shows are beginning. That's the most crucial time of our day."

"Well, let's think about this," he said. The governor paused. He was a father, a mentor, and a problem-solver and he was searching for a solution that could work to benefit both of us. "Maybe somehow we could move the office closer to you," Mario Cuomo said.

"That's very kind of you, Governor, but it won't be necessary," I said, laughing. "We'll deal with things just the way they are."

I thanked him for calling, and after hanging up felt even better about working with him. Not every one in the Administration, however, was as understanding or felt the same way after my *Working Mother* piece appeared. Some colleagues used it as an opportunity to test my commitment to the Cuomos, my work ethnic, or my manliness. I was packing up my briefcase to leave the World Trade Center office late in the afternoon on the day we returned from Columbia

University, when John Iaccio, one of Andrew's young "turks" who was part of my original interview team, came into my office. Iaccio, usually upbeat and friendly, acted as if he had a chip on his shoulder.

"Andrew wants you to do some polling for us tonight," he said.

With the beginning of the governor's 1986 re-election campaign just a few months away, nightly polling was a staple of the Cuomo team. It had to be done after work hours, on your own time, to avoid using State employees on State time to do the task, a violation of State law.

"Well, I'm sure you can get someone else for tonight, John," I said. "I've just been with the governor the past few days up at Columbia and am going home to see my son tonight. Sorry."

Iaccio was incensed by my refusal.

"Then you'll have to answer to Andrew," he said sharply.

"Fine," I said. "Give me his number. I'll call him. I'm sure Andrew will understand."

Iaccio glared at me. He picked up a piece of paper from my desk, scrawled Andrew's direct phone number on it, and threw it at me.

"There!" he said. "Call him!" He stormed out of my office.

I dialed Andrew Cuomo's number and recounted my conversation with Iaccio, mentioning that he told me that the polling command was coming from Andrew.

"I didn't tell him to say any such thing," Andrew said calmly. "Sometimes, Stephen, these guys use my name because they think it will make people jump higher. Go home and be with your son, tonight. You've earned it."

I was moved by Andrew's considerate tone of voice, and his kindness, which mirrored his father's. He did not reference my *Working Mother* piece, but understood what this meant to me and my son. Maybe, I thought, just maybe, a part of him wished that his own father placed him ahead of an all-consuming career a few more times while he was growing up. But, Andrew Cuomo never had to doubt his father's fierce loyalty for him. In fact, it was that loyalty, that visceral protective instinct for his children and his family which was at the core of Mario Cuomo's decision to never run for president. One of the most telling moments came in September, 1986, well before the boomlets for his presidential candidacy in 1987 and again in 1991.

At the beginning of 1986, Andrew, working as a partner for the law firm of Blutrich, Falcone & Miller, following his stint in the Manhattan DA's Office, launched a non-profit organization named HELP—Housing Enterprise for the Less Privileged. It was a homeless housing and assistance program that became a model for the nation. For the first nine months of HELP's existence, Cuomo ran his nascent non-profit from his law office, on a pro-bono basis. The exploding number of homeless in New York—nearing 80,000 by the mid 1980s—had a deep impact on Andrew, as it did upon many other New Yorkers.

While the concept and implementation of HELP received rave reviews from most quarters, Andrew's short-lived tenure at his law firm did not. He was uncomfortable with the firm's lack of mandates prohibiting family members of elected officials, or the officials themselves, of doing business with the State. Cuomo wrote in his memoirs that:

I wanted to go further, so the firm, at my request agreed that we'd avoid controversy by turning down any representation before the State...still there was speculation and gossip...And the Albany media loves to foment "scandals." (*All Things Possible,* Andrew Cuomo, Harper Collins 2014, p. 88).

Those controversies reached a fever pitch in early September, 1986. The Governor was already in a testy mood. His re-election campaign was never in doubt, but he was no longer having fun. The press, led by the *New York Post,* was pummeling Andrew's law firm for allegedly doing business with State agencies and for accepting clients who were seeking to curry favor with the governor by hiring a law firm in which his son was a partner. Halfway to the speaking event, the car phone rang. It was Andrew.

Mario Cuomo picked up the phone, and listened quietly to his son for several minutes, deeply massaging his forehead with the large hand that wasn't cradling the phone to his ear. Suddenly, the governor starting shouting into the receiver.

"What do you mean you're a liability to me? What kind of talk is that? You're tired, you're working too hard on this campaign and you need some rest. *Don't let me hear you talking like that,"* Mario Cuomo said, slamming down the car phone into its' cradle.

There was complete silence in the car for a few moments. Finally, the governor spoke, seething with anger.

"Imagine that. My own son, thinking he's a liability to me. *This is some god-damned business,"* Mario Cuomo said. "You go into government because you try to do some good, and what do they do? They attack your kids. They spread rumors that somehow you must be connected to the Mafia because your name ends in a vowel. *And for what? All because you want to serve? At what price? And when did my kids ever agree to pay the price?"*

I watched him look out of the passenger-side window of the black, unmarked State Police car, his anger barely contained, and knew at that precise moment that Mario Cuomo would not run for President of the United States; he would never subject his children to the brutality of a presidential campaign.

"Aaaah, the whole thing stinks," Mario Cuomo said, waving his right hand as if chasing away a fly, swatting his frustration into the air, brushing away the stench of stories which hurt his son, and his family, and gagged him. With one wave of his large hand, he pushed aside any of the tightly reasoned arguments being advanced in favor of a "Cuomo for President" campaign in the next presidential election.

Mario Cuomo understood how news, rumor, and innuendo worked better than any American politician of his time. He knew that a story, no matter how untrue or far-fetched, took on a life of its own, once reported and repeated. Any link between his name or Andrew's name to questionable clients—even if the story later proved false—would linger in people's minds for months, or in some cases, years. The damage was often subliminal, a mere suggestion to a jury quickly withdrawn, and it became impossible to erase from public consciousness despite detailed rebuttals or outright denials. All that was necessary for the phony charge to pass for fact, was for it to be repeated over and over again, until it became one with the Cuomo name, indivisible.

Above all, he would not allow his children to be maligned by *anyone* or used as props in the no-holds barred, media reality show, which political campaigns were quickly becoming. His family had not asked for a life in public service, he had; and he would stand as a bulwark against their being bullied. I loved him for leaping to Andrew's defense, admired his certainty in being an unflinchingly protective father. And, deep down to the marrow of my bone, I felt safe in his presence, similar to the sense of safety my brother's calm manner often gave me.

6 ▫ Saggital Man

Mario Cuomo won his second term as New York State's Governor in 1986 with sixty-five percent of the vote. His re-election
should have been a cause for celebration and a source of great joy
and gratitude. Instead, a full week after election day, he was still furious with reporters for making his son's law practice a political issue.
Only the unrelenting drumbeat of state business pulled him out of
his self-imposed seclusion.

The Governor travelled to New York City to open a new, affordable housing project in Brooklyn—the kind of feel-good story every
public official loves to tell. The carefully chosen event was Cuomo's
first New York City-based appearance since his re-election, an example of how well Cuomo Administration policies were working to
move families from homelessness into permanent housing. We drove
down the crowded central Brooklyn street in the Governor's unmarked State Police car and spotted more Manhattan-based television crews than customarily met us for outer-borough events. Usually, it took a major crime story or a massive public demonstration
to get midtown-Manhattan-based media crews to cross one of the
bridges into the Bronx, Queens, or Brooklyn, and rarely into Staten
Island. Their large presence, camped out in front of the Brooklyn
house we were visiting, signaled that the press' focus was going to be
much broader than housing.

Cuomo, sitting in the front passenger seat, became noticeably tense.
We exited the car, and walked up the stairs into the renovated housing unit, where the Governor sat down on a comfortable sofa and
chatted quietly with the young Black mother and her children, while
TV cameras rolled. The new home, like the children's wide eyes, was

bright and hopeful. Mario Cuomo would have preferred to stay there all day, exchanging smiles and jokes with the kids rather than head back downstairs to face the press, without the buffer of a beautiful, young Brooklyn family blessed with a sparkling, new place to live.

We climbed down the building's front stoop and waded directly into a media maelstrom. WNBC-TV Correspondent Ben Farnsworth ignored the housing announcement and went right at Cuomo about his on-going feud with the press:

Cuomo: I don't have a feud. I was candid about the press, not the whole press, that's silly. I mean to condemn all politicians is wrong; to condemn all of the press is wrong. There were some reporters in some situations who did some things which I thought were not the best kind of reportage, and I made that statement and I repeat it. What's wrong with that? What the press, I gather, is saying, is, 'Oh, you musn't ever criticize the press or they'll call you churlish; they'll call you Nixon. You know, that's interesting. What that suggests to me is that maybe we should have been criticizing them earlier, and more fiercely. If reporters criticize a politician, the politician says "You're all against me." But that's what the press is doing now.

Farnsworth: So, you did not criticize the unfair reporting of the *Times*, the *News* and the *Post*?

Cuomo: I just got 65% of the vote; how unfair could they have been? And I made that point very, very clear. As a matter of fact, here's something you didn't report. What I have said over and over again for four years is that I don't know many politicians who did as well as I did with the press. They were very kind to me. That overall, they were much fairer to me than I probably deserved. I have never said that the press is unfair to me. That's the press because that's a good way to ward off the criticism. "See, he's condemning all of us." I don't. I'm not like that.

Farnsworth: Governor, have you seen the story this morning quoting several unnamed sources in the National Democratic Party who raised the possibility that after your resounding re-election victory you were a little nervous with all the talk about the Presidency?

Cuomo: Did they quote anybody? Did they quote the politicians?

Farnsworth: No, they didn't.

Cuomo: Then why do you believe it?

Farnsworth: Well, you can understand that politicians aren't going to say it for the record.

Cuomo: You've just made my point. You want to argue with me, suggesting that there was a report in the paper; you don't know the reporter, there was no evidence, the reporter made the charge and you want the politician to defend against the charge by a reporter you don't know who made a charge without any evidence. That says something about that report.

Farnsworth: Well, I just want to know how you feel about it.

Cuomo: What I feel about it is that people who read that paper should read it very carefully. The way you listen to politicians you should listen to reporters. You should say: 'Should I believe this person? Is this person credible? Is this person giving me evidence?' I think the test they apply to politicians should apply to you. That's fair.

Farnsworth, a consumer reporter, was new to the political beat for WNBC-TV, and Cuomo humiliated him in front of a crowd of his colleagues, all looking for a piece of the same story. The human interest story of previously homeless Brooklynites moving into clean, permanent places to live was lost, and Mario Cuomo was still seething when he climbed back into the front passenger seat of the unmarked State Police car. I got into the back seat and the Governor immediately turned his large head around toward me:

Cuomo: What did you think about this business with the press?

Villano: I don't think you should have gone into things again with Farnsworth, Governor. I think you should have simply said, 'I've already discussed that. Let's turn the page and look at what we've accomplished for these families.' Then, he would have been forced to focus on the housing story.

I looked away from the Governor, out toward the Brooklyn storefronts we were passing as the car pulled away. I expected him to come roaring back at me and simply wanted to get out of the car and take the subway home. Cuomo glared at me:

Cuomo: He was wrong on the facts. He didn't even have the facts. He hadn't read the story he was asking about. Who'll call them on it if I don't? Who'll tell them when they do something wrong?

Villano: The press has to do that to themselves, and to a certain extent, they do. *Newsday* has Tom Collins, the *Washington Post* has an ombudsman. Granted, what they do is by no means enough. But for a public official to criticize the press… You're going against hundreds of years of history, of an institutional relationship between the press and government. Here, the issue is the public's right to know."

I was pulling arguments out of everywhere to slow him down; I'd use anything that popped into my head from past journalism courses or my years as a labor journalist. When you challenged Mario Cuomo, you needed to grab every life preserver available. Cuomo's eyes grew larger, bearing down on me.

Cuomo: Doesn't the public have the right to know if the press is telling them the truth?

I did not flinch. Sometimes, when debating Cuomo the best tactic to use was to throw questions right back at him, in a kind of Socratic-dialogue on speed. It was a technique he taught me.

Villano: Of course they do, but who determines it? Does the Press? Do you? Everytime you get into a disagreement with the press it results in a sideshow and takes attention off the main issue we want the press to cover. Just like it did today with housing…

Mario Cuomo shook his head vigorously and abruptly cut me off.

Cuomo: No sir. No sir. I think you're wrong. We have to keep hitting them on this. I want to do all the Sunday morning talk shows. Somebody's got to show they are not afraid to criticize the press. I want to keep hitting, keep hitting them…"

I was dumbfounded by Mario Cuomo's raw, blind anger on this issue. I could scarcely believe that this highly intelligent human being who measured each word and thought carefully, as if hand-tailoring a Saville Row suit, could be so closed-minded and self-destructive. I was desperate to get him onto a different, more high-minded track, which is where I believed he excelled.

Villano: Why not try a different approach, Governor? Change the playing field. Give a major, Notre Dame-like speech at someplace like the Columbia School of Journalism, focusing on some of the very issues we've raised: who determines the public's right to know? What obligation does the press have to monitor itself? You could lay out the issues and raise the entire debate to a higher level, like you did with abortion. I think that approach would be far better than 30-minute back-and-forths on Sunday mornings."

Again, the Governor quickly shook his head.

Cuomo: No. No. No! I want to continue doing it my way. I want to hit this every way possible, every day. I want to get on all the Sunday morning talk shows as soon as possible."

I was exasperated with Mario Cuomo, convinced his months' long war with the press had warped his view of reality. By targeting the Governor's family during the campaign, the press pushed Cuomo beyond his own ability to control himself. His anger erupted like Mt. Vesuvius, and I immediately remembered what the great writer Murray Kempton said, when asked if he thought Cuomo should run for President:

"Oh, I hope so," Kempton chuckled, his pixie-ish eyes twinkling with delight. "I can't wait to see him explode during a Presidential campaign the first time someone attacks his family."

If my service was worth anything to Cuomo, I had to try to put the brakes on what was becoming a run-away train, powered by temper. I looked straight back at the Governor. I had seen all this before. These tirades against invisible forces were commonplace in my own family where we were always engaged in fights to the death with the mysterious "they," a power out there beyond the boundaries of the family, controlling everything; unseeable, but unquestionably evil, as far as anyone could tell. It was a primal, bound to an intestinal, instinct to protect those closest to us, and I understood it all too well.

To cope with the constant culture of chaos in my family, the histrionics and rants against the all-powerful "they," and my father's frequent fits of rage, I developed an observer's shell; a trance-like calmness that enveloped me as a means of protection and escape. It happened when I watched, motionless, as my father seized his shotgun, or when he upended a fully-set dining room table one Thanksgiving Day because my brother and sister were quarreling. I had that same feeling, looking directly through Mario Cuomo. Nothing he could say or do could unnerve me; my trance took over. I had offered a constructive suggestion for him to give a major First Amendment speech, offering to draft it for him. But, he was the Governor; if he chose not to do it, there was nothing more I could do except set up the television interviews he was demanding and gird myself for the fight, or resign. My mantra kicked in one more time:

Villano: You may be right on the facts about this, Governor, but there's no way you can win. The press has the last word, the last edits. It's a no-win situation for you.

Cuomo stared right back at me, even more intensely than before, as if I blocked a shot he wanted to take at a basket. He hated to be told he could not win.

Cuomo: That's what people said to me on the death penalty; that's what they said to me on the 'Mafia' issue. Don't you think this is the same as the flap over the 'Mafia?'

Cuomo's use of the term 'Mafia' in the heat of our discussion was like a punch in my stomach, knocking me out of my calm, trance-like state. Was he intentionally using that word with me to simply win the argument, which the Governor had been known to do from time to time? Did he know more about my brother and my family than he had ever let on? No, no, no, that couldn't be it. I had no evidence of that at all. None. In fact, leading up to the campaign he pulled me closer each day, did not push me away. He relished our disagreements, especially when my colleague, Stephen Schlesinger, and I told him he was sounding just like Richard Nixon in his attacks on the press. He slammed the phone down on us when we suggested he was becoming "Nixonian."

Mario Cuomo was still in battle mode, having come off a grueling year of constantly defending his family, and having beat back allegations of favorable treatment concerning the clients of his son's law firm. Cuomo blamed himself, and his choice of pursuing a career in public service, for the unfair focus on his family, and the media was the source of that intense focus. The New York press, and increasingly, national reporters, were possessed by the trajectory of the public lives of two diametrically different New York Italians throughout 1986: the rapid rise of John Gotti to the top of the Gambino Crime Family, and, at virtually the same time, the growing fascination with the prospect of Mario Cuomo as a candidate for President—the first Italian-American in U.S. history to be talked about seriously as the nation's top public official, and the first to be subjected to an endless flow of insidious innuendos associated with having a vowel at the end of his name.

Political operatives, in both parties, began to cook up their own conventional wisdom, that "Italians from the Northeast can't win," as Cuomo told the *New York Times* reporter Jeffrey Schmalz on January 18, 1986, just a month after a *New York Daily News* poll gave him a 79% approval rating for the job he was doing as Governor of New York. Tellingly, 66% of those polled said it would be fine with them if Cuomo ran for President—an astronomical level of popular support coming only three years into Mario Cuomo's first term. The *Daily News* headline from the first Sunday in December, 1985, shouted out their poll's findings: "NEW POLL OK'S CUOMO'S PREZ BID." I sucked in a gulp of air when I opened up the *News'* Sunday edition, never expecting the calls for Cuomo to step forward to move that fast. How long could I survive a presidential campaign before someone, somewhere, found out about my brother, and my family's links by marriage to both the Genovese and Gambino crime families?

I had no time to formulate any kind of a strategy—to exist on the Governor's staff or to exit from it—before NBC Nightly News ran an explosive story on December 4, 1985, during its evening newscast—the day after the *Daily News* poll results were announced. NBC reported that "five companies identified by authorities as mob fronts have made contributions to a campaign fund for New York Governor Mario Cuomo."

The NBC report lasted for several minutes and contained video of the Governor and Mrs. Cuomo at a Friends of Mario Cuomo fund-raising dinner, walking around and shaking hands with people, as they did at every event. When the company names were mentioned in the audio of the report, a graphic appeared on the television screen of the five corporate names, followed by a quick camera cut to a letter bearing "Executive Chamber" stationary, containing unreadable words. The visual implication was clear: an Italian-American governor was accepting money from alleged "mob-front" companies.

There was so much completely wrong with the story and the way NBC presented it: the allegations about the "mob front" companies, the insinuation that somehow Cuomo knew, the visual smear that he was shaking the hands of mobsters (even though they were hands of other supporters) as if to seal the deal, and the completely misleading freeze-frame on the official government stationary of the "Executive Chamber." The least little research by NBC would have revealed that no political business was conducted on official State stationary, since all political correspondence—particularly concerning donors—was handled by the political organization, the Friends of Mario Cuomo. It was a distinction about which both the Governor and Andrew Cuomo were fanatical, and they underscored it again and again with all staff and campaign operatives.

Here it was, I thought, the first salvo in the national media campaign against Mario Cuomo, and it represented the first time that a national television network mentioned his name, and the word "Mafia", in the same sentence.

My internal sirens sounded. Instinctively, I wanted to rush to Cuomo's defense, shout out his innocence and call all my friends in the press and let them know that I knew first-hand that Mario Cuomo had no connections to the mob, because I did. Everything was spinning so fast, completely out of control. I knew the Governor would want my reaction to the story, so I sat down and drafted a response immediately, in the form of a scathing letter to Lawrence Grossman, President of NBC News:

By using the terms "Mafia," "mob" and "mob-front companies" to establish the tone of your report, and then mentioning but one public official—one of the most highly respected Italian-American public officials in the nation— the message you communicated was that, somehow, Mario M. Cuomo was linked to these "Mafia"-run companies.

Although the facts of the story clearly contradicted your underlying message, your selection of ethnic code words and the linkage of those slurs with the name of an Italian-American leader has done enormous damage to Italian-Americans across the nation...

To reinforce the damage done by the NBC report, I used a quotation from Professor Richard Gambino's *Blood of My Blood* (Anchor Books, Anchor Press/Doubleday, 1974, to underscore the case:

Italian-American politicians, businessmen and career men are frequent targets of whispering attacks initiated by their non-Italian rivals. Insinuation or brazen lies about "Mafia" connections are enough to rouse know-nothing fears of Americans and torpedo the career of an Italian-American. (p.305)

Nearly 100 years earlier, similar canards and lies were spread by the White Nationalist League of Louisiana about Italian immigrants, resulting in the lynching and shooting of 11 innocent Italians. It was a brutal story from our own past, brilliantly documented by Professor Richard Gambino, in his book *Vendetta: The True Story of the Largest Lynching in U.S. History* (Doubleday, Garden City, NY., 1977). Cuomo personally felt the lash of ethnic bigotry when he was shut out from white shoe Wall Street firms, despite receiving a top score on the New York State Bar exam. There simply weren't that many "Marios" working at established Wall Street law firms, and none were willing to take a chance on one, no matter how gifted.

He intuitively understood the deep roots of xenophobia and bias toward Italians, and how the catastrophic lessons of anti-immigrant fervor were lost on many Italian-American families, as well as upon respectable American media outlets, academic and legal institutions, which should have known better. Instead, many found it easier—and more profitable—to perpetuate destructive ethnic group stereotypes, rather than research and analyze the facts of each individual case, or merely pay attention to history.

One clear exception was the gifted Irish-American writer, Pete Hamill. In his book *Why Sinatra Matters* (Little Brown and Company, 1998, pps 44-46), —aimed at reaching a middle-class audience of Sinatra fans—Hamill clearly explained the circumstances of the visceral racial hatred toward Italian immigrants that resulted in the 1891 New Orleans slaughter of 11 innocent men:

In New Orleans, the garish myth flowered in the imaginations of newspapermen. There were gangsters among us, who were different from American gangsters; they were darker, swarthier, spoke a different language and were bound together by blood oaths....When a trial of Italian immigrants for murder, resulted in the acquittal of eight men and no verdict on three more...that verdict did not satisfy the respectable Americans of New Orleans...Two days after the verdicts, a mob of several thousand, led by 60 leading citizens...surrounded the jail where the Italians were awaiting the final bureaucratic disposition of their cases....

The Americans stormed the jail, dragged the Italians out of their cells, and murdered them. Two were hanged screaming from lampposts. One of them tried climbing the hangman's rope with his free hands and was riddled with bullets. Seven were executed by (vigilante) firing squads in the yard of the jail, and two more were discovered hiding from the street mob and shot to pieces. It remains the single worst lynching in American history...The lynchings were approved by the editorial writers of the New York Times, Washington Post, St. Louis Globe-Democrat *and* San Francisco Chronicle*, along with about 50 percent of the other newspapers in the nation. Theodore*

Roosevelt, one of the leading younger Republicans, said the lynchings were a "rather good thing," and bragged that he had said so at a party to 'various Dago diplomats.'

Cuomo knew deep into the marrow of his bones that most Americans—and shockingly most Italian-Americans— knew nothing of this inbred, nationalist animosity against Italians, which manifested itself in the single, biggest mass lynching in the United States. By contrast, the execution of Sacco and Venzetti, some 36 years later, while more broadly known, was far less consequential in the nation's history of hatred and violence aimed a single ethnic immigrant group.

That history was behind my draft letter to NBC, and when it was finished, I faxed it to Mario Cuomo in the Governor's Mansion in Albany. He called me immediately, surprising me by his calmness

"This is terrific, Steve," the Governor said. "Let's send it out right away."

I hesitated. It was one thing for me to defend Mario Cuomo's integrity; it was another to put the name "Villano" on a public letter condemning the Mob when my family was connected to organized crime. I had to persuade Mario Cuomo to take another tack.

"I don't think I should send it out under my name, Governor," I said. "It would be far more effective and much more powerful coming from some national Italian-American organization, rather than one of your staff people, who will automatically be discounted as biased."

Cuomo agreed and mentioned William Fugazy, the President of the Coalition of Italo-American Associations as the logical choice. I sent the letter off to Fugazy, and within days, NBC received a powerful protest from a prominent Italian-American organization, with the names of Lee Iacocca, Al D'Amato, Geraldine Ferraro, and Jeno Paolucci on the official letterhead. Mario Cuomo rewarded me for performing well under pressure the only way he knew how: pulling me closer and giving me more assignments that merited his trust. It was positive professional feedback full of pitfalls, serving to increase the tension on my tightrope. The Governor's support-ive actions made it impossible to entertain any notion of leaving the Cuomo Administration for fear of my family's own mob con-nections being exposed. I was in the trenches with Mario Cuomo and we were both fighting for our lives. Destiny? Perhaps. Why else would I have been placed along side of Cuomo to clear the stain of the mob-related slurs from his family, mine, and the names of other Italian-Americans? Who better to understand what it was to bleed from the psychic stab wounds Mobsters inflicted on the people who loved them, than someone who intimately knew of their power to demean, and make us think less of ourselves? My family prepared me well for the challenge.

Less than one week later, the issue of Mario Cuomo's Ital-ian-American heritage was ignited again, this time by Cuomo's first press secretary Tim Russert and former Nixon dirty-trickster, Roger Stone. The Governor asked me to sit in on a six-week series of seminars at the New School for Social Research being conducted by the author Ken Auletta, a columnist for the *New York Daily News*. Auletta's classes focused on Mario Cuomo's tenure as Governor, and the kind of job he was doing, with Cuomo slated to appear during at last class session. Stone appeared at Auletta's second-to-last class on December 10, paired with Tim Russert, who as an NBC News correspondent, was fully aware of the NBC news story linking Cuo-mo to "the mob" which ran just the week before. When Auletta asked both panelists to talk about "Mario Cuomo as a public leader and national figure and how he communicates with different levels and the public," Russert and Stone wasted little time talking about Cuomo as a prospective presidential candidate:

Russert: "If you look at the *Daily News* poll and his 79% approval rating, you can see that it cuts across all the demographics of any polling data. The key is his ability to say to people: "These are the problems. You may not agree, but I'm doing the best I can." Add to that the notion of family and values. If you listen to the beginning of any Reagan speech and the beginning of any Cuomo speech, there is almost no difference. They make the same appeal to family values, patriotism. Only at the conclusions do they drift apart.....in a Presidential campaign, the rap will be: "Is Mario Cuomo too New York, too Italian, too liberal?" But, I'll tell you, if Mario Cuomo goes to Birmingham, Alabama and Abilene, Texas, and gives the same speech about family he gives in Buffalo, he'll do very well.

So there it was, like a rotting corpse unearthed in the back yard, and it was first introduced by former Cuomo Press Secretary Tim Russert: "Is Mario Cuomo too New York, too Italian?" What was that supposed to mean? With Russert opening the door, it took only seconds for a bottom-feeder like Roger Stone to spit out what his stomach bile created:

Stone: The problem is that in a presidential campaign there is a much greater focus on the person. Did you carry your own garment bag off the plane?...The press in a national campaign looks at everything. Is he bright enough? Moral enough? Tough enough?... There's still a lot people don't know about Cuomo. We know how he plays in a controlled environment. But, I saw a poll from Texas a week ago where three people asked if Cuomo was an American name.

That was how they did it, the amoral bomb-droppers, and Stone was a master at matter-of-factly maligning people. Just toss out the inflammatory phrase in a normal sentence, a casual discussion, without raising your voice and let it sit there, to see if it gets challenged. If it doesn't meet with resistance or rebuttal, drop another, and then another, until the drumbeat of despicable lies and shadings takes on the patina of fact since they've been repeated so frequently— the poison fruit of a pathological political mind who understands precisely what he's doing.

I felt my anger rise up through my neck. I amended Stone's sly slur to myself: "Three fucking people asked if Cuomo was an American name." It took all my strength to stop from jumping out of my seat, grabbing Roger Stone by his necktie and strangling him.

"How dare you repeat that ethnic slur about Mario Cuomo, you slimy little prick," my eyes said, silently shooting stilettos across Stone's throat, slicing his jugular veins. I struggled to force the words back down my throat. I was there as Auletta's guest, and taking copious notes for the Governor, but for a split-second, I imagined calling my brother Michael to test my family's mob connections to control the raw sewage known as Roger Stone.

The slimy Stone was not quite finished. He would make it appear that he was covering his tracks in response to a question from the audience about whether the United States was ready for an Italian-American president, when, in fact, he subtly suckered Tim Russert in to deliver the latest droppings of his dirty work.

Stone: "I think if the voters get the measure of a man, regardless of his ethnicity, they'll vote for him—unless it comes into the larger question of being a New Yorker."

Russert: "There's the Jackie Robinson syndrome of politics which will be at work. Being the first Italian-American there is a different standard of application. They'll come at him with everything. A lot of it has already begun. I believe they'll be a knee jerk attempt to link him with the Mob or Mafia."

Russert's remarks froze me in place. I repeated them again and again, and wrote them down: "I believe they'll be a knee jerk attempt to link him with the Mob or the "Mafia." Of course "a lot of it has already begun," since Russert's own network, NBC, started it, without any basis in fact.

I didn't hang around to chat with Russert after the class ended. I was as angry with him for introducing the words "mob" and "mafia" into the seminars, as I was with Roger Stone. I expected slime to ooze out of Roger Stone's every opening, since it had been seeping out for years, like excrement from a colostomy bag, but Russert was another story. He had worked closely with Senator Daniel Patrick Moynihan for six years and then with Cuomo for almost two more. He knew the caliber of human being he was so loosely throwing into the same sentence with two words Cuomo was furthest from: "Mob" and "Mafia." He knew how Cuomo would react to those words. Whether Russert was still trying to prove his independence to NBC from his work with high-ranking Democratic public officials, a year after he left Cuomo's staff, or whether he didn't realize how physical proximity to Roger Stone had infected his mind and his own discourse, he should have know better.

I quickly packed up my tape recorder and my notes, pulled my heavy winter coat over my shoulders, left the New School classroom and headed down to the cold West 4th Street subway station. While I waited for the #1 train to take me up to Penn Station, I stared down at the tracks, watching two fat rats scurrying underneath, scavenging for food. "Russert and Stone", I thought, both scratching for tidbits of gossip to slip in-between the canapés and cocktails at chic West Village parties. It was a miserable business, and I hated it more than Mario Cuomo did.

A few days later, the Governor appeared on a statewide call-in show where he debated whether the "Mafia" existed with the *New York Post* columnist Frederick U. Dicker. The press ridiculed Cuomo for days, overlooking his clarification that he meant "not all organized crime was Italian-American, as the Italian word, 'Mafia' connotes." His nuance was lost.

Cuomo's parsing of the language was too fine and too fragile, in the face of what was happening on the streets of New York City. The night before Mario Cuomo was scheduled to give the guest lecture at Auletta's final class, Gambino Crime Family boss Paul Castellano was shot and killed in front of Sparks' Steak House on East 46th Street in Manhattan. The New York City media was orgasmic over the Castellano killing. Cuomo tried to turn the temperature down by holding an Albany Press conference the following morning to confront the issue of ethnic stereotyping and the saturation usage of the word "Mafia" in every single news report. Jeffrey Schmalz of the *New York Times* reported on the Governor's comments in a December 18, 1985, article entitled: "Cuomo Condemns Use of 'Mafia' For Describing Organized Crime:"

"'The conservatives who attack me with great regularity—think about it—whenever they get really annoyed at something I'm doing and they want to write a piece that's negative, it almost always mentions *The Godfather*, always mentions ethnicity,' Cuomo said."

Schmaltz went on to write that "Mr. Cuomo's comments, in a discussion with reporters, were primarily aimed against the use of the word 'Mafia' to describe organized crime. The word was used repeatedly yesterday and today in relation to the slaying on Monday of Paul Castellano, the reputed organized crime leader. The Governor wound up speaking for 45 minutes, describing what he sees as an overall stereotyping of Italian-Americans: 'As I have gotten older, this has become more significant to me,' Mr. Cuomo said."

In his passion to explain that not all organized crime was Italian, the Governor asked if other ethnic groups—Chinese, Israelis, Cubans, Blacks, Jews, Russians could also be linked to organized crime. Then, in driving home his point, Cuomo went too far:

"You're telling me that 'Mafia' is an organization, and I'm telling you that's a lot of baloney," Mario Cuomo said.

The Governor, surfing on the wave of his own passionate arguments, doubled-down on his statement, making matters worse by saying he was surprised that Rudolph W. Giuliani, the United States Attorney for the Southern District of New York, used the term "Mafia." Schmaltz reported precisely what Cuomo said: "You call him up today and say the Governor of the State of New York is surprised that he would use the word 'Mafia' to describe organized crime."

Schmaltz, a meticulous *New York Times* reporter, did just that. He called Giuliani who sawed off the rhetorical limb the Governor had climbed out onto. The fine rhetorical point of distinction Cuomo was making had crashed to the ground.

"You can't go so far as to suggest that the Mafia doesn't exist," Giuliani said to the *Times*. "There is indeed a group known as the "Mafia" that organizes itself around the fact that it is Italian or Italian-American."

Still, Mario Cuomo persisted in pointing out the damage the uttering of the very word did to Italian-Americans. The thought was out there, breathing and growing stronger like a brushfire, with each new story about the Castellano killing, and Mario Cuomo knew he needed to work mightily to suffocate it:

"'Mafia' is an Italian word and every time you say it, you suggest to people that organized crime is Italian—it's an ugly stereotype. I've lived with this notion all my life."

The wall-to-wall tabloid and television coverage of the killing of Castellano, made Mario Cuomo into a sagittal man, not just a sage, on the subject of the "Mafia," splitting in two what he was trying to accomplish with his precise definition of organized crime. The media frenzy surrounding the Mob killing, and the rise of John Gotti as the heir apparent to head the Gambino Crime Family, overwhelmed the delicate distinctions of Jeff Schmalz's story, both erasing and proving Cuomo's argument simultaneously. New York's tabloids were filled with charts and graphs of the "Mafia" families, with speculation as to who was now in power and who was out. Every name on the Org Charts of organized crime ended in a vowel.

I could not sleep for days. It was impossible to escape the coverage of the assassination of Castellano, and equally difficult for me to rid my mind of the picture of John Gotti at my brother Michael's wedding 18 months earlier. Everywhere I turned, I faced images of Gotti, my brother and Mario Cuomo.

What made matters worse was having to accompany the Governor to Ken Auletta's final seminar at the New School—that day after the Castellano murder—following his press conference held earlier the same day in Albany. I was consumed with thoughts of my family, my brother and Carmine Fatico; with evidence of my family's mob connections exposing itself in front of my eyes. I knew Cuomo was mistaken about the existence of the "Mafia"; I *knew* it existed for much of my life. It's shadow hung over my family for decades, and "Uncle" Charlie Fatico, the man who god-fathered Gotti into the Gambino Family, was my brother's admission ticket as well.

I could not hear a word the Governor said in Auletta's class. I stared at the stage, but kept replaying the news reports of the Castellano killings and the speculation about John Gotti. My mind rewound Tim Russert's warning: "I believe they'll be a knee-jerk attempt to link (Cuomo) with the mob or the "Mafia." I looked at Mario Cuomo on the stage of the New School that evening and felt like my chest had been split right down its center, with each of my limbs stretched to their sinewy limits, in opposite directions. I wanted to disappear, to flee from Mario Cuomo as quickly and invisibly as I could; at the same time, I wanted to fling myself onto the stage to protect him, if he were threatened by anyone, especially my family's connections.

I struggled to wish away the existence of the "Mafia" as much as Cuomo did. I wanted to burn every tabloid in New York that glorified the latest, gory gangland killing, wiping out any chance that the Governor could be vilified by the name Villano. I looked at Mario Cuomo, holding his head up high on the stage of the New School, his integrity unshakable, and knew that the only choice was to fight along side him. Two days later, December 19, 1985, Senator Ted Kennedy of Massachusetts announced that he would not seek the Democratic nomination for President in 1988. Mario Cuomo, six vowels and all, was all anyone in politics wanted to talk about.

7 ▫ Money As God

A bizarre tale of two cities, and contrasting Christmas Eves, un-folded on opposite coasts five days after Teddy Kennedy's withdrawal as a candidate for President pushed Mario Cuomo to the top of everyone's short list of potential Democratic presidential candidates.

In New York, John Gotti, the new reputed head of the Gambino Crime Family—following the murder of Paul Castellano the week before—threw a Christmas Eve party at the squat, brick-fronted Ravenite Social Club on Mulberry Street in lower Manhattan. Hun-dreds of guests packed into the darkened club, its two small front windows shuttered by old-fashioned white Venetian blinds, to greet Gotti, pay their respects and wish him luck. My brother Michael was among the well-wishers, and upon entering the Ravenite that unho-ly night, was photographed by FBI agents staking out the notorious Mob hangout. The photos would be used against my brother in his sentencing hearing three years later, as evidence of his connection to Gotti, either as a friend, or a business associate.

Across the country in the clean, bright sunlight of Irvine, Califor-nia, I was celebrating Christmas Eve at precisely the same moment with my parents, my sister Vera, my brother Vinnie and their families. Michael told our parents he would not be with us for the holiday because he had business in New York, but did not share with them where in New York he had business, or what that business was. My mother, as usual, accepted what her first-born son said as Gospel according to Michael, consistent with her Panglossian view of the world and anything he did.

California was as far as I could get from my brother and the news of John Gotti, Paul Castellano and Mario Cuomo. Flying over the ocean as we circled back toward land, I imagined jumping into the pristine Pacific, playing with my son, and feeling the waves wash every trace of the Mafia away, cleansing it from my family, and watching it shrivel and die on the sand the way jellyfish do, when they've been out in the sunshine too long. Then, I envisioned the tide coming in to wipe away every trace that we were there, every footprint on the beach, every sign of what existed moments ago.

When we arrived at Orange County, California's John Wayne Airport, I made the mistake of buying the *Los Angeles Times* and the *Orange County Register*. Both papers were filled with long stories about John Gotti, the Castellano killing and Gotti's ascension to the top of organized crime in the United States. I quickly read the stories and threw the papers in the trash, believing that, somehow, by tossing them away, the stories, too, would disappear, and my family in California would be unaware of what was happening in New York.

I wanted to lose myself in California and Christmas Eve, escaping from the unending tension of covering up one life, while living another. I wanted to be in one place, whole, as one person, known and loved by everyone around me, and not pretending to be someone entirely different, at odds with myself. Since childhood, the holiday served as a zone of safety for our family, despite financial pressures humming at a high pitch like highway noise in the background. Everything swirling around, threatening to swallow us would be put on hold for that one night. Weeks of preparation, of shopping and arguing about money, of putting up holiday decorations and wrapping packages—all were aimed at making Christmas Eve as near-perfect as possible, just for a blink of time each year.

Christmas Day was an anti-climax; Christmas Eve was showtime and everything had to be ready for the curtain to rise. All differences and difficulties were tossed together in a huge bowl of steaming hot linguine with crabs, drenched in a marinara sauce so sublime it swamped thoughts of everything else.

Distance, divorce, fights, failures, money woes—all faded away with each mouthwatering bite of *baccala* smothered in fresh tomatoes or friend shrimp, delicately buttered scallops or octopus salad that made you forget who you were.

My mother was the master chef, with culinary disciples in all of her children except me. As the oldest, Michael came closest to matching her innate skills and confidence in the kitchen. When he cooked, his stubby fingers moved as effortlessly as hers, despite the paralysis of my mother's right arm. She guided her right fingers with her "good" left hand, making each meal all the more miraculous. Since my parents' move from New York to Southern California when my son was a toddler, each year became increasingly more important for me to have him experience Christmas Eve with my family. Matthew was being raised Jewish, and after my conversion from Catholicism to Judaism in 1980, we stopped having a Christmas tree, despite it being a small, symbolic piece of perfection for me; a tangible thing of beauty I could carve out of a chaotic life.

Not having a Christmas tree heightened the urgency of having my son experience the rituals of the Italian side of his family on Christmas Eve. Sitting down at my mother's dining room table, extended by two heavy wooden leaves, was the closest we came to Nirvana, cracking open the first delicious crab-legs drenched in marinara sauce that my mother had prepared.

I held the family record from a previous Christmas Eve for sitting for five consecutive hours and consuming every last crab in the large pasta pot. I was just beginning to crack open my first crab shell when my brother Vinnie punctured my own outer covering, which I mistakenly thought I made impenetrable.

"I can see the headlines now," he said, "BROTHER OF CUOMO AIDE TIED TO GOTTI."

I pretended not to hear him, which was not always possible, since his comments were often in your face and purposely outrageous to gain maximum attention.

We argued politics frequently. He was an Orange County, Republican and supporter of Ronald Reagan. His Gotti comment had no political content, but was meant to make light of a circumstance about which he knew I was deadly serious. Vinnie was well aware of how much I detested our brother's wise-guy friends. At Michael's wedding the year before, he was titillated by Gotti's presence at the same table with "Uncle" Charlie Fatico, trying to get me to go over and "shake John's hand."

I refused. To my brother Vinnie, Lucky Luciano, Vito Genovese, Pat Eboli, "Uncle Charlie," John Gotti, and my brother's association with some of them, was all a long-running family joke—part of a narrative of family folklore. When our Aunt Josephine tried to tell us what "nice men" Vito Genovese and Tommy Eboli were since she cooked for them, it was Vinnie who quickly coined the tragic/comic phrase, "Nice men who kill people." He loved getting my participation in the mockery, even if it meant making me the butt of his humor.

Usually, I was entertained by my brother's outrageousness, and the quickness of his mind, and took pleasure in lacerating his lunacy. Somehow, whether by intention or accident, he broke open my deepest fear: of a public connection between Cuomo, me, my brother and John Gotti. I pretended to ignore him by changing the subject. I focused on how delicious the crabs were, and how happy we were to be away from the bitter cold of New York. I turned to my father to discuss former New York Yankee star, Roger Maris, who died just a few weeks before Christmas, counting on his anger at learning of Michael's regular Sunday visits to "Uncle Charlie's" years earlier helping me steer the conversation away from Michael and his sketchy friends.

My father was a different person now at age seventy, having retired and moved out to the West Coast seven years earlier. He and my mother were squeaking by on Social Security, and on a few extra dollars he made working part-time in the mailroom at Vinnie's electronic parts company. They were living in a modest, clean, Section 8 Federal Housing garden apartment complex in Irvine, amidst the ostentation and over-the-top wealth of Southern California. Never one to refuse a handout, my father appreciated some of the benefits of Michael's connections, and was not about to, as he would say in his garbled Brooklynese, "bite the fuckin' hand that feeds me." To my father, money was viewed as the savior, Don Quixote's Golden Helmet of Mambrino, the gilded key to open the prison's padlock. The people they admired, whether in the Mob or not, were people with money. Mario Puzo put it this way in *The Fortunate Pilgrim*, (Random House, 1964, p. 87):

> *But money was God. Money could make you free. Money could give you hope. Money could make you safe... Money guarded the lives of your children. Money lifted the family out of darkness. Who has not wept for lack of money? Who has not wept for money? Who comes when money calls? Doctors, priests, dutiful sons...Money was a new homeland...*

When he was still working full-time, the highlight of my father's work year came around the Christmas holidays, when the wealthy lawyers and accountants on the upper floors of the Manhattan office building he worked in as a maintenance workers, gave him cash tips for his personal services throughout the year. A "good year" of tips from the upper-floor tenants meant a good year for all of us, since my father's good fortune would trickle down to his children in the forms of gifts, or feasts of hard salami, fresh Italian bread and chunks of provolone cheese.

Once a year before Christmas, (it was always around Christmas when money achieved the glow of the Savior) my father packed us up in his old Plymouth and drove the family to the elite Port Jefferson community of Bel Terre, where his boss, Mr. Douglas, lived. We never knew his first name; it was always "Mr. Douglas;" money bought him that respect. The boys were required to wear jackets and ties for our ritual visit, and my sister a skirt, which could not be too short. A housekeeper opened the large wooden door, and, after my father removed his grey fedora hat and held it in his hand, ushered us into a huge foyer, where we stood at attention in front of a grand old mahogany grandfather clock. The clock watched us with its single large eye, making sure we didn't touch anything or make it dirty, loudly ticking off the minutes before Mr. Douglas and his wife entered the room bearing Christmas cookies and gracious upper-class Protestant smiles. After commenting on how much we had grown over the past year, Mr. Douglas handed each of us a sealed envelope.

We thanked the Douglases and, smiling, backed out the front door, with my father placing his grey fedora on his head once we stepped out into the cold air. We were not permitted to open the envelopes until we were in the car, and safely out of sight of the Douglas mansion. Year after year, we'd open our envelopes gingerly, careful not to rip the ten dollar bill which we knew was inside. We felt flush, and secretly, longed to live with the Douglas' where money flowed like sweets, and the entry hallway was nearly as big as our split-level house in North Babylon, purchased on a GI mortgage.

It was a blink of a glimpse into another world, and, to us, the streets of Bel Terre were paved with gold, even if there were no Italian-Americans living there. What was left for each of us to figure out, if we wanted to, was how to find our way back to that "new homeland" of money, without holding our hat in our hand.

For my father, now seventy, it was too late to worry about any of that. He had done what he had to do to raise four kids on a paltry salary, provide a home and a yard in a working-class suburb of New York, and have a little money left for booze and playing the ponies. He was an immigrant's son, who came of age during the Depression, with nothing more than a ninth-grade education, and achieved more than he ever thought possible; amazed at how far he'd come from where his own parents were back on Union Street in Brooklyn. What mattered most to him now was money—*the thing itself*—as Harriet Beecher Stowe once wrote about slavery. He could care less how it was obtained.

Rather than rescue me from Vinnie's merciless teasing about the Mob, me, and Mario Cuomo, my father prolonged my discomfort by bragging about Michael's "friend" at Universal Studios, Gene Giaquinto. Giaquinto was a former top executive at MCA-Universal. He headed the company's Home Entertainment Division under

Lew Wasserman until he was put on paid leave of absence in late 1988. Giaquinto once sent a limo down from Hollywood to pick up my sister and my nieces, treating them to a VIP tour of Universal Studios.

Kathleen Sharp's book *Mr. & Mrs. Hollywood: Edie & Lew Wasserman and Their Entertainment Empire* (Carroll & Graf Publishers, N.Y., an imprint of Avon Publishing Group, Inc., 200, p.395) is packed with allegations of Giaquinto's connections to criminal enterprises and extensively quotes Organized Crime Strike Force Prosecutor Richard Slavin about Giaquinto's dealing with a mob-owned company in New Jersey beginning in 1983 (p.396). The Giaquinto connection to my brother Michael did not merely consist of limo rides to LA & free tours of Universal Studios. A *New York Daily News* story a few years later ("Mob in the Movies: Feds probe Gotti's starring role in killing Hollywood deal", by Jerry Capeci, April 8, 1990) would detail Michael's involvement with Giaquinto in a story based upon FBI reports and testimony. The story focused on a dispute allegedly between actor James Caan, backed by the Genovese Crime Family, and MCA-Universal, which owned the rights to a film about the legendary crime boss, Meyer Lansky. Capeci, the Organized Crime reporter for the *Daily News*, writes:

> *The key players included Eugene Giaquinto, a former top executive of MCA-Universal, who boasted that he had known (John) Gotti as a boy, and allegedly worked hand-in-glove with the mob; Michael Villano, who also knew the kid Gotti and became a businessman with a penchant for partying with him; Martin Bacow, a would-be screenwriter who boasts of a long friendship with the late Lansky, and of course, Caan, a star who's played wiseguys on screen and makes no secret that he plays with them in real life.* (p. 7, Sunday, April 8, 1990)

Capeci went on to write that the battle for the right to make the movie came down to James Caan wanting to do it, and Martin Bacow having a completed script and a four-million guarantee from

Giaquinto for MCA's home video rights. The FBI affidavit filed on the incident reported:

Giaquinto said that if they (the Genovese Family) wanted war, that he had had a meeting in New York and had been promised anything he wanted, and it came from number one. Bacow then asked if number one "was the G guy," meaning Gotti. "Yes," said Giaquinto. (p. 43)

Then, Capeci's story on the Lansky movie and my brother's Michael's involvement with Giaquinto, according to FBI affidavits, got as specific as a wiretap could get:

Giaquinto also told Bacow that he had been trying to reach Michael—presumably Villano—adding that "he could have them all on planes "to Los Angeles at a moment's notice.

On July 8, 1987, Giaquinto connected with Villano via a transcontinental phone call, according to the affidavit: 'They (Genovese mobsters) are all over the place', he complained.

"Shame on them," replied Villano, who promised to send someone to Los Angeles to get "all the facts." Minutes later Giaquinto called Bacow to reassure him.

"Villano told me to tell you that it will be resolved in one minute, no matter where the move was coming from," said Giaquinto, according to the affidavit."

A similar story which appeared a year earlier in the Orange County, California Edition of the *Los Angeles Times* ("Mob and the Movies: Life or Art—Who Plays Lansky?", Sunday, March 19, 1989, pps. 34-38) recounted the same conversation involving my brother from the FBI affidavits. However, on a page summarizing "Meyer Lansky's Cast of Characters" (p. 38), Michael is included in a line-up of ten, which included Meyer Lansky, John Gotti, James Caan, Vinny (Jimmy Blue Eyes) Alo of the Genovese crew, and Eugene F. Giaquinto, the MCA-Universal executive.

The *LA Times* story described my brother this way:

Michael Villano: New York businessman who the FBI believes is Giaquinto's link to the Gambino Crime Family, and who declared "shame on them," when informed by Giaquinto that the Genovese family was laying claim to the Lansky film. (p. 38).

I sat there in stony silence and stared at my father. His eyes bulging from all the booze he drank, his puffy face flushed. I expected wisdom, compassion maybe, or a shared commiseration over Roger Maris' death. I expected him to sense my discomfort and guide the conversation away from Gotti or my brother's gangster friends. But, there was no comfort forthcoming. Instead, my father was locked in a loop of genuflection over Gene Giaquinto's generosity. He told me, several times, how much money my brother Michael sent him for Christmas, and how expensive the bottle of wine was that Michael bought when he came to California and treated my parents to dinner. My article on Roger Maris' death stayed in my suitcase, since my father's concentration on cash made it irrelevant and impossible to share. Different things mattered to us.

"I'm seventy years old, Steve," my father reminded me, over and over again, slurring his speech as he usually did. "I just want to be taken care of from here on out."

The escape route through my father was blocked. He was oblivious to my pain, and I, intolerant of his. Too much whiskey had numbed him to feeling any more pain, his own or mine. Too much torment blinded me from seeing who my father was and what he needed.

"Money is no object, Rock, with dese guys" he kept repeating to me. "Money is no object."

My father had convinced himself that his small, personal sell-out was of no consequence, since, in his mind, he wasn't either. I was too sad for both of us to contradict him. Despite his girth, there was nothing left of my father. He was tired of struggle. His fire was out, his fight, gone; his sense of dignity, disappeared...at least for now. I glanced over at the modest but meaningful gift we carried across country—a book on the history of horseracing—wrapped neatly and resting inconspicuously under my parents' Christmas tree. It might have gotten noticed if a $100 bill was sticking out of the book's cover. Otherwise, I knew it would be tossed aside as soon as my father opened it, never to be read. Mario Puzo was right. Money was God—especially on Christmas Eve.

8 ◻ Scylla & Charybdis

I could not get far enough away from my family, fast enough, following that unnerving bi-coastal Christmas Eve which brought little peace or comfort. Returning to New York, I prepared to bury myself completely in Mario Cuomo's re-election campaign to escape my family, even while Cuomo touted the strength of family as the bedrock of society. All of the Cuomo Administration efforts were aimed at advancing that vision, while my actions toward my own kin were designed to put them out of sight. I was not embarrassed by them; I just wished I was not related to them.

The harder I worked, I reasoned, the less time or energy I would have to think about my family, and the easier it would be to immunize myself against the stupidity of one brother, the insensitivity of the other, and my father's ignominious surrender to the bums he belittled all his life. If any of them called on me for help or understanding, I could use that trite, but justifiable, excuse of being "too busy" to become involved in their troubles, which were perpetual. Distance from them was essential to my own survival. Two decades earlier, the drumbeat of family dramas led me to a lame, half-hearted adolescent attempt to take my own life, as an avenue of escape. Time and changing circumstances, like the birth of my son, made that route unthinkable. Now, I was lost again, and before I could recalibrate my compass, a sloppy suicide attempt by a prominent public official slapped me to my senses.

Nine days into 1986, Donald Manes, Queens Borough President for 15 years, was found bleeding with knife cuts on his left wrist and left ankle, in a city-owned vehicle pulled over on a shoulder of Grand Central Parkway in Queens, NY. Manes, Queens Country Democratic Party Chairman and a close political ally of Mayor Edward I. Koch, was a powerhouse in New York politics for more than a decade

Initial news reports of what happened to Manes on the evening of January 9 were suspicious. Just two days earlier, he had been inaugurated for his fifth term as Queens Borough President—of which he won with 85% of the vote—one week after Ed Koch was sworn in for his third term as Mayor of New York City. Manes left a dinner party at Queens Borough Hall in Kew Gardens that night in an unusual manner. He sent his chauffeur home for the evening, got behind the wheel of a plain city carpool vehicle, drove onto Grand Central Parkway and was spotted weaving eastward along the wide Parkway for two miles, before finally getting pulled over by an NYPD patrol car. Manes told the police officers who stopped him, according to a chronology published in the *New York Times* on January 19, 1986:

...he had been abducted by two men, hidden in the back seat of his car and was ordered to drive around Queens and ultimately slashed on his left wrist and ankle.

When pressed by police at the scene, Manes could not identify his abductors or explain his knife wounds. Hospitalized that night at NYU Medical Center in Manhattan, Manes lost one-third of his blood and was moved into the coronary care unit, where physicians could monitor his heart.

The following day, news of Manes curious accident was all over New York's tabloids and television stations. Mayor Koch, strongly supported by Manes' Queens political organization in each of his own elections for Mayor and his 1982 Democratic Statewide Primary election campaign for Governor against Mario Cuomo, immediately rushed to the Borough President's bedside. Koch, with great fanfare, fawned all over Manes, kissing him on the forehead and telling him: "Don't worry about anything, Donny. We all love you." Two days later, Pulitzer Prize-winning columnist Jimmy Breslin reported in the *New York Daily News* that Queens lawyer Michael G. Dowd was personally instructed by Manes to pay a $36,000 bribe to Geoffrey G. Lindenauer, a Manes friend and associate. Lindenauer, a rotund man who fit the Thomas Nast cartoon caricature of a back-room political hack, was strategically placed by Manes in the position of Deputy Director of the NYC Parking Violations Bureau, where he could act as the Borough President's "bagman," collecting bribes. Breslin wrote that Dowd was providing United States Attorney Rudolph Giuliani's Office with the information about the bribe Donald Manes directed him to pay. When the news broke about Dowd—the first domino to fall for Manes and others in a massive political corruption case that unraveled over the next few months—Mayor Koch's hospital-room kiss on Donny's forehead turned into a bitter kiss of death. James S. Kunen, writing in a *People Magazine* story of March 31, 1986, entitled "Mayor Ed Koch Tries to Survive as NY, NY is Plunged into Scandal, Scandal," noted:

> *Koch, who had frequently described Manes as his 'good friend', quickly denounced him as a 'crook.' And, even though Manes hadn't been charged or convicted of any crime, Koch said he should go to jail.*

Rumors ran rampant in the City's political circles of a massive kickback scheme centered around private company contracts with the Manes-controlled NYC Parking Violations Bureau. As the federal investigation widened in the weeks ahead, the web of corruption grew to include an elaborate bribery and extortion ring involving Citisource, Inc., a company that made hand-held computerized ticketing devices. Masterminded by Manes, the money-laundering logistics were worked out with Lindenauer and Bronx Democratic Party Chairman Stanley Friedman, who's wife served as Koch's $47,500 per year Deputy Director of the Office of Special Projects and Events. Friedman successfully represented Citisource before the

City when the company was awarded its $22.7 million contract. In return, Manes and Friedman received thousands of shares of Citisource stock. The US Attorney Office labeled the operation a "racketeering enterprise," with the Parking Violations Bureau ripping off the City for more than $2 million during the Koch years.

Desperate to avoid blame, Koch began flailing out at everyone, dumping on Manes and his Queens cronies to distance himself from the exploding extortion scandal. Frantic to steer the public's focus away from himself—a completely unfamiliar move for Koch, who craved attention and adulation—the Mayor tried to tie Mike Dowd to Mario Cuomo. In a classic example of Koch's litany of lies and histrionic efforts to pull anyone he could into the cesspool of city corruption he enabled, Koch began ranting that Dowd managed Cuomo's Mayoralty campaign against him in 1977, as if somehow implicating Mario Cuomo into the Queens crowd by association. In truth, Dowd had been a volunteer on Cuomo's campaign for Mayor, which Koch won, and he stepped in as acting coordinator for a few weeks when the full-time campaign coordinator became ill.

In the same way many of Mario Cuomo's political opponents, like Roger Stone, were slyly suggesting that Cuomo's Italian heritage made it likely that he was Mob-connected, Koch tried to insinuate that since Cuomo was from Queens, he was part of that corrupt crowd. It was a wild claim, so far removed from reality, that it collapsed almost as quickly as Koch's credibility. In fact—and Koch knew this better than anyone, because he was its prime beneficiary—Mario Cuomo was anathema to the Queens County Democratic Organization, which Manes chaired.

Cuomo began his public career as an outsider, brought in as a skilled, independent lawyer to mediate the Forest Hills housing dispute by Republican/Liberal Mayor, John Lindsay in 1972. He disdained politicians and politics, especially the clubhouse "pols." New York's City's political establishment roundly rejected Mario Cuomo when Koch ran against him for Governor in the 1982 New York State Democratic Primary. The City's political bosses reached the same conclusion about Cuomo that my brother Michael's friends in the Gambino Crime Family did: he was "unreachable."

Every single Democratic County Leader in NYC—most prominently Queens' Donald Manes, the Bronx' Stanley Friedman, and Brooklyn's Meade Esposito—lined up behind Ed Koch, who was the odds on favorite to win. Cuomo surprised them all by winning the primary and then the general election. Since he hadn't made deals with the City's political bosses, he owed them nothing—unlike Koch. Even when the powerful triumvirate of Manes, Friedman, and Esposito tried to force a deal down Mario Cuomo's throat to enable him to get on the ballot for Governor at the NYS Democratic Convention in 1982, instead of having to go the laborious petition route—Andrew, acting on his father's behalf—refused to take it. Andrew Cuomo wrote of that turning point in his book *All Things Possible* (Harper Collins, NYC; 2014, pps. 65-66):

I'd been summoned by the New York City Democratic bosses; Meade Esposito from Brooklyn, Donald Manes from Queens and Stanley Friedman from the Bronx...

Friedman and Manes were my father's contemporaries; Esposito was my grandfather's age. It really was a smoke-filled back room. Each man was nursing a fat cigar...

Koch said "we're giving your father the 25 percent he needs to get on the ballot," Manes said.

...I looked at Manes and said, "I don't want your votes."

"What do you mean you don't want our votes?" he barked. "That's the only way you'll get on the Democratic ballot."

"I'd rather get shut out by the convention," I said. "Then I could say the Democratic bosses shut us out." They knew it was true, but brazen to articulate.

"Kid, nobody's asking you," Manes said. "We're telling you. You've only got enough delegates to take 15 to 20 percent of the votes. We're going to make up the difference. Our delegates will cast enough Cuomo votes to get you to 25%. Do you understand that, kid?"

I said, "Well, I don't accept it."

"It's not up to you," Esposito said.

"What do you mean, it's not up to me?"

"We're going to have our people vote for you."

I said, "I won't accept their votes."

He said, "Nobody's asking if you accept."

"I'll reject the votes at the convention."

"There's no way to reject votes."

I said, "Well, if you are going to have your people vote for us, I will have my people vote for you."

Not only did Andrew Cuomo tell Manes, Friedman and Esposito to take their back-room deal for Mario Cuomo's nomination and shove it, but he out-maneuvered them on the Convention floor, winning a delegate chess match that resulted in his father receiving 39% of the vote, nearly double what the NYC political bosses had him pegged at getting. Mario Cuomo was on the ballot in the Democratic Primary for Governor via the Convention route, and the Cuomos had shown Manes, Friedman, and Esposito that—unlike Ed Koch—they weren't in their pockets and didn't need them. This was heresy, and it stuck in Koch's craw for years.

Breslin and a few other New York reporters, including Murray Kempton, saw right through Koch's shrieking sideshow on the Manes case, done to deflect attention from his own accountability for what was happening under his nose. Breslin told Kunen at *People Magazine*:

How could he not know? By making a deal with all the (party organization) leaders—Brooklyn can have this job, Queens can have this—he gave the City away. He allowed them to steal millions.

Murray Kempton, also a Pulitzer Prize-winning journalist like Breslin, was no less damning when asked about Koch by Kunen:

You're talking about a man who is really basically un-aware...He did not realize that these guys (from the political club-houses) are in business. Their outlet is buying houses, collecting money. His outlet is going on The Tonight Show.

If Koch's claims were being viewed with skepticism and disbelief, Donald Manes' story was being shot full of holes. Nothing added up: not the stab wounds, not the lack of blood outside the car, not the victim's inability to identify his attackers. New York City's Chief of Detectives Richard T. Nicastro rejected the Borough President's account of the incident, stating that, "Our opinion at this time, is that injuries were self-inflicted." A few days later—the same day that Michael Dowd appeared before federal prosecutors to reveal the bribery operation—Manes issued a statement from his hospital room at NYU Medical Center, admitting that he tried to kill himself.

I was traveling to an event in New York City with the Governor on January 28, —six days after Manes' mea culpa—when Cuomo raised the subject of Koch's appalling actions. With Claire Shulman, Deputy Queens Borough President taking over at Queens Borough Hall that day, the conversation turned to the scandal surrounding Donald Manes, his attempted suicide and Ed Koch's Captain Queeg-like behavior. Cuomo had every reason to rip Koch apart, especially in private, but he did not. Nothing Koch did surprised him anymore. Other people's lives were at stake, and Cuomo respected the fragility of life and relationships better than most in public life. His observations were subdued and thoughtful; his voice was level and almost morose.

"When the heat gets turned on, you really begin to see who melts," Cuomo said, referencing Koch.

The Governor asked me what I thought of the whole "unseemly mess."

I found Koch's behavior as despicable as Breslin and Kempton did. The Manes mania caught me, like most New Yorkers, off guard, and it made politics and political corruption seem just as distasteful and dishonorable as the work of the Mob. Life in public service was, to me, a constructive counterpoint to the ways of the wise guys we witnessed growing up, an altruistic alternative to the fishy business of the boys my brother visited at the Bergin Hunt & Fish Club, or the Ravenite. What was happening with Manes and his twisted web of organizations was worse, in certain ways, since public officials owed us much more than could be expected from gangsters.

For those of us who believed in government as a force for good, it was a terrible time. Political bosses and crime bosses were becoming indistinguishable from one another, except in the products they exchanged and their methods of enforcement. In both cases, there were shakedowns, bagmen, bribery, extortion, kickbacks, and racketeering. What struck me was that if the Mob could have come up with such a sophisticated scheme of siphoning money *from* the city under the guise of collecting fines and penalties *for* the city, they'd have it in operation all across the country. It seemed small consolation that at least those who stood in the way of the public officials caught abusing their power—whistleblowers like Mike Dowd—didn't end up face down in a pool of blood on the sidewalk in front of Sparks Steakhouse. I took a deep breath and looked straight at the Governor.

"Well, Governor," I said, "for the first time in a long-time I've thought about what my mother said to me: 'Be a writer. Forget politics.'"

That's all I wanted to share with Mario Cuomo, since I knew the my mother's advice did not imply she was recoiling from corruption. She had lived with the Mob through marriage in her family for decades, and learned, as we all did, to accept tainted goods with quiet disgrace from members of our family.

But suddenly, things were far different for her, with her oldest son "mixed up with those guys," and her youngest working for an Italian-American politician who was the antithesis of everything the Mob represented. Her instinctual maternal fear was that my business of serving the public, and my brother's business of taking from it, would, inevitably collide and break the family apart. She didn't care less about John Gotti, Donald Manes or Ed Koch, or even Mario Cuomo, whom she admired. All that truly mattered to her were her children. Whatever happened, she wanted us to all get along.

Cuomo shook his head, and flashed a gentle smile at me. "No," the Governor said. "This is what makes things challenging for people like us."

People like us. I loved that Mario Cuomo included me in the same phrase with him. I found it difficult to do that myself, knowing my family's history and my own failings. I wanted to be more like him, only without my baggage—without the mess of my brother's involvement with "Uncle" Charlie and John Gotti, the complicity of my knowledge of those relationships, and the danger I knew they contained for Mario Cuomo and me.

The Manes mess grew far more tragic over the coming months. Donald Manes' associate and bagman, Geoffrey Lindenauer, at the center of the corruption scandal, was indicted on charges of extortion, racketeering, and mail fraud on February 24. He faced twenty-five years in prison, if convicted. To avoid such severe punishment, he pleaded guilty in exchange for his testimony against Manes. Lindenauer revealed the extent of the corruption, in exchange for what would eventually be a two-year prison term. His guilty plea and agreement to testify against his boss, pushed Manes over the edge.

In mid-March, Marlene Manes, worried about the her husband's deeper descent into despair, made a frantic phone call to his psychiatrist, Dr. Elliott N. Wineburg, to discuss voluntarily admitting Donald Manes to a mental hospital. According to the *New York Times* story by Richard J. Meislin, entitled: "Manes Death: A Frantic Call, A Fatal Threat," (March 15, 1986), Manes picked up the downstairs phone and listened in on the conversation between his wife and his psychiatrist. When Dr. Wineburg asked Marlene Manes to hold on while he answered his doorbell, Donald Manes "pulled a 14" Ecko Flint Knife with an 8¾ inch blade from the kitchen drawer and thrust it into his chest."

"Mrs. Manes," the *Times*' Meislin wrote, "rushed into the kitchen and, as Mr. Manes slumped to the floor, she withdrew the knife from his chest and hurled it across the kitchen. Hearing screams over the dangling kitchen phone, Dr. Wineburg ran the five blocks from his home to the Manes residence...Two EMS units responded but found no vital signs. Manes was rushed to Booth Memorial Hospital in Flushing, where he was pronounced dead at 11:00 pm."

New York's political world was shaken by the news of Manes' suicide and reports of the horrifying scene Marlene Manes and her daughter had witnessed. While there was universal condemnation of Donald Manes' crimes, there was widespread sympathy for his family. Mario Cuomo attended Manes' funeral at Schwartz Brothers-Jeffers Memorial Chapel in Forest Hills, paying his respects to the Manes family. Even Ed Koch was there. Throughout the entire sordid ordeal which consumed the first three months of the year in which Mario Cuomo was up for re-election, the Governor emerged with his dignity and personal integrity as unshakeable as ever. He and Matilda Cuomo had known the Manes family for years and expressed deep compassion for Marlene and their daughter Lauren, who endured the worst of her father's nightmare, and separate ones of her own.

It would have been too easy and safe for Mario Cuomo to remind the press and public of his distance from the Democratic bosses and Koch's coziness to Manes and Friedman—"cheap grace" he would have called it, and he refused to do it. He simply operated at a higher level. The Governor, like Manes, was from Queens, and that sudden political poison, coupled with the rise of John Gotti, an Italian-American mobster from the same borough, could have made Cuomo a target for guilt by geographic, as well as ethnic, association. Mario Cuomo bought into none of that. Secure in who he was, Cuomo had nothing to prove or disprove, and nothing to hide.

Writing in his memoir years later, Andrew Cuomo underscored precisely who his father was (*All Things Possible*, Harper Collins Publishers, 2014, p. 79):

Nothing and no one can shake him. Public affection or disaffection doesn't move him. Wealth doesn't define him...He has never spoken to me about money...His sense of right and wrong and his pursuit of principle are paramount. He is exactly in private as he is in public. There is no 'public persona'. It's just him. The ultimate fight is being at peace with oneself. My father had won that battle before he ever began.

During this cascade of calamities in the first quarter of 1986, I closely studied every single nuance of Mario Cuomo's mannerisms and behavior and every line and expression on his face. I observed how he handled the report of Manes' first suicide attempt, the news of the spreading scandal surrounding the City's Parking Violation Bureau, the tragic circumstances of Manes' horrible death and its inhumane impact on his family.

Cuomo was steady, almost stoic, throughout the ordeal, with his face and his voice revealing deep compassion and reservoirs of emotion and grief. Watching him was an instruction in how to behave, how to comport oneself under intense pressure. It made me admire the man even more, apart from his politics—and feel far worse about the tightrope I stradled that could, somehow, if it came loose, ensnare him and carry down both of us. It also made me feel safer being in his presence, by his side.

Cuomo's moral strength drove me to work harder for him. I pretended that my brother's Mob connections, and my family's longtime links to both the Genovese and Gambino crime organizations, were a mirage, a figment of an overactive imagination. I would simply ignore them out of existence, allowing nothing—neither my family nor my fears—to distract me from public service, or pursuing Mario Cuomo's policies. If the Governor could resist everything thrown his way, so could I. I would dedicate every ounce of my energy and commitment to advancing his agenda, and protecting the Governor from any kind of political or personal attack. I had scrutinized his behavior under pressure, and was drawn even closer to what I witnessed.

Cuomo rewarded my loyalty and work ethic with high praise and more work, pulling me closer to his inner circle. It was a powerful aphrodisiac. I craved more of it, as if it were cocaine, ignoring the risks of my family's links to organized crime. I was seduced by Mario Cuomo's compliments and kindnesses and by the promise of using political power for the public good. I was exactly where I always wanted to be, doing what I always wanted to do. I loved being pulled closer to the center of things, and, at the same time, loathed my weakness for allowing it to happen.

Westchester County Executive Andrew O'Rourke surfaced as a potential Republican candidate to run against the Governor for re-election. As he exhibited a frightening ignorance about the Shoreham Nuclear Power Plant on Long Island, my role in the Administration, as the one Executive Chamber staff member living within proximity to the nuclear facility, took on a whole new dimension. Fabian Palomino, Mario Cuomo's oldest and closest friend and the Governor's top advisor on Shoreham, came into my World Trade Center office to inform me of what Mario Cuomo had in mind.

"The Governor told me we've got to find a better way to use your talents," Fabian said, matter-of-factly.

Within days, I was working more closely with Palomino. My lengthy commutes back and forth to Long Island each night finally had a policy-related purpose. But I was consumed with trepidation, as my star rose within the Administration, over the issue of Shoreham, since my brother knew many people involved with work on the plant.

Ironically, and unrelated to Michael's involvement in the circles of the NY Metropolitan-area trade unions, an article in the *New York Times* by Michael Oreskes entitled "Corruption is Called Way of Life in New York Construction Industry" (4/25/82)—appearing in the midst of Mario Cuomo's first campaign for Governor— revealed the depth of the intertwining of organized crime with the New York City construction industry.

"I've never dealt with an industry that has more pervasive corruption than the construction industry," James F. McNamara, Director of Mayor Koch's Office of Construction Industry Relations told the

Times. "When I say corruption I'm using a very broad term. Some of it is labor racketeering. Some of it is political influence. Some of it is bid-rigging; some, extortion."

The *Times'* Oreskes went on to report that "Organized crime figures have infiltrated many important construction unions, from truck drivers to carpenters to blasters. Sixteen of thirty-one union locals in the City that represent laborers, the backbone of any construction job, are described by law enforcement authorities as being under influence of organized crime." Some builders and developers throughout the five boroughs of New York, including The Trump Organization, paid whatever extra costs were exacted through organized crime's control of the cement industry, drywall, or other aspects of the construction business.

In *Trump: The Deals and the Downfall* (Dec. 1991, Harper Collins, NY. NY), Wayne Barrett wrote that Donald Trump met with Genovese Crime Family boss Anthony "Fat Tony" Salerno in the apartment of their mutual attorney Roy Cohn in 1983. The book appeared less than a year after the Oreskes' *New York Times* article had detailed organized crime's infiltration of New York's construction industry. Salerno, along with then-Gambino Crime Family boss Paul Castellano, tightly controlled the NYC concrete industry through their company, S & A Concrete. Cohn's client list—since he moved to New York from Washington, DC in the mid-1950s, following his work as a prosecutor, an Assistant U.S. Attorney, and Chief Counsel to U.S. Senator Joseph McCarthy during the Army/McCarthy hearings—included celebrities, Studio 54, alleged mobsters like Salerno, and later, John Gotti.

Barrett documented that Cohn also represented Trump in meetings with another key New York construction industry player, convicted labor racketeer John Cody, another former associate of my brother Michael's. Cody, at the peak of his power in the mid-1970s through 1982, when he was dealing with Cohn on Trump's behalf, was no small operator. As President of Teamster Local 282, Cody controlled 4,000 drivers of delivery trucks in New York City and

Long Island. He had the power to bring to a grinding halt the $2.5 billion construction industry, which employed 70,000 people. He could shut down any construction project in New York, including Trump Tower, by pulling out his drivers. Cody told Barrett: "Donald liked to deal with me through Roy Cohn." Barrett reported that Trump did, however, have to deal directly with John Cody's girlfriend, Vernia Hixon, to whom Trump gave a sweetheart deal for several apartments, just under his own, in Trump Tower.

Despite his posturing as a New York power player, Trump cowered in front of John Cody. As recently as 2016, Cody's son, Michael, told Christopher Dickey and Michael Daly of *The Daily Beast* (October 13, 2016, "The Swiss Connection: The Party Girl Who Brought Trump to His Knees,") how Donald gave Cody whatever he wanted:

"Trump was a guy who would talk tough, but as soon as you confronted him, he would cry like a little girl. He was all talk, no action."

Cody made sure Trump took good care of his special friend Hixon, even funneling some $500,000 to her for renovations of her apartments, while he was in jail for racketeering and income tax evasion. When Trump balked at fulfilling some of his promises to Cody's girlfriend, Barrett reoorted that "Cody and Hixon cornered him in a nearby bar and got his agreement. 'Anything for you, John,'" was Hixon's recollection of Trump's comment. Trump was so terrified of crossing Cody that at one point, when Cody called Trump from prison to complain about construction problems on Hixon's apartments, Barrett reported that "Trump greeted him nervously on the phone. 'Where are you?' Trump asked. "Downstairs?"

"My father walked all over Trump." Michael Cody told *The Daily Beast. "Anytime Trump didn't do what he was told, my father would shut down his job for the day. No deliveries. 400 guys sittin' around."*

To John Cody and his colleagues, Donald Trump was just another puffed-up, pasty patsy.

Indicted by a Brooklyn Grand Jury on charges of racketeering, extortion, and tax evasion, Cody was sentenced to five years in prison at the end of 1982. His sentencing Judge, Jacob Mishler, was the same federal judge who sentenced my brother Michael to federal prison six years after Cody's conviction. With Cody's ability to wield such vast economic power and choke off Trump's flow of cash, there was little wonder that Donald Trump asked Roy Cohn to meet with Cody to keep him happy. They were *in business* with these guys. They had buildings to complete, and fortunes to make. Cooperating with the FBI or Federal and State law enforcement officials to clean up the construction trades industry was not a priority for Donald Trump. Making money was.

"There are no heroes in this industry in terms of helping law enforcement officers," McNamara told Oreskes of the *Times.*

Had Mario Cuomo, *anytime* between 1985 and1992, when the presidential boomlets for him reached their peaks, attended a private meeting in a posh New York townhouse with the boss of one of New York's biggest crime families under investigation by the FBI, his political career—at the state or national levels—would have been finished. It's unlikely that the media—grasping for any shred of a link between Cuomo and organized crime—would have ignored such a meeting if it had occurred between the head of a Mafia crime family and the nation's first Italian-American candidate for President. The vowel at the end of his name would have been Cuomo's indictment, regardless of the circumstances of the meeting.

Raised just a few miles from each other in Queens, N.Y., Cuomo and Trump were worlds apart. Mario Cuomo grew up atop his father's modest little grocery store in South Jamaica, where he didn't learn to speak English until he was eight years old; Donald Trump grew up in his father's opulent, twenty-three-room mansion high on a hill in exclusive Jamaica Estates where working class Italians were not welcome.

That was years before the Trumps would do all they could, which included violating federal and state anti-discrimination laws, to keep working-class families of a different color out of Trump-built working-class housing in Brooklyn. Unlike Cuomo, who lived among struggling immigrant families from diverse backgrounds, Trump lived a gilded life, a sheltered, elite existence where he was chauffeured to his privileged private school in his mother's rose-colored Rolls Royce.

Each family had far different views of their own histories: the German Drumpfs Americanized their name to Trump for business reasons; the Italian-born Andrea and Immaculata Cuomo, proud of their lineage, language and land of origin, were interested in what other immigrant families wanted: putting bread on the table for their children. They had nothing to hide, no names to change.

The differences between Mario Cuomo and Donald Trump went far beyond the separate universes into which each was born. Vast chasms of values, beliefs, character, and respect for all people and cultures separated the two. Cuomo led a life of great integrity, with zero tolerance for injustice, and profound reverence for the law, for all faiths, families, and human dignity. Addressing an NAACP conference at the New York Hilton, on December 11, 1991—just one week before declining to run for the Presidency in 1992—Cuomo's voice quaked with emotion when he came to the subject of racism:

The truth is that the ugly and dangerous instinct still lives among us...the instinct to stigmatize, to stereotype, to scapegoat, to malign people because of the tint of their skin, the God they pray to, or the place their parents came from...

A few months later (June, 1992), in a speech before New York University's Urban Research Center on Immigration, Cuomo spoke of his own family's history of battling discrimination against immigrants:

I thank God the country didn't say to them, "We can't afford you; you might take someone else's job, or cost us too much." I'm glad they didn't ask my father if he could speak English, because he couldn't; I'm glad they didn't ask my mother if she could count, because she couldn't...I'm glad they didn't ask my father what special skills he brought to this great and dynamic nation, because there was no special expertise to the way he handled a shovel when he dug trenches for sewer pipe. I'm glad they let him in anyway.

Cuomo knew, from personal experience, of the damage also done by stigma and negative stereotyping, fighting the ugly lies of "mob connections" for years. "My whole life has been a statement against that crap," he argued passionately when a *Newsday* editorial questioned why he refused to deliver a JFK-style "Houston Ministers" speech to squash the rumors.

Donald Trump's life expressed exactly the opposite statement. His "incestuous intertwining with organized crime,"—with mobsters like John Cody and "Fat Tony" Salerno—had been documented for decades, according to Barrett in *Trump: The Deals and the Downfall.* Trump took his counsel from shrivel-souled sycophants of the mob like Roy Cohn, and, for years, did business with the New York and Philadelphia crime families. Writing in *Politico,* (May 22, 2016) author David Cay Johnston put it bluntly: "No other candidate for the White House…has anything close to Trump's record of repeated social and business dealings with mobsters, swindlers, and crooks."

Trump was a punk among punks: an amoral actor doing business with amoral peers. No souls, no hearts, no nothing—the complete antithesis of Mario Cuomo. As John Cody's son observed, my brother's friends had zero respect for Trump. They knew they could squeeze him for as much as they wanted, since all that mattered to Trump was money. That's a language organized crime understood. Conversely, although they knew he opposed everything they represented, even the mob guys could see that Cuomo—the anti-thug—pointed the way toward a better life for their children, and, in their gruff way, they admired him for it.

Federal investigations into the Mob's infiltration of the construction trades was not limited to New York City. Law enforcement officials took a long look into the Long Island portion of the industry in a Justice Department /FBI Investigation dubbed "L'IL Rex" or the Long Island Racketeering and Extortion Investigation. While intending to focus on Long Island, it gave law enforcement authorities a detailed look at how tightly interconnected the construction industries were in NYC and its suburbs. In *Shoreham and the Rise and Fall of the Nuclear Power Industry* written by former Federal prosecutor and Deputy State Attorney General Kenneth F. McCallion (Praeger Publishing, imprint of Greenwood Publishing Group, Westport, Conn., 1995), the author explains what first brought Shoreham to his attention:

> *My first brush with the Shoreham issue had come while I was serving as a Special Assistant Attorney General with the Department of Justice's Organized Crime Strike Force in Brooklyn. After I had completed the investigation and trial of Daniel Cunningham, who was convicted in 1982 of racketeering, bribery and embezzlement charges, Forbes Magazine ran a cover story in February, 1983, raising the specter that Cunningham's effort to organize the security guards at Shoreham and other nuclear facilities, including what might give organized crime access to nuclear fuel. Ed Bradley of CBS' "60 Minutes" interviewed me about organized crimes connections to Cunningham's union. What interested me most about that investigative report, however, were the interviews of local law enforcement officials who detailed Shoreham's sad history of no-show jobs, kickbacks and cost overruns.* (p. xiv, preface)

McCallion and some of his colleagues in the U.S. Attorney's Office in Brooklyn's Organized Crime Task Force referred to the East End of Long Island, where Shoreham was located, as "The Wild East," because it was wide open to organized crime. An NPR "Week-end Edition" story by Steve Henn (November 17, 2012) summed up the concern of law enforcement officials during the early 1980s:

> *McCallion realized that a number of unions and contractors working at the Shoreham Nuclear Power Plant construction site were the targets of other organized crime investigators. Several union leaders ended up in prison. "We noticed that the construction seemed to be going on forever," McCallion said. They'd build part of the plant and then literally some of it was ripped out and reconstructed. The rumors among the trades (unions) at Shoreham, was that they never really wanted the project to finish because it was just a tremendous boondog-*

gle for everyone, except the consumers of electricity on Long Island.
The organized crime-related corruption in New York's construction industry, the enormous cost overruns at the Shoreham Nuclear
Power Plant, and Long Island's burgeoning anti-nuclear movement,
had been bubbling during the decade *before* Mario Cuomo was elected Governor in November, 1982. Cuomo lived a life apart from all
this, narrowly focusing on his family and a quiet life practicing law,
as far removed from the vast amounts of money changing hands between mobsters, real-estate developers, and construction contractors,
as he was from the old-boy political clubhouses of Donald Manes,
Stanley Friedman and Meade Esposito.

Lesser mortals, operating in the middle of that mayhem, might
not have been able to avoid one temptation or the other, let alone
both. Manes, Friedman, and Esposito loomed like the multi-headed
beast Scylla on one side of a narrow straight, extracting flesh or financial gain—as they did with Ed Koch—if one traveled too closely
to them, or allowed them to define the course. On the other side
of the narrow passageway to sunlight, whipped the unceasing whirlpool of the organized crime Charybdis, involved in legitimate and
illegal operations, purchasing public officials and business leaders as
easily as it sold cement, bringing everything it touched down to the
bottom of the sea. Mario Cuomo—like Odysseus—steered clear of
both perils, emerging at a higher, but far more personally punish-
ing level of public service. He preferred being entirely on his own,
owing favors to no one.

The Governor's strength of character in the face of the dual dangers of organized criminal behavior inside and outside of government, presaged the description of another working-class hero living
on a different plane of existence in a grubby, brutal world, brilliantly
written by Actor/Writer Stanley Tucci a decade later in the screenplay for his break-out movie, *Big Night*. In a compelling scene toward the end of the movie, Tucci's character Secondo, the younger
brother of the star chef, Primo (played by Tony Shalhoub), confronts
the mercenary merchant from the restaurant across the street (played

by Ian Holm) who plotted against Primo and Secondo's business to force the talented chef to work for him:

"You would never have my brother. He lives in world above you! What he has…what he is…is rare. You are…nothing."

It was a description that perfectly fit Mario Cuomo threading his way through tumultuous times, and creating his own unique path through persistence, duty and faith. But Cuomo's unique worldview did not include the anti-nuclear protests that erupted on Long Island after the Three Mile Island accident. At that time, 15,000 demonstrators blocked the gates to Shoreham. About 600 protesters were getting arrested for scaling the chain-link fence around the facility. Taking to the streets to protest public policy was simply not Cuomo's style; reason and debate were, with courtrooms often providing the venue.

Immediately upon being sworn in as Governor on January 1, 1983, his lack of identification with the anti-nuclear movement would abruptly change. The Suffolk County Legislature passed a resolution by a 15-1 vote in February, asserting the County's refusal to participate in an evacuation plan for Shoreham, a condition required of all U.S. nuclear facilities following the Three Mile Island accident. The Shoreham plant, nearing completion, was the most expensive non-operating nuclear power plant in the nation's history, with costs ballooning to almost $6 billion, or more than 80 times projections.

Later that same year, Cuomo came face-to-face with the heart of the opposition to the operation of Shoreham, the Shoreham Opponents Coalition, led by the tenacious and articulate Nora Bredes. A bright Cornell University graduate pursuing her Masters in Education at Columbia University, Bredes spoke in calm, measured tones and always came armed with facts. Attending a Hauppauge fund-raiser for NYS Assembly Member Patrick Halpin, Cuomo stopped outside the catering hall and devoted most of his time talking to Bredes and some 1,000 anti-Shoreham demonstrators.

"Instead of coming in to endorse me," Halpin later said, "Mario Cuomo spent the evening talking to the protesters outside. He was really engaged with that movement."

Cuomo was taken with the intelligence, persistence, and passion of Bredes. The Governor would point to Bredes, after she became pregnant the following year with her first son, Nathaniel, as one of most powerful reasons to keep the people of Long Island safe in the event of a nuclear accident. Additionally, his experience of getting caught in "beach traffic" on the Island convinced him of the impossibility of evacuating several million people west through New York City if Shoreham had an accident like the one at Three Mile Island. To Cuomo, a pragmatic humanist, the issue of public safety that was most tangible to him. The problem was clearly identifiable, and ultimately within his authority to solve.

From 1981 to 1986, the year Cuomo ran for re-election, public opposition to Shoreham's operating as a nuclear power plant nearly doubled. Over two-thirds of Long Islanders wanted to put their health and safety first, above any issue of rising electric rates, even *after* a decade of climbing utility rates and the failure of LILCO's transmission system during Hurricane Gloria the year before. If the power company couldn't even respond to an anticipated act of nature like a hurricane, how could anyone expect it to handle all of the exigencies of an emergency evacuation of 2.7 million Long Islanders brought about by a nuclear accident?

The Governor gave a keynote address at a Suffolk County Democratic fundraiser in late April, 1986, on the same day his eventual Republican rival O'Rourke met with the *Newsday* editorial board. A *Newsday* reporter, covering the Shoreham controversy, informed me that at the meeting O'Rourke told the paper's editors, "He believed it was too difficult to maintain a 10-mile evacuation zone around nuclear power plants."

My eyes grew wide. I asked the reporter to repeat what the Republican candidate had said, since I could scarcely believe it. O'Rourke, seeking to curry favor with the pro-nuclear power Reagan Administration and the mostly-Republican business and trade labor interests on Long Island that were pushing hard for Shoreham to go on-line, had missed the biggest issue on Long Island, since the Three Mile Island accident: public safety. Proposing a smaller evacuation zone was going against every single study, proposal, and resolutions advanced by State and local officials for protecting the public from a nuclear accident. It completely ignored the overwhelming wishes of Long Islanders. I walked over to where the Governor was sitting on the dais and whispered to him what the reporter told me. Cuomo's eyes danced with delight.

"He really said that?" the Governor asked.

"That's what the reporter told me, Governor. I wrote it down," I said, showing him my notes.

I could see Cuomo's mind working at warp speed.

"He's not officially a candidate yet, so I shouldn't respond. You handle it," the Governor said. And, just like that, I was thrown into the forefront of the Shoreham fight—me on one side, my brother Michael's friends on the other. In an instant, the elaborate walls I had constructed between my brother and me were breached.

I went back to the *Newsday* reporter and told her that O'Rourke was either "woefully misinformed on the Shoreham issue, or was completely insensitive to the health and safety concerns of 2.7 million Long Islanders." With Cuomo's encouragement, I was going for O'Rourke's jugular, relishing my being in the thick of the battle. The following morning, when the *Newsday* story appeared, the Governor was so pleased with the way it came out he called me at home.

"Has anyone spoken to you about your role in the campaign, Steve?" Cuomo said.

"Not specifically, Governor, although I did attend a meeting in Andrew's office on Wednesday evening about it," I told him.

"Well," Mario Cuomo continued, "I'd like you to consider being Chief Spokesman for the campaign. I haven't quite worked it out yet about when you'd start and I want to make sure that the operation of the New York City News Unit continues without interruption, because its' work is very, very important to us."

The directness of the Governor's request took my breath away.

All week long, since Fabian came into my office and talked about finding a new role for me, I had played mind games. How could I do more for Cuomo and not be too visible? If I did more for the Governor, became more of a newsmaker, would I become more of a target for the press? I flip-flopped on my decision with each thought: one moment, I knew I had to keep everyone in the Administration at arms length; the next moment, I'd say "fuck it," I needed to finally distance myself from everyone in my family if I was going to achieve anything. There was no solid ground under my feet, and I teetered back and forth, shifting my weight from side to side. I prayed that an irresistible opportunity to take a more public role in Mario Cuomo's campaign or Administration would not be dangled in front of me. Until it was. Then I wanted to seize it before it disappeared, or I changed my mind yet again. The Governor sensed my reticence.

"We have to start thinking about your future, Steve," he said. "We can't keep you in the News Unit forever. If God is good to us, and we win this election, we have to talk about another more important position for you."

"Th-Thank, you, Governor," I stammered, frightened and exhilarated by what was happening.

"So how does the role of Campaign Spokesperson sound?" Mario Cuomo asked me.

"It-it sounds exciting, Governor, and I'm gratified to have your confidence," I said. And mortified, I did not say. And terrified, I thought. What if the press starts to focus on me, and my brother, my family and the Mob?

I hung up the phone with Mario Cuomo and began to sweat. What if the Republicans hit me as hard as I hit Andy O'Rourke the night before? What if they did their customary dirty tricks and dug up everything on my brother? It would be such an easy thing for them to do, since my brother ran in political circles with lots of Republicans on Long Island. His friends in the Building Trades gave large donations to local, State and National Republican campaigns and I could picture him going out to lunch with a few of his cronies, bragging about the important new role his "kid brother" had with Mario Cuomo. I could hear him bragging about me because he was genuinely proud, but also aggrandizing himself in the process, to show his friends that if anyone could reach the "unreachable" Cuomo, he could, elevating his status among them still more. I knew that if his associates could do anything to hurt Cuomo they would, especially now, since Cuomo was opposing them on bringing Shoreham into operation—actions that could cost them millions in cash.

Why *shouldn't* they try to bring him down? What if I became campaign spokesperson, and *Newsday* did a local boosterism story about a home-town boy who made good? Somebody, somewhere could easily put out another story about another Villano whose friends were making money hand-over-fist on Shoreham.

I closed my eyes and shuddered as I saw another version of the headlines haunting me: "CUOMO CAMPAIGN SPOKESMAN HAS MOB TIES." It was the nightmare story my brother Vinnie teased me about on Christmas Eve at my parents' home in California, when Michael was embracing John Gotti at the Ravenite. I wanted to dive headlong into the campaign, and swim as far and fast from my family as I could. My fears froze me in place. I would not pursue it; would not follow up on the conversation with the Governor. I'd let him think I was not interested. If it materialized, I would do it, but not actively campaign for the post as campaign spokesman for the Governor. News of my appointment could be the bomb waiting to be detonated to derail the Cuomo campaign. I would not light that fuse.

The next day there *was* an explosion, but it did not involve my brother, the Mob, or me. The force of the blast, heard around the world, changed the subject for a while, putting Mario Cuomo on a clearer path toward re-election, and making my personal decision less relevant. The Chernobyl Nuclear Power Plant in Pripyat, Ukraine exploded, belching huge quantities of radioactive particles into the atmosphere across the Soviet Union and Western Europe, immediately killing 31 people and causing the emergency evacuation of tens of thousands of human beings from their homes. An accident at Shoreham on overcrowded Long Island was no longer an esoteric exercise, and Mario Cuomo became—overnight—a worldwide champion of public safety in the face of nuclear disaster. Cuomo was taking on the Reagan Administration, the Nuclear Power industry and utility companies at the peak of their power. The dangers of Scylla and Charybdis were behind us; random events were in control.

9 ▫ Passionate Indifference

There were no random acts of God or man, like Chernobyl, that caused a crescendo of commentary and citizen support for Mario Cuomo to run for President of the United States. It was simply a question of how far above everyone else he was as a thinking, feeling public official of towering personal integrity. He was, indeed "rare," as Secondo said about his older brother, Primo, in Stanley Tucci's *Big Night*, and everyone, even his political adversaries, knew it.

It was what drove many of us to go to work for him, laboring long hours for low salaries. Cuomo revealed himself to me, and many others, in his unique *Diaries of Mario M. Cuomo: The Campaign for Governor* (Random House, New York, N.Y. 1984). When I first read his words while eating a grilled cheese sandwich in a down-on-its-luck luncheonette in Centereach, Long Island, I sat straight up; this was the kind of high-minded, high-quality public official I wanted to work with. He didn't care about money, unlike many politicians, and I found that compelling. He wanted to use political power to achieve some good for others in this life, not for self-enrichment, aggrandizement, or ego gratification.

What I especially loved about working with Mario Cuomo was that we shared the same passion to immerse ourselves in the problems of the world and find constructive solutions while, at the same time, detaching ourselves from our daily duties to think about why we did what we did, and why it mattered. We were continually weighing what needed to be done, against what it was we were doing, and what difference it was making in the lives of others and our own. Inspired by Teilhard de Chardin, Cuomo's actions were tempered by a profound recognition of the need to achieve balance between possessing worldly goods and renouncing them, and harmonizing the conflicting pulls of passion and indifference

No matter what Cuomo said to dissuade the deepening discussion of his being the great Democratic hope against the Reagan/Bush crowd, his own words, to many, were far more than words. In his 1986 re-election campaign, the Governor did not side-step controversial national issues. He relished debating them, whether they were nuclear power, the deductibility of State and local taxes—for which he crusaded throughout New York State in stark opposition to the Reagan Administration's effort to eliminate the mortgage-based, middle-class tax benefit—or, on the crucial matter of nominations to the U.S. Supreme Court.

President Ronald Reagan's first Supreme Court appointment, coming just six months after he took office in 1981, was the politically moderate Justice Sandra Day O'Connor. The first women nominated to serve on the nation's highest court, O'Connor was ratified by a 99-0 Senate vote in September, 1981.

Five years later, with the US Senate controlled by Republicans, 53-47, Reagan was presented with a unique opportunity to redirect the philosophical direction of the Supreme Court for generations to come. Chief Justice Warren Earl Burger, who had served since 1969, announced his retirement in the Spring, 1986. Losing no time, Reagan held a press conference on June 17, where he announced Burger's pending retirement, and nominated Associate Justice William H. Rehnquist to succeed him. In a rare "two-fer" for a President, Reagan also announced he would nominate Antonin G. Scalia to replace Rehnquist.

Liberals around the country were outraged at Reagan's blatant move to push the Supreme Court sharply to the right, especially on the issues of abortion, gun control, free speech and the rights of the accused. Mario Cuomo, as the leader of the more progressive wing of the Democratic Party, was expected to condemn Reagan's nominations on ideological grounds, since they represented a view of government which Cuomo vigorously opposed. Accordingly, Cuomo was invited to address more than 4,000 members of the American Bar Association at its annual meeting held in Radio City Music Hall in mid-August, 1986. He was an outstanding lawyer who finished at the top of his class at St. John's University Law School, and clerked for two years for New York State Court of Appeals Justice Adrian Paul Burke. As Governor, he won bi-partisan praise for the caliber of the judges he selected for New York's highest court.

Cuomo delivered his 28-minute speech—with U.S. Supreme Court Justices Berger, Willliam J. Brennan, Jr., and Lewis F. Powell, Jr. in the audience—surrounded by speculation that he was speaking out on the court nominations in preparation for a pending Presidential run. Armed with copies of his prepared text, we anticipated his words to the high-powered ABA audience, with major national media in attendance, would garner widespread attention.

Cuomo's speech made national headlines when he warned of the danger—for a President from either party—selecting Supreme Court nominations on ideological grounds first, with merit as an afterthought:

Most of the nominees of the current Administration have been from the same party and are distinctly branded as leaning hard to the right in their political outlook. That's not a coincidence. It is not unusual for a President to try to bend the Court to fit his own ideological, social or political beliefs... The present effort, however, is a particularly emphatic one.

While he challenged Reagan's criteria for selecting Supreme Court—and lower court—nominees, Cuomo did not challenge the merit or ability of either Rehnquist's or Scalia's nominations, although he did believe "character" was fair game. Regarding Rehnquist's record of discriminating against Black voters in Arizona when he was a political operative for Richard Nixon during the 1968 Presidential campaign, Cuomo argued:

Character is always a relevant subject. So, the investigation into whether Justice Rehnquist has told the truth about events in his past, whether he ever approved of bigotry or violated the canons of ethics, cannot be called extraneous.

The *New York Times* (August 12, 1986) gave the story ("Cuomo Sees Peril in Picking Judges on Ideology Basis,") the most prominent top-of-the fold position in the newspaper, with a center front-page photograph of Cuomo speaking as the three sitting Supreme Court Justices sat listening behind him. Following the speech, only Justice Brennan spoke to the press, telling the *Times'* Jeffrey Schmalz that Cuomo's speech was "very, very significant." In an impromptu, streetside press conference after his presentation, the Governor tantalized the national press even more about a prospective presidential campaign, when reporters asked how the present situation could be remedied:

All you need is an event and you could change it in Washington. And that event is 1988. Some candidate can come forward and make it an issue, saying 'I'm going to depoliticize it. I'm going to appoint the best judges.

When the inevitable follow-up questions came about Cuomo's ambitions to be that candidate in 1988, several of us on staff tried, unsuccessfully, to pull him away from the conversation and the circle of national reporters crushing in on him. But Cuomo enjoyed the give-and-take, and the attention being paid to his ideas. The growing national fascination with Mario Cuomo was cutting both ways. Everything he did and said was weighed against the backdrop of a potential presidential candidacy.

After his landslide victory in 1986, and with few other powerful progressive voices speaking out against the palpable damage Reagan Administration policies were doing to working families and the poor, speculation about a future Cuomo candidacy for president intensified. That attention, while useful in raising his profile among New York voters, had a shadow side as well. It magnified every action by the Governor and his family and, as Cuomo viewed it, was partially responsible for the abuse heaped upon Andrew by the press during the gubernatorial campaign.

He buried the hatchet with the media by delivering an eloquent, constitutionally sound, yet challenging speech on the First Amendment before the members of the New York Press Club in the weeks followed his re-election.

In the immediate aftermath of his blistering Brooklyn blow-up with NBC's Ben Farnsworth and other reporters, a few of us on staff were convinced Mario Cuomo had lost all reason on the subject of the press. When I told my fellow staff member and political soulmate Stephen Schlesinger about Cuomo's tirade against reporters, Schlesinger shared a confidential memo he wrote to the Governor a few days earlier. Schlesinger, the co-author, with Stephen Kinzer, of *Bitter Fruit: The Untold Story of the American Coup in Guatamala*, (Anchor Books/Doubleday, New York, N.Y., 1982), an expert on the United Nations, and the son of historian Arthur M. Schlesinger, Jr., the former White House Assistant to President John F. Kennedy, was never cowed by Cuomo. He had grown up around the Kennedys and had been privy to high-level battles of policy, the press and political personalities. He was blunt with the Governor:

I think you are hurting yourself with your attacks on the press over the past few days. They make you look like a sore loser. After a record-breaking landslide election, observers would expect that you would be savoring the fruits of victory. Instead, you appear to be dwelling on the pettiness of the press...journalistic mayhem comes with the territory in political life.

I left Schlesinger's office on one side of the 57th Floor in our World Trade Center offices and headed back toward the Press Office, running into Marty Steadman.

"I think he's lost it on this Andrew issue with the press, Marty," I said to Steadman. I recounted to Marty how badly Cuomo's exchange with reporters went in Brooklyn a little earlier.

"No, no, he's got a great new idea," Steadman said, motioning me into his office.

I sat down in the stark office chair next to Steadman's desk, while he sat behind it.

"He's gonna give a big speech at the Press Club," Steadman said. "High-minded; he sees it on the scale of another Notre Dame speech."

"*Son-of-a-bitch*," I said to Steadman. "When I suggested that approach to him this afternoon I caught hell from him over it."

"Well, he's determined to do it now," Steadman said, smiling.

He got up from behind his desk and tapped me on the side of my shoulder with a folded newspaper as he headed off to the bathroom.

"Good work," Steadman said.

Cuomo called me at home at 10:30 pm that night to tell me of his decision. His tone of voice was fatherly, almost conciliatory—maybe even a bit apologetic, for losing his temper with me earlier in the day in Brooklyn.

"I'd like you to be involved with this speech, Steve," Mario Cuomo said.

"Sure, Governor, sure. I'd be honored to work on it," I said, amazed by the quick turn about in his tone on the topic.

I hung up the kitchen phone and laughed; Mario Cuomo's way of apologizing for his churlish behavior was to give you more work. I was up well into the early morning hours crafting a two-page outline containing my suggestions for his speech. When I arrived at the World Trade Center office early the next morning, I faxed copies of the memo to the Governor, Steadman, and Gary Fryer. Fryer called me immediately to tell me it was a terrible idea, with too much risk involved that would backfire on us. Then, after acknowledging the Governor was now "hot to do the speech," Fryer gave me his characteristic arms-length send-off.

"You're on your own with this, pal," he said.

"That's fine, Gary," I replied. "I'm comfortable there."

I could not comprehend Fryer's fear of failure. The subject matter was first-rate, the tactic was smart, and there was much historic precedent to draw from. Mario Cuomo was the best orator in the country, with a keen sense of himself, his audience and history. A formal speech, unlike an impromptu press conference on the streets of Brooklyn, was an environment we could control, and would win points from the press just for tackling the issue.

Dozens of draft versions of the speech circulated around to staff members for the next ten days. Cuomon was seeking suggestions, quotations, input and revisions from his staff. Ideas came pouring in, and even the great constitutional lawyers Floyd Abrams and Victor Kovner were consulted on the text. The project became a full Cuomo-team effort, imbuing each of us involved with a strong sense of mission. We were passionately defending the First Amendment *and* advancing Mario Cuomo's future. This was exactly the kind of meaty stuff many of us who worked for Cuomo longed to do.

"I want a Blitzkreig review of this,"Cuomo wrote in black magic marker on a thick speech packet circulated to all."Someone needs to start checking all the source materials and citation forms."

Cuomo's speech, entitled "A Brief on the Freedom of the Press," was delivered before a packed audience of the New York Press Club on November 25, 1986. Reporters from around the nation jammed the room. He opened his talk by admitting past sins:

My discussions—of the press, with the press—have occasionally produced unexpected reactions. That happened a couple of weeks ago around election time.

I looked over at Steve Schlesinger and rolled my eyes. Cuomo began with a self-effacing joke, then found his grove by tracing the early history of the Constitution and "the geniuses who designed this wonderful ship of state":

Having provided for the right of free speech for the whole citizenry, they went further and provided separately for 'Freedom of the Press.' **As broadly as possible.** *Not tentatively. Not embroidered with nuances. Not shrouded and bound up in conditions. But plainly, purely.*

Cuomo was in full swing now, and couldn't resist taking a carefully drawn shot at the Reagan White House, undergoing the burgeoning

Iran/Contra scandal, which it had tried to keep under wraps:

The Press' insistence on forcing the White House to begin to tell the truth about the Iranian transaction is the most recent dramatic reminder of how the press works incessantly to assure our liberty by guaranteeing our awareness.

In a scholarly, lawyerly fashion—sounding almost as he did in his American Bar Association speech a few months earlier—Cuomo cited a string of legal cases to underscore the Supreme Court's changing interpretations of press freedoms: *NYT v. Sullivan, Westmoreland, Sharon,* and the more ominous lower court decision in the *Tavoulareas v. Washington Post* case. Cuomo noted that in Tavoulareas, Judge Antonin Scalia—then a member of the lower court's three judge panel that ruled on the case—"would have made the *Washington Post* liable."

"Scalia," Cuomo warned, "is now a member of the highest court and has been added to those already unhappy with *NYT v. Sullivan.* He does not share the reluctance of the majority in *Sullivan* to threaten the Press with vulnerability to libel judgements."

Cryptically, or maybe not so, Cuomo addressed some of his own staff's criticism of him of being perceived as "Nixonian" for criticizing the media. Then, he went on to cite other presidents who had difficulties with the Press, from George Washington to Thomas Jefferson, Teddy Roosevelt, Woodrow Wilson, Franklin D. Roosevelt, and John Kennedy:

And of course President Kennedy tore up all the White House subscriptions to the Herald Tribune *because he didn't think their coverage of him was fair.*

The room full of tough, seasoned New York reporters laughed. Cuomo couldn't resist turning an oft-used line about him on its head:"Frankly, I think all of those guys were a bit thin-skinned."

It was Cuomo's JFK moment; he had the press corps purring. With a few more flourishes about what New York State did to protect press freedoms, the speech was a triumph. It had succeeded beyond expectation, quelling Cuomo's quarrels with the press, and making him sound like the statesman we knew he was. The only liability of the speech, if it were one, was that it elevated Cuomo even more in the eyes of the national media. Despite his protestations that he was not interested in running for President, and had "no plans to make plans" to run for President, the sweep of his intellect and the sweetness of his ability to persuade a crowd as tough as the New York Press corps, made journalists salivate over the possibility of a Cuomo campaign against the Reagan/Bush Administration.

The pull by the press and many national Democratic Party activists for the Governor to begin to take even the slightest steps toward putting together a Presidential campaign for 1988 became almost gravitational at the beginning of 1987. The Iowa Caucus and New Hampshire Primary were less than one year away. It was becoming impossible for Mario Cuomo to go anywhere, or discuss even the most mundane of State issues—like rebuilding crumbling infrastructure of the State's roads and bridges—without the conversation turning to the presidency. The topic teased Cuomo: on the one hand, it gave him a greater platform to discuss the issues of economic justice and jobs, subjects which mattered most to him; on the other, it colored everything he did, threatening to box him into an untenable position, of having to run, whether he wanted to or not.

In the minds of many people impressed by Cuomo's intelligence, compassion and clear capabilities, it was unthinkable that such a talented individual *did not* want to rise to the top of his field. With a name ending in a vowel, the assumption, often said aloud, was that he was concealing a family connection to the Mob.

The clamor for him to become a candidate for president grew louder in early 1987, convincing Cuomo to clarify his passionate indifference on the subject. He loved serving the people of New York State, and the preoccupation with his feints and nods toward the presidency was beginning to interfere with our ability to communicate about the Administration's programs. He found the perfect venue to address the issue on his monthly call-in CBS Radio program "Ask the Governor."

The program was hosted by long-time CBS Radio Newsman Art Athens, a popular and distinctive radio voice in New York City. The biggest news of the day, at a press conference we held earlier the afternoon of February 19, 1986, in the Governor's Conference Room on the 57th Floor of Two World Trade Center, was when, whether and where Cuomo was going to make up his mind about running for president. In the Socratic way he often responded to reporters, Cuomo asked them what made them so sure he would say anything to *them* about the presidency.

"What makes you guys think you're so important that I should announce it to you, first? Maybe, I go right over your heads, to the people," Cuomo said.

The Governor looked at the reporters packed into the meeting room with a deadpan defiance. My eyes went wide and I looked over to Marty Steadman, standing off to the side. We shared one thought: he'll do it on the CBS "Ask the Governor" radio show scheduled for that evening. Cuomo often expressed the sentiment that he loved talking on the radio, not only because he had "the perfect face for it," but because he could directly talk to the people, without anyone editing his words.

The press conference ended, the Governor walked back to his office, and I ran down the hallway to mine. That evening, Carol, Matthew and I had tickets to go see the Tony Award-winning musical, *The Mystery of Edwin Drood*, with good friends from Long Island. I had picked up the tickets earlier that day. We had looked forward to seeing *Drood* for months. Since being turned into a smash-hit musical, *Drood*—Charles Dickens last unfinished novel—pioneered the use of multiple possible endings, with each night's audience determining the outcome.

My son and his best friend, Brian Goldman, were buzzing about the show for weeks, and I did not want to run the risk of their missing

the performance because of my crazy work schedule. I sensed Mario
Cuomo had a few surprise endings of his own for that evening that
were not crowd-sourced, like the endings to *Drood*. I quickly called
Carol to work out some contingency plans.

"Uh—I think you'd better come into the city just a bit earlier
tonight," I said.

"Why?" she asked, sensing something a little off in my voice.

"I—uh—have a hunch the Governor is going to say something
momentous on his radio show tonight."

"Uh oh," she said. "Sounds like a long night ahead for you."

"I think so. *The Mystery of Mario Cuomo* may unfold tonight before
The Mystery of Edwin Drood does."

An hour before the radio program began, Marty Steadman divided
up a list of local and national reporters for our Press Office team to
call. We were to "strongly suggest" to reporters that they tune into
the Governor's show on WCBS-AM that night. Nothing else. If we
were asked, "Is this IT?" we were to simply tell them to stay tuned.

"The Governor wants to make sure nobody gets burned," Steadman said.

The show proceeded as it normally did, with Athens opening up
by asking the Governor a few questions, followed by phone calls
from the listening audience, and screened by CBS Radio producer
Terry Raskyn to prevent pranksters from tying up the phone lines
or filibustering an issue. With a few minutes left until the end of the
program Mario Cuomo paused, took a deep breath, and read the
text of the announcement he had prepared:

*I have been telling people for a long, long time that I had no plans to run
for the presidency and I didn't have any plans to make plans to run for the
presidency.*

*Despite that, there was an awful lot of speculation about it, and I promised
I would make a statement on this subject before the end of February, and
this is as good a time as any to do it as I've had, with so many New Yorkers
listening in…..*

In my opinion, the Democratic Party offers a number of presidential candi-

dates who can prove themselves capable of leading this nation toward a more sane, a more progressive, a more humane future. I will not add my name to that list. I will not be a candidate.

But I will continue to work as hard as I can to deal with those problems in New York and to support the selection of our party as vigorously as I can in my role as Governor here in the State of New York. I'm very, very grateful to a lot of people who suggested that I might adequately serve as a candidate myself. But, the decision I've made I think is best for my state, best for my family and, I think, also best for my party.

And, I make the statement now so that no one, no one will be disadvantaged by the false expectation of candidacy on my part. There were some people who were developing expectations. I don't want them to be damaged as a result of that, and so I choose this moment to make my position clear. I will not be a candidate."

Within seconds of Mario Cuomo uttering the words "I will not be a candidate," every single phone line on the 57th Floor of the World Trade Center Press Office was jammed. Private citizens called, crying in disbelief, pleading with us to change the Governor's mind. Reporters from across the country and around the world were calling, desperate for the complete text of Cuomo's withdrawal statement. Our single fax machine strained to keep up with the demand for copies. Right next to it, the Associated Press teletype machine clattered away, non-stop, until it ran its scroll of paper down to the end. There was no time to breathe, or barely to go to the bathroom, between phone calls. For two solid hours, calls poured in, from public and press alike. It was like working a phonebank at a nationwide Telethon. Around 10:00 pm I left the Trade Center and headed up to the Imperial Theatre on West 45th Street where *The Mystery of Edwin Drood* was playing. When I walked in, ticket in hand, the theatre manager stared at me.

"The show is almost over," he said.

"I know," I said, my voice strained from being on the phone non-stop for several hours. "I just got out of work. My boss just said he wasn't running for President tonight."

The theatre manager came to life.

"You work for Mario Cuomo?" he said.

I shook my head "yes."

"How could he *not* run," the theatre manager argued. "He *has* to run."

I held up my hand.

"Please, please," I said. "I don't want to talk about this anymore tonight. Just show me to my seat; I want to be with my family."

The theatre manager personally showed me to where Carol, Matt and our friends were seated, and I slipped quietly into the darkened row, kissing Carol as I sat down.

"Well?" she whispered.

"He's not running," I said quietly.

My attention was snapped around to the stage, where two of the main characters, John Jasper, Drood's uncle, and Mayor Sapsea, who also served as a narrator, were singing a duet called "Both Sides of the Coin." The words could have been written by Mario Cuomo, or Teilhard de Chardin:

Sapsea: *Nature seldom ever fails to most obligingly provide, an undisclosed opposing side to one's dismay.*

Jasper: *There's shadows in the shining morn—*

Sapsea: *If there's a rose it bears a thorn—*

Jasper: *You're good as dead as soon as born—*

Sapsea & Jasper: *And yet, we smile!*

Sapsea: *But, luck's division is perverse,*

Jasper: *It seems to work more in reverse—*

Sapsea: *If things are better, they'll be worse in just a while!*

The audience of nearly 1400 people roared with laughter at the lyrics to "Both Sides of the Coin," the double meanings contained in every word, and the over-the-top performances of the actors playing Jasper and Sapsea. I squinted to look at my *Playbill*, making certain

I was in the theatre, watching *The Mystery of Edwin Drood*, and not back in the Governor's Press Office, listening to Mario Cuomo play with words, still witnessing *The Mystery of Mario Cuomo*.

I already had one surprise ending for the night, after spending months anticipating a few others, including one where I headed off stage if the Governor decided to pursue the presidency. Sitting in the dark coziness of a Broadway theatre, watching unrestrained madcap and mindlessness in front of me, all sense of time and place suspended, and surrounded by the people I loved, I didn't want to deal with any more plot twists. Everything else could wait for morning. Until then, like the rest of the audience in *Drood*, I'd have to come up with my own closing scene.

10 ▫ Slack

I devised a few *Drood*-like endings to my own developing drama
between my work for Mario Cuomo and my loyalty and love for
my family. In one ending, Cuomo went on Art Athen's radio show
and announced he was running for President, and the following day
I quietly resigned without telling anyone why. In another, I held a
press conference at the World Trade Center the week after Cuomo's
announcement that he would run for President, and told reporters
that I *knew* Mario Cuomo had no mob connections because I *did*,
and *then* resigned, throwing myself on not one, but two swords for
the great Italian-American hope. In yet a third scenario, I told Cuomo of my brother's association with John Gotti, and our family's
historic links to both the Genovese and Gambino Crime families,
and he told me it didn't matter and decided to run for President,
notwithstanding.

With one big twist, that presaged what *actually* happened a year
later, when Cuomo found out about my brother, praised my work,
and stuck with me *and* his decision *not* to run. I imagined I could
have singlehandedly silenced the slurs against the Governor by
reporting "Live-from-Inside-the-Gambino-and-Genovese-Crime-
Families" that Mario Cuomo had no connections, *zero*; that he was,
in fact, a persona non-grata with the Mob, or, as my brother's friends
put it, "unreachable." On the other hand, my eyewitness testimony
could have had no impact at all, since the national media already had
its own more mysterious and colorful narrative, more consistent
with the public's prejudices—and far better for ratings.

Cuomo's never-ending, open-ended endings spared me my con-
fession. He was out of the presidential race for now, so I was still in.

If he was in, I would take myself out—or so I wanted to believe. The overlapping mysteries of Mario Cuomo and Edwin Drood demonized me. If Cuomo tipped the other way, and I was able to put his interests—and the interests of the country— above my overwhelming desire to do penance for the sins of my family and be part of his national campaign, I would be out of a job. I had no contingency plan, no other crowd-sourced endings.

The Governor's "not-a-candidate" pronouncement on Art Athens' radio show panicked me. A simple nod the other way and my family's Mob connections could complicate, and potentially kill, a Cuomo candidacy. I struggled to steer events in another direction, and began to look for other opportunities outside of the Cuomo Administration, flirting with running for local public office, reasoning that I could still do public service, without putting the Governor at risk.

Almost simultaneously with my flirtation, a Rand Corporation Study, *Racketeering in Legitimate Industries: A Study in the Economics of Intimidation,* by Peter Renter (Rand Corporation, Santa Monica, CA, 1987) found two specific crime families extensively involved in the Long Island garbage carting industry: the Lucheses and the Gambinos. New York State's head of the OCTF, or Organized Crime Task Force, Ron Goldstock, asked Rand to examine racketeering and collusion in that industry on Long Island. This request was prompted by wiretaps obtained by the OCTF between organized crime leaders controlling garbage collection in Nassau and Suffolk Counties. These new revelations complicated matters. As long as my brother lurked around Long Island politics, and the often invisible seam between organized crime and local government existed, that door to local elective office was closed. For me, there was no other public service option.

While not savvy in business or as tough as the punks he ran with, Michael was expert in subtly manipulating those of us who loved him. He intuitively understood that we wanted to believe what he was selling out of his briefcase was inherently good, because *he* was selling it, and *he* was good. Love him, love his work, whatever it was. Every generous act became a down-payment on forgiveness for his other actions. His kindness made him masterful at milking the family's mantra: whatever was done by any family member was accepted; all transgressions were forgiven.

It was such an uncomplicated, compromising concept: my brother right or wrong, above all. The narrower the frame of reference or breadth of experiences among each family member, the easier it was to be conned: blood of my blood, no matter how reprehensible his actions were. To question that equation, made *you* the aberration, the outsider. Was there any *higher* moral obligation than backing a family member? What if your family member broke the law? Placed peoples lives in danger, including members of our family? To whom were you more responsible: your siblings and parents, or to the larger universe out there? Do you close your eyes and pretend that nothing at all is going on, or going wrong?

Arthur Miller, the Pulitzer Prize-winning American playwright, posed the same questions in his classic drama, *All My Sons,* (*Arthur Miller: Eight Plays*, Nelson Doubleday, Inc., Garden City, N.Y. 1947) when the younger son in his play, Chris Keller, finds out that his father, Joe Keller, knowingly produced defective aircraft engines to meet the incessant demands of government contracts being filled during World War II. Chris, who returned home from the war, discovers that the defective engine heads his father sold to the Air Force were responsible for the deaths of 21 bomber pilots—the news of which caused his older brother Larry, another pilot, to end his life by crashing his plane—destroying his love and loyalty for his father:

Chris: (to his father) "You had 120 cracked engine heads, now what did you do?

Joe Keller: You're a boy, what could I do! I'm in business, a man in business; 120 cracked, you're out of business…what could I do; I never thought they'd install them…I did it for you, a business for you!

Chris: "For me! Where do you live, where have you come from?

For me! I was dying every day and you were killing my boys and you did it for me? ...What is that, the world—the business?...Don't you live in the world? What the hell are you? You're not even an animal, no animal kills his own; what are you?

Joe Keller: Then...why am I bad?...A man can't be Jesus in this world!"

Chris: "I know you're no worse than most men but I thought you were better. I never saw you as a man. I saw you as my father... You can be better! Once and for all you can know there's a universe of people outside and you're responsible to it..."

My brother hadn't knowingly sold defective engine parts that caused American fighter pilots their lives. He wasn't selling narcotics or "whacking" anyone. Yet, he knew that the cash he was carefully counting out into neat little piles had not been earned by him, or by those to whom he was delivering it. He knew he was operating outside of the law, a line which, for him, had long since been erased. He lived in a parallel universe with its own planets, its own order and a separate set of rules. To stay in orbit, and avoid crashing and burning, he had to keep rotating on the trajectory chosen for him, as the best use of his loyalty, likeability and limited skills.

I knew how deeply he had fallen in over his head, with tough, hard people, far more brutal than he pretended to be, who would brook no excuses for not bringing in money. Carmine Fatico was revered among the Gambino organization for his prodigious earning abilities, and as a protégé of "Uncle Charlie's," I could smell my brother's hunger to produce or feel his fear if he did not. What he did was not simply business for Michael—he had morphed it into his life and a new personality.

I didn't expect him to be a Jesus, nor thought he was worse than most men. But, as Miller's Chris Keller viewed his father, I thought he was better; I never saw him as a man; I saw my brother as *the man I once wanted to be.* Now, that man was unrecognizable to both of us. He disappeared; gone behind a stack of cash, or ignorant Guinea swagger which was a put-on for him, but essential, he believed, for surviving in a deadly business. Far more slowly and painfully than Joe Keller did with a single gunshot, Michael was killing himself in front of the people who loved him, and money, approval and self-importance were his weapons of choice.

Like Mario Cuomo, I attributed no special meaning to money. I had no idea, or inclination, how to commodify things, how to cash in on influence, or how to turn every encounter into a transaction. My brother and his friends harbored no such illusions; there was no public interest, only theirs. In their minds, they were businessmen, or as Ian Holmes' callous character in *Big Night* put it, they were "whatever they needed to be."

Cuomo could read me as well as I learned to read him, and he picked up on my unease, my need for a change, and my desire to be closer to my family. Within weeks of his first decision not to run for President, and before I could line up another position outside of his Administration, the Governor asked me to set up the Mineola-based office of the Long Island Power Authority, the public power entity created by the New York State Legislature as a mechanism to shut down the Shoreham Nuclear Power plant. It meant a move closer to home and an opportunity to help set up and run a brand new public entity on an important public policy matter. It also took me off of Mario Cuomo's personal staff, creating an extra layer of protection for the Governor. I seized the offer and ran with it, securing office space for the new State Authority a short distance from my alma mater, Hofstra University Law School. Ironically, the new location was also just down the block from the Federal District Courthouse in Uniondale.

I cast a casual glance at the courthouse on the way to the new offices, never imaging that within twelve months I would be observing Federal Judge Jacob Mishler, one of my heroes from law school, send my brother off to jail. My manic efforts to create some slack, some distance between Cuomo, my brother, the Mob and me, backfired. Events and circumstances had the opposite effect, binding me closer and tighter to each side of the divide. I longed for a loosening of the tension; the slightest sign of space and time to catch my breath; a period of balance where I could steady myself and find some peace. I knew the high wire could snap at any moment, recoiling sharply, and sending me tumbling without end, or a safety net to ease my fall. That momentary period of grace would have to wait; first there were powerful currents to contend with.

Overnight, I became a key Cuomo spokesman in our fight to shut the Shoreham Nuclear Power Plant. I lived on Long Island, was friends with members of the Long Island press corps, and now, I would work on the Island. Geographically, I was farther from Mario Cuomo than I had ever been since beginning work in his Administration two years earlier. However, on policy and political issues, and matters that would affect his legacy long after both of us were gone, I was now closer to him than I had ever been. My contact with Cuomo increased as his stature grew, and he became the strongest voice to speak up against the extremism of the Reagan Administration on economics, education, taxes, environmental issues and energy—with particular emphasis on nuclear power.

The national nuclear power lobby declared Mario Cuomo to be their Public Enemy Number One, clearly seeing that the closure of a fully finished nuclear power plant could be the death knell for an industry already struggling financially, and lacking acceptable solutions to issues of safe evacuations and disposal of nuclear waste.

The Governor and I spoke nearly every morning, before I left for work. Shoreham consumed us; Cuomo had given his word to Nora Bredes and other activists that he would do everything in his power to shut down the Nuclear Power Plant to protect public health and safety. In the Governor's system of values nothing mattered more than human life and human dignity, public safety and justice. Within the span of a few short months in my new position, I spoke more with Mario Cuomo than I had spoken with my own father over several years, catching myself wishing that *he was my father*, and his family, untainted by the Mob, also mine.

We developed a routine for Sunday mornings, starting when I was in the NYC Press Office, and continuing during my time fighting Shoreham. I would watch the pertinent public affairs shows, and the Governor would call me soon after the programs ended to get my perceptions of them. Sunday morning, October 4, 1987, was no different. Mario Cuomo had taped an interview with Leslie Stahl of CBS' *Face the Nation* late that week. The show was running during prime Sunday morning, public affairs time in New York. We did not know how the show would be edited, but knew that one line of her questioning was certain to make headlines: Stahl's repeated questions about whether Mario Cuomo had any "skeletons in your closet," concerning Organized Crime. She badgered him about whether there was any "truth" to the rumors that his father-in-law Charles Raffa was connected to organized crime— unfounded rumors which the writer Nick Pileggi demolished in scrupulous detail in a *New York Magazine* article two weeks later.

Mario Cuomo had been answering such insulting questions repeatedly over the past two years, seething at the fact that he was even asked such questions, which assumed that because of his "ethnicity" he must, somehow, be connected. John Gotti's rise to power, and Cuomo's nearly simultaneous rise in national political polls as a presidential possibility, made reporters feel that such insidious inquiries were fair game, even though similar questions were never asked of any other national figure in either political party. *Face the Nation* was the first national news program to give a platform to the unproven rumors about Cuomo since NBC had produced the first unsubstantiated story almost two years earlier.

Coming a few weeks after the *Face the Nation* interview, Nick Pileggi's *New York Magazine* article destroyed all the mob innuendos fact-by-fact. Pileggi did what no electronic news reporter bothered to do: he ran down each rumor, interviewed police, prosecutors and others, and punched holes in every single lie being systematically circulated about Mario Cuomo by his political opponents. Every rumor and piece of gossip surrounding the assault on Charles Raffa was disproved by police records, and by a thorough checking of the facts by Pileggi, in a November 2, 1987, *New York Magazine* article entitled "Cuomo and Those Rumors: Getting to the Bottom of all the Mob Talk."

Pileggi carefully scrutinized every single rumor and innuendo and found that none of them stood up to scrutiny and could be easily proven false. For example, he found that despite claims to the contrary by anonymous sources, every piece of information about the assault on Charlie Raffa was still on NYPD computers. If the Cuomos wanted to make that information disappear—with Mario Cuomo as Governor and Andrew in the Manhattan DA's office at that time—they could have easily done so. It was all right there, for any enterprising reporter to find. By running down every rumor, Pileggi's piece set the record straight on the smears about Mario Cuomo having a personal connection to organized crime. The writer found nothing supporting them. His interview with Edward McDonald, the head of the Organized Crime Strike Force of the U.S. Attorney's office in Brooklyn should have put the matter to rest:

"I have never heard of Cuomo connected with any wiseguys in any way whatever," MacDonald told Pileggi in the *New York Magazine* piece. "It shouldn't be worth denying, but still, the calls keep coming in."

But, the anonymous calls kept coming in, Pileggi, told WOR Radio Host Sherrye Henry on October 27, 1987, because of the "simple vowel at the end of the name which made the link." "Just the vowel" Pileggi told Henry, "makes the tie."

The "calls" started pouring in to reporters like Pileggi and law enforcement officials after the keynote address Mario Cuomo delivered at the 1984 Democratic National Convention in San Francisco, less than two months after the brutal beating of his father-in-law. The electrifying *Tale of Two Cities* speech contrasted the wealthy, walled-off America of Ronald Reagan's supporters, with the desperate lives of the majority of the nation's working families, and catapulted Cuomo into a progressive, cultural figure at the height of Reagan's popularity. Overnight, Mario Cuomo became the first Italian American public official seriously talked about as a potential Presidential candidate. The buzz cut both ways: inspiring thousands of Italian-American professionals, like myself, to enter public service, and sounding off alarm bells among frightened political opponents, who kept the Mob-related rumor mill churning in order to keep Mario Cuomo contained. Cuomo, an eloquent, educated working-class hero from an electorally-rich State, was potentially dangerous to the wealthy oligarchs of the Republican Party, who worked hard at convincing blue-collar Democrats that the rich man's pitch man, Ronald Reagan, was one of them.

I had grown fiercely protective of Cuomo. I was willing to sacrifice my relationship with my brother, and my own family for him —even my own life, as I discovered during the death threat against him during the 1986 campaign. Nothing mattered more to me than keeping Cuomo's integrity intact, and proving that the rumors about organized crime were politically motivated lies. Stahl's story outraged me. I shouted at the television, legal pad on my lap as I wrote down her quotes and the Governor's.

"You son-of-a-bitch," I screamed at her through my television set. "You fucking son-of-a-bitch—how dare you ask him those questions."

I shook with anger, picked up the phone and dialed the Executive Mansion in Albany, identifying myself to the State trooper who answered.

"Steve Villano, calling for the Governor, trooper." My voice was still quaking.

"Hi, Steve, how are you?" Mario Cuomo said, coming on the line. His voice sounded subdued.

"I'm furious, Governor," I blurted out. "I just finished watching *Face the Nation* and I'm outraged at how she treated you. I won't let them get away with such slurs against you and your family. I don't know how you remained so calm throughout."

Cuomo was quiet for a few moments, allowing what I just said to sink in, and giving me time to calm myself. He and I both knew how he could remain so calm during the interview: he had nothing at all to hide; he could not be shaken. With great restraint, he refused to fall for the bait of becoming a "hot-headed Italian." His anger, as expressed in later interviews, was framed in terms of how the presumption of guilt by ethnicity, slurred all Italian Americans, more than 99% of whom had no Mob connection.

I turned my anger into a letter to CBS News President, Howard Stringer, asking whether Leslie Stahl "would have raised the same question in exactly the same manner to a public official whose name did not end in a vowel," specifically citing Senator Bill Bradley and the Reverend Jesse Jackson. The letter, which I signed, was a milestone for me. It was the first time I went public using my own name on the subject of organized crime, and sent copies to then-CBS owner Laurence Tisch, the *New York Times*, the Chairman of the FCC, and Ken Auletta at the *New York Daily News*. A few days later, I phoned Auletta to get his reaction, and to ask him the question I did not have the courage to pose in print.

"Ken, the question no one is asking is this: *So what?*" I said. "So what if his father was Vito Genovese or his brother was John Gotti? What difference would it make so long as Mario Cuomo is clean?"

I heard the desperation in my own voice, caught myself and stopped, waiting for Auletta to respond. In his signature soft voice, he agreed it would make no difference at all. We ended the conversation, and I hung up the phone, wondering if I had protested too much. I was inserting my own family's circumstances for Cuomo's, and worried that I may have aroused Auletta's suspicions. Two weeks later, the stock market crashed, with the Dow Industrial Averages dropping over 500 points, overshadowing innuendos about Mario Cuomo and the mob.

I immersed myself in the battle to shut Shoreham over the next six months, drafting op-ed pieces and position papers for the Governor on public power and energy conservation. The stakes for Cuomo, for Long Islanders, and the nationwide nuclear power industry, could not be higher. Each day ratcheted up the confrontation another notch. Just as the politics of the moment were hitting a fever pitch, my brother Vinnie called me at my office.

"Stephen!" he said, in his usual upbeat fashion. "How are you and your pointy-headed bureaucrat friends doing?"

I was too overwhelmed with work to appreciate his playful political digs, but came back at him with the work that consumed me each day.

"We're trying to get your friends in the Reagan Administration to stop shoving a nuclear power plant down our throats," I said.

"Well, I'm sure Mario will give them a good fight," he said. Despite my brother's support of Reagan and other Orange County, California conservatives, he liked Mario Cuomo because of his Italian heritage. He trusted Cuomo, and the fact that I worked with the Governor of New York, solidified that trust.

"What's up, Vin?" I asked, sensing there was another purpose to the call.

"Well," Vinnie said, "I just wanted to let you know that I'm doing a letter of personal reference for Mike on his upcoming tax hearing."

I was silent. For months, I had worked hard to pretend that my brother Michael no longer existed. Vinnie sensed my discomfort.

"If would probably be helpful if you did a character reference for him too," he said.

I asked Vinnie to fax a copy of his letter to me, indicating that I was not making any promises. His fax came over in a few minutes. I dashed over to the fax machine to make certain no one else would see the letter, written on the corporate stationary of Wyle Laboratories, and signed by my brother as "Vice President, Military." It was straightforward, like Vinnie. He called Michael "the Rock of Gibraltar" for himself and the rest of the family, writing that he "was always available to help in every way. He is a really good guy!" Vinnie wrote emphatically about our older brother.

I read that last line over and over, and recoiled each time. I no longer felt the same way Vinnie did about Michael, yet I also knew that anything I did would be for my mother, not Michael. I wanted to be able to look into her eyes and say "yes" if she asked me whether I wrote a letter on behalf of her oldest son, but needed a way to tell my own truth about my brother. The letter I drafted was on my personal stationary, not on any official State letterhead, which both brothers would have preferred. Consciously, I wanted to ensure there was no link that could be made between my brother Michael, the Mob, me, and the Cuomo Administration: a decision which ended up being prescient.

A few months later, Nassau County Labor Commissioner William Pedersen, asked for "compassion and leniency" for my brother in a letter written on County stationary, an act of poor judgement which constituted the main thrust of a *Newsday* story on my brother's eventual sentencing, on Saturday, September 17, 1988 (Tom Renner, "Clemency Letter Raises Ethics Query in Nassau," p. 5). A letter of support for my brother on New York State stationary would have overshadowed Pedersen's stupidity, and put the focus on my letter as smoking-gun evidence of a link, no matter how tangential, between Cuomo, Villano and the Gambino Crime family. The *Newsday* investigative team, of which Renner was the key reporter on organized crime, had, for months been looking into whether Mario Cuomo had any organized crime connections. My employment for the Cuomo Administration—if used to influence any judicial proceeding—would have been impossible to ignore, even though Mario Cuomo had no involvement or knowledge of either the case, or my brother.

The only way I could justify doing a legal character reference for Michael was to ignore what I knew about him in recent years, and focus on what I remembered about the person he used to be. I wrote that my brother was a "responsible, hard-working, dedicated, kind and loyal human being," a "devoted loving father," and a "respectful, compassionate son to our 73-year-old parents who revere him." That much I knew to be true, and would swear under oath about my brother's character. Anything more, would have compromised my own.

From virtually the day after I sent a character-reference letter of my brother to Judge Mishler through mid-July—a period of three months—there was no let up in my schedule. Cuomo and I spoke several times a day about the Shoreham controversy. The Administration entered a period of intense negotiations with the Long Island Lighting Company to shut down the Nuclear Power plant, in exchange for a State buyout of the utility. The Governor, knowing I communicated to all sides in the growing dispute, placed me squarely in the middle between staunch public power advocates on the left and more moderate anti-nuclear leaders who simply wanted to use the threat of a public takeover as a means to shutdown Shoreham.

It was a balancing act I had plenty of practice performing, and an easy one in comparison to what I had been living each day for years. What I loved about being the man-in-the-middle on *this* issue, was that both sides were enormously intelligent and committed to using the power of government to do good; defining what constituted that "good" was where they differed.

There was a parallel for Cuomo, between the battle Franklin D. Roosevelt, as Governor of New York, faced over public power nearly sixty years according to Kenneth Davis in *FDR: The New York Years, 1928-1933* (Random House, New York, NY., 1979). FDR, like Cuomo, threatened the private power utility interests by having the State go into the transmission business in competition with them. He stopped short of supporting state-owned transmission facilities, angering Socialist leader Norman Thomas and his followers who wanted a total public take-over. Cuomo, like FDR, also selected a compromise position.

"Roosevelt referred to a complete public takeover as a 'birchrod in the cupboard' Governor," I reported back to Cuomo after researching the matter. "He held it behind his back, like a stick, to beat the utilities over the head with, just in case he needed it."

Cuomo loved the "birchrod in the cupboard" imagery and used the phrase repeatedly during his efforts to sell the Shoreham settlement. The Governor was personally involved in hammering out the agreement to shut down the Nuclear Power Plant, an enormous accomplishment that defied the odds, the powerful Reagan Administration, and a well-funded nuclear power industry. We were exhilarated by our efforts after a year of grueling work: we had stopping Shoreham and the public health threat it posed on an Island with a population of nearly three million people. From the Governor's perspective, I passed through another crucible and he was grateful for my work. Now, with one crucial job done, it was time to move on to the next. Within weeks, Andrew Cuomo called offering me a senior position at the Division of Housing and Community Renewal, at a significant increase in salary.

"Stephen," Andrew said, again pronouncing my name exactly as my mother did, "we need a first-rate team for Housing, and we'd like you to be part of it. The issues are very complex; we're going to have a whole new thrust. Think about it."

Minutes later the Governor called and repeated Andrew's offer. It was simply how the Cuomos rolled. One month passed without another word from either Andrew or the Governor, and, I was relieved by the delay. In that time, Michael matter-of-factly informed me that the "income tax hearing" for which I had written his character reference was actually a "sentencing hearing," on the charge of federal income tax evasion, for which he could be sentenced to up to four years in prison.

"*Are you fucking kidding me, Michael?*" I said when he called to tell me the news. "Federal Income tax evasion? Are you fucking kidding me?"

"It's what the government got Al Capone on," he said, as if I would be impressed by the comparison.

"How stupid could you be, Michael?" I blurted out. "How goddamned stupid could you be?"

Boom. Just like that. Income tax evasion. Jail time. Sentencing hearing. Another one of my brother's smug, wise guy scheme's gone awry. I was reeling; tossed between my obsession to work harder for the Governor and move up in the Cuomo Administration, and my gut instinct that to do so, would make me, and my brother's connections, a bigger target for an enterprising reporter, or a political enemy. I was driven to learn more about my brother's case, angry with myself for ignoring his circumstances for months while his legal problems grew, unnoticed, like a hidden cancer. Now, the tumor had burst open, spreading rapidly and become visible; impossible to pretend the growth did not exist. Working five minutes from Judge Mishler's courtroom, and in control of my own daily schedule, I attended every hour of my brother's hearing with the express intention of learning as much as I could about his involvement with the Mob, who he really was, and how to deal with the outcome of his sentence. It was time to stop pretending, like Voltaire's Professor Pangloss in *Candide*, that all was for the best, or that the problem would simply go away over time.

On the morning of the first day of my brother's hearing before Judge Mishler, July 7, 1988, Mario Cuomo called me at home, just before I left for the Federal Courthouse. The Governor praised my work and my ability, talking about my "great" future within his Administration. Ninety minutes later, I was sitting in Federal District Court in Uniondale, at the start of several months of hearings in Michael's income tax evasion case, where I heard our family name repeatedly linked to John Gotti's. Each time it was repeated, over the course of the next several months of the "income tax hearings" in Judge Mishler's courtroom, the slack went out of the tightrope across which I was tip-toeing. I felt certain that it was only a matter of moments before everything came tumbling down.

I avoided giving the Governor or Andrew a response to their offer for the Housing position as long as I could, and quietly contacted a private sector head-hunting firm to begin looking for permanent positions outside of government. Only a few weeks remained before Michael's prison sentence would be decided, and I was crazed to find a path away from Mario Cuomo—despite desperately wanting to accept the Governor's offer to perform even more public service, at a higher level. A lifetime of thinking of myself in only one profession was rushing to a brusque conclusion; as quickly as my brother's life before prison was coming to an end. It hadn't mattered how hard I worked to push myself away from him, from his friends and their Guinea arrogance and stupidity. I was tethered to my brother, whether I liked it or not. We shared the same blood, the same name, and nothing could ever alter that.

The *Newsday* story I warned the Governor about, when I called to tell him about my brother's jail sentence, appeared on Saturday, September 17, 1988. It was accompanied by a full photo of Michael, nattily dressed in his dark, double-breasted blazer and light slacks, striding out of court. The photo was captioned: "Michael Villano leaves court yesterday."

He spared me the embarrassment of being photographed with him, by telling me to leave the courthouse earlier than he did—a small, gentle gesture for which I was grateful. Immediately after Judge Mishler sentenced my brother to ninety days in jail, with three years probation, I followed him and his lawyers into a conference room off to the side of the main Chamber. Mike Rosen, Michael's lead attorney, made sure the door was securely shut.

"Congratulations, Mike, Congratulation," Rosen said, patting my brother on his back.

Smiles and handshakes circulated between my brother and his other two lawyers, who expressed relief that he had "dodged a bullet" of a four-year sentence. I stood quietly, my back against the door of the small, windowless conference room; my body language pleading for freedom; struggling to grapple with the idea of my brother going to jail. I leaned hard against the closed door, trying to force my way out through the solid wood. Michael noticed my growing discomfort.

"You don't have to wait around anymore, Steve," he said. "I really appreciate your being here."

Our eyes made contact, but I did not speak.

"There's a *Newsday* photographer waiting outside to take Mike's picture," Mike Rosen said to me. "You don't need to be in any photograph, Stephen, so why don't you leave now, before us."

I hesitated. I did not want to be in any *Newsday* photo, but also didn't want to run out on my brother, despite knowing his prison sentence would not begin for thirty days. I had come this far and wanted to see this thing through. Michael broke the awkward silence, telling me to leave.

I grabbed his hand with both of mine, my throat straining for air, and walked out of the tiny conference room. I wanted to run down the steps, out of the courthouse, as fast as my legs would carry me, but knew I could not. I strolled slowly out the front door of the Federal Courthouse when a young, thin woman with long brown hair—the *Newsday* photographer—snapped my picture. I wanted to stop and shout at her: "Stop! I'm not him; I'm his brother; I'm the good guy." Instead, I walked straight ahead, composed and quiet, carrying my briefcase, the prop I brought to every hearing so no one would confuse me with Michael. I was wearing my blue and white seersucker suit, with brown penny loafers and my wire-rimmed glasses: Harvard yard vs. Prison yard, I thought. They could not possibly confuse us.

Finally, I reached my car, a sub-compact Plymouth Horizon with a "Dukakis for President" sticker on the rear bumper. My hand trembled as I unlocked the door. I climbed in and slowly drove past the photographer, making certain she could see my poor man's car and Dukakis sticker. How many organized crime figures drive around in Plymouth Horizons and are liberal Democrats? Surely, she'll see that.

"She snapped my picture," I muttered to myself, driving away. "She snapped my fucking picture."

Fortunately, the Nassau County Labor Commissioner's careless act of writing a character reference for my brother on Nassau County government stationary, had made Commissioner Pedersen the lead of the story, and kept the name "Villano" out of the bold-faced headlines. The story went on to detail my brother's failure to pay more than $130,000 in federal taxes on money he collected from several businesses in Queens. Pedersen told *Newsday* that "he asked me to write the letter for him…He told me he had some income tax problems…that he was convicted of income tax."

Apparently, Pedersen's letter, and those from Vinnie, me, and others, did help reduce my brother's sentence. Judge Mishler originally considered giving Michael a four-year jail sentence, with five years probation, but said he was "impressed by the people who wrote on Villano's behalf." I could look at myself in the mirror and my mother in the eye, even if I had to look away from Mario Cuomo.

The story appeared on a Saturday morning and the day remained eerily quiet. It must be like this after death, I thought: No more calls, no more thoughts, no more contact. The following day, I made my weekly Sunday call to my parents in California and pretended that nothing had happened—no prison sentence, no court appearance, no tax issues, no newspaper story; nothing. My brother asked me to keep everything a secret from them, using my mother's high blood pressure to handcuff me in hiding the truth. I felt dirty, like an unindicted co-conspirator for participating in another of my brother's cover-ups. It was a position he placed me in more than once. In court, during the sentencing hearing, I listened as Michael's attorney advanced my brother's make-believe story of a life-long friendship with John Gotti, which I knew was untrue.

My brother had not met John Gotti until "Uncle Charlie" Fatico introduced them to each other, when my brother was in his early thirties. We *never* knew Gotti as we were growing up; we knew the Ebolis, Vito Genovese, Carmine Fatico, other, more senior mobsters—but *not* John Gotti. My mother would never have allowed it, since Gotti was a street hood, and my brother Michael, a model son. I was trapped by his lies, my love for him and my mother, and had compromised my own ethics and integrity so my brother would not spend any more time in jail.

The next day, Monday, September 19, 1988, a reporter friend at *Newsday* called me. He told me that my brother and I were the talk of the newsroom that day and that *Newsday*'s Investigative Unit knew that Michael and I were brothers.

"John McDonald came up to me, and said, 'It's weird—Steve is straight as an arrow,'" the reporter told me.

I had known *Newsday*'s McDonald for four years when he was covering Suffolk County Community College, where I worked as an Administrator and Instructor, before going to work for Cuomo. A careful, fair and solid journalist, McDonald was promoted to *Newsday*'s Investigations Unit, a group of top-flight journalists who won a number of Pulitzer Prizes for reporting on crime and corruption across Long Island. According to McDonald, the Investigative Unit devoted many hours and resources looking into rumors of Mario Cuomo's alleged mob connections, coming up with nothing. Tom Renner, *Newsday*'s lead organized crime reporter who covered my brother's sentencing hearing each day, and wrote the Saturday story about his sentencing, worked closely with McDonald. Learning that the Villano brothers were the "talk of the newsroom" at *Newsday* destroyed me. I called my sister Vera that night to tell her the news, that my public career was finished. She tried to comfort me.

"People won't hold you responsible for what Michael did," she said.

"It doesn't matter, Vera," I counterec. "It doesn't matter that I am not Michael, don't you see? Politics is a miserable, nasty business. And this is not like Billy Carter being an alcoholic or Kitty Dukakis being an addict. *This is Mafia*. Even the hint of "Mafia" near anyone with an Italian name is politically fatal. The reporters at *Newsday* and their Investigative Unit already know all about me and Michael."

"How do they know?" Vera asked.

Her instincts to protect her baby brother were kicking in. Once, as a child, when a neighborhood bully grabbed an ice cream cone from my hands and left me crying, Vera leapt to my defense, buying another cone, and shoving it into his face, sending the bully home in tears.

"Because a reporter friend of mine told me that the Villano brothers were the talk of their newsroom," I said. "Reporters who have known me for years couldn't believe how I could be so law-abiding and have a brother alleged to be a bagman for Gotti."

"But the Governor said it doesn't affect you; he told you not to worry," she protested.

"Would you have expected him to say anything else?" I said. "That just shows you the kind of person he is. Why do you think I work for him? If he were somehow tainted by Michael's link—by a Villano's link to John Gotti—I couldn't live with myself. No, Vera. I've got to get away from him."

Two weeks later, I interviewed for a position at a small, liberal arts college on Long Island. The next day, Matilda Cuomo's father, Charles Raffa, died. He had never recovered after having been badly beaten and left for dead four years earlier in a mugging outside of a property he owned in Brooklyn. Now, he would be laid out in a funeral parlor in Williston Park, Long Island, just a few minutes from my office. The appropriate thing to do was to go, quickly pay my respects, and leave. For weeks, I was trying to distance myself from the Governor. When he saw me at the funeral parlor, he greeted me with a quick "How are you doing?" I didn't know how to answer. Did he mean, in general? In the aftermath of my brother's sentencing? Was he grateful that I came to the funeral parlor, or was his abruptness telling me to get lost?

I carefully measured everyone's response, feeling isolated, until Andrew Cuomo rose from the wooden folding chair on which he was seated. He walked over to me, gave me a warm welcome, and introduced Kerry Kennedy, his fiancé, and the daughter of one of my first political heroes. His gracious action was too much to grasp; my mind separated from my body and floated someplace up on the ceiling of the funeral parlor, looking down on everything, and everyone below. Nothing was real. My eyes observed the three of us standing there—me, Michael Villano's brother; Andrew Cuomo, the son of Mario Cuomo, and Kerry Kennedy, the daughter of Robert F. Kennedy. I was overwhelmed with the impossibility of it all. I heard myself say "Excuse me," to Andrew Cuomo and Kerry Kennedy;

I watched myself genuflect in front of Charlie Raffa's coffin; felt myself kiss Matilda Cuomo good night, and shake Mario Cuomo's hand. I observed myself go through all the motions before I left, feeling nothing, unconnected to my body. Exiting the funeral home, I took deep breaths in the crisp, October night air, calmed myself and drove home.

The following week my brother went off to serve time. I wasn't sure at which prison. Like everything else with Michael, information was obscured. It could have been Brooklyn or the Manhattan Correctional Center for a short time, with an eventual move to some federal facility someplace. That's usually how indefinite things were with him. He could be tight lipped for business reasons or mysterious for his own purposes. In this case, he wanted people to believe he was being sent away where all the big time wise guys were sentenced—to the United States Penitentiary in Lewisburg, Pennsylvania, which had housed Whitey Bolger, Henry Hill, Jimmy Hoffa, and John Gotti at different times. Instead, Michael landed in Loretto, Pennsylvania, a minimum-security Federal Correctional Institution—a place for lower-lever mobster wannabes—half-way across the state from Lewisburg. I offered to come and visit him in prison.

"Nah, that's not necessary, Steve," he said, "It's a long drive on one-lane, back country, winding roads. Plus, I'm only gonna be there a short time; not less than thirty days; not more than ninety days."

He made his time in prison sound as harmless as a product warranty. To me, it was 30-90 days that changed my life; to him he was simply "goin' away on business for a few weeks," as he told our parents. His life of lies would continue in jail and after.

"I'm worried more about the three years of probation when you get out of jail, Michael," I said to him over the phone, the night before he left for prison. A key condition of his probation was that he not associate with any members of organized crime for three years.

"Your every move is gonna be watched. The Feds have invested too much in you now to let things drop," I said. "If they catch you near any of those guys, they'll throw the book at you. You've got to stay away from those people, those places."

"What am I supposed to do? Become a hermit?", Michael said. "Have three lawyers accompany me wherever I go?"

There it was again: that old Guinea arrogance, which got him into trouble in the first place. No way is this man gonna change. No fucking way. Still, as furious as I was with his pig-headedness, I could not sleep for the first three nights he was in jail; the thought of my brother in a barracks-like cell with nine other men kept me awake. My brother—who used to sleep in the big room at the top of the stairs with Vinnie and me, each in our own single beds, each with our own lives, yet connected by the roof over our heads and something else. I stared up at the ceiling in my darkened bedroom on Long Island and wondered if, in the dark and quiet of the night, my brother's eyes were open, looking at the ceiling in his cell. I wondered if he asked himself how he got there; how his life got away from him; if he looked into the darkness and saw himself as he was before, wanting to grab the innocent, unlined face he saw, slip it on, like a fresh new suit of clothes, and start over.

On my final day of work for the Governor, the night before I was to begin my self-imposed exile working at the small college, Michael called me at home. In prison, he was allowed one-five minute phone call a day. I was surprised to hear from him, although I could not get him out of my mind. Leaving public service and my work with Mario Cuomo sent me spiraling into a deep depression. I despised my brother's arrogance and carelessness one minute, and felt sympathy for him the next; chastised my own stupidity and willful blindness for pretending my family's Mob connections neither existed nor mattered, and felt sorry for myself the next moment for leaving my work for the Cuomo Administration. I was surprised to hear my brother's voice on the phone. Had he remembered that my work for the Governor ended that day? Instinctively, I asked him how he was doing; how he was surviving prison.

"I'm doin' good," Michael said. "Doin, ok. It's comfortable here; I made a lot of friends; I work in the dining room for lunch and dinner. I'm helping to set up computers here, too."

I informed him that Mom and Dad were coming into New York from Southern California to spend Thanksgiving with us the following week, and to celebrate my son's Bar Mitzvah, which would be a few days later.

"I'm sorry I'll miss it," he said.

I told him I invited his wife and their young daughter to attend, and also to join us on Thanksgiving, since I didn't want them to be alone, while he was in prison.

"Thank you, Stephen, that's very nice of you," my brother said. "I'll try to call your house on Thanksgiving Day to talk to everyone, if I can get a free phone."

Trapped again, only this time by myself, trying to do the right thing to limit the collateral damage from my brother's crimes. That Thanksgiving Day was the first time in his thirteen years of life that my son was celebrating a holiday with both sets of his grandparents. Christian and Jewish holidays were carefully carved out between each family, with Thanksgiving alternating from place to place each year.

This year would be different. My parents came from California and Carol's from Florida, to be present at their grandson's Bar Mitzvah. It was a milestone for all of us, validating my decision to convert to Judaism eight years earlier. Now, every member of the family on both sides would share in a week full of celebrations, kicking off with Thanksgiving. Midway through dinner, the telephone rang. I excused myself from the table and picked up the kitchen extension.

The connection was poor, but I could make out Michael's voice, sounding as if he was calling from far away. We exchanged brief holiday greetings, and then he asked to speak to his wife and young daughter, and our mother and father.

He wished all a "Happy Thanksgiving," informing our parents he was in Korea on business and would not be able to be back in time to see them at Matt's Bar Mitzvah. My mother's eyes brightened when she heard his voice, visibly delighted that he had remembered to call during the holiday, from the other side of the world. Even from prison Michael had sucked me into yet another cover-up, using my mother's joy to silence me, and my desire to protect my parents from pain perpetuating his intricate web of lies. I felt dirty again, an undiscovered co-conspirator, and the day I wanted to be perfect ended up being ruined.

11 ▫ Agita

My hasty hiatus from Mario Cuomo was no break from the forces pulling in opposite directions. Two Christmas cards that year framed the tension perfectly: one, from my brother, postmarked from Loretto, PA, was signed, "Love, Inmate Michael;" the other, from the Governor and Mrs. Cuomo, and sent from the Governor's Mansion, its' front cover emblazoned with Mario Cuomo's favorite quote from Teilhard de Chardin: "All that really matters is devotion to something bigger than ourselves."

My brother was released from prison three days after my 40th birthday in mid-January. Carol, Matt and I had tickets to see a Broadway show, and a complex mixture of compassion and curiosity compelled me to call my sister-in-law and arrange a sort of "welcome home" dinner for Michael on his first day back, at Carmella's Restaurant in Greenwich Village. As the only family member present when he was sentenced to prison, I needed to see his face when he came home; he had completed his sentence, and, in an odd way, so had I.

How had he survived? I thought that by looking into his eyes and studying his face, it would help me understand. All anger toward my brother was gone. His fatigued face yielded no answers. There was no trace of the brightness in his eyes, ever-present when he was younger, that once encouraged me to embrace the future. I wanted to hug him, but I did not. I wanted to tell him that I would help him rebuild his life, but I did not.

Instead, I listened quietly as he railed against "the god-damned government," and realized his ways, hardened by years of self-deception, were not likely to change easily, if ever. But, I had closed the loop; I saw him off and welcomed him back; that circle, for me, was complete. Michael's imprisonment and my six-month, self-imposed sentence away from Mario Cuomo, liberated me. It was time to start anew. I called the Governor and asked to come back to work with him.

"I think I left public service prematurely, Governor," I said. "I find myself fiercely defending our policy initiatives at every turn. I belong working back alongside you"

Cuomo's response was enthusiastic.

"You have all sorts of energy, Steve," Mario Cuomo said, "all kinds of desire to say and do important things. We should consider doing a book together on Shoreham, put down our main ideas, why its worthwhile reviewing, its implications—give it some thought. I spoke to Jason Epstein (Cuomo's literary agent). He'd like to see a book outline. Meanwhile, see what Andrew has in mind for you."

I was elated. The end of my exile was in sight. Within days, Andrew Cuomo called to tell me he was pleased I wanted to come back, and that I ought to think about running the Governor's NYC Press Office. I told him I would, but needed to tie up a few things where I was working. In the interim, Mario Cuomo and I worked directly with each other, faxing outlines on the Shoreham book back and forth. The Governor treated me as his colleague, his co-author. At last, I felt free from the Mob's stench, and out from my brother's shadow, until a few days later when an unexpected guest sat directly behind my family at my nephew Michael's wedding.

I happily anticipated my brother's son's wedding for months, looking forward to my own son celebrating an occasion with my entire family. Now, every generation of the Villano family would be present, and to me, it carried a great deal of meaning. My nephew was a sweet and loving copy of my brother Michael, with layers of years and duplicity peeled away. A kind, thoughtful kid, he silently stood by his father throughout some of the most tumultuous times over the past decade. I berated myself for never rescuing him from my brother's life, knowing that his overwhelming desire for his father's love and approval would not have allowed that to happen. After the short wedding service we left the church and drove a few miles to the Holiday Inn in Plainview, Long Island, for the wedding reception. As we entered the party room, I noticed a long, large empty table directly behind us. Everyone in the room stood while the wedding party entered. My nephew and his new wife were introduced and welcomed with a warm round of applause, as the bandleader invited everyone to join them on the dance floor. When the music stopped, we returned to our seats and the table behind us was full. Seated at it were twelve bulky men, wearing tight-fitting dark suits. Still exhilarated from dancing, I hadn't paid too much attention to their faces, but my brother Vinnie did.

"Stephen," he whispered across the table to me, "Do you see who's sitting behind us. It's Big John—Gotti."

I stared at Vinnie's wide eyes and then turned to look, spotting Gotti's silver grey hair and unmistakeable face. I jerked my head back quickly, looking away from Gotti and straight across our table at my brother Michael, seated next to my father. Furious, my eyes flared with anger. How could he be so careless and stupid? How could he put his entire family in the direct line of fire if some group of punks from a rival mob blasted their way into the wedding, gunning for Gotti? Whether he knew it or not, he was using my son, and all the rest of us, as Gotti's human shields. Not only had the presence of the Mob boss endangered all our lives, but also my brother was flagrantly violating his parole by not keeping away from these wise guys for three years.

Did he want to end up back in jail, this time for far longer? I glared at him. He caught my look and quickly looked away. He had entrapped me again. Not only did our parents not know of his imprisonment, or the terms of his parole, but my brother knew our parents were staying at my house. They were dependent upon me for transportation to and from the wedding, making it impossible for me to simply get up and leave. Besides, *I did not want to leave*; I was crazy over my nephew and his sister and wanted to share a joyous occasion with them. Before Gotti and his crew arrived I was enjoying myself; dancing with Carol, seeing my parents healthy and enjoying themselves, and watching my son laughing and smiling with his older cousins. *I belonged there; John Gotti did not.* My brother Michael motioned for Vinnie to join him.

"Vinnie, you ought to go pay your respects to John," Michael said, nodding in Gotti's direction.

Vinnie dashed over to Gotti's table, titillated by the entire experience. I stared straight past Michael, daring him to make the same request of me. He knew I held his secret from our parents; knew that I specifically warned him to stay away from these hoods for the duration of his probation; knew how I detested every one of them, especially Gotti. He said nothing to me. After a brief appearance, Gotti and his henchmen left my nephew's wedding.

I was so angry with my brother Michael that five months passed before I spoke with him again, at our parents' fiftieth Wedding Anniversary party in California. During that time, I was back working with Mario Cuomo and wanted nothing to do with my brother or his "friends." We were seated next to each other on a dais which included our parents, along with our brother Vinnie and sister Vera. While everyone was enjoying dinner, Michael attempted to break through my silent hostility toward him.

"They're giving me trouble, Steve," he said.

I continued eating, not bothering to look at him.

"Who is?" I asked.

"The god-damned government," my brother said. "They had a probation officer at Michael's wedding, disguised as a bartender."

I stared at him, closed my eyes, and shook my head.

"You remember the rolling bar behind our table and in front of the table where John was sitting?" Michael said.

I hated the way he casually dropped the name "John" as if Gotti were just another member of the family attending a family event. Just another one of us.

"No, I really don't," I said.

"Well, the bartender worked for probation," he said. "He was sent to keep an eye on me. Now they're claiming I shouldn't have been there if I knew Gotti was gonna be there."

I looked at my brother without speaking. He answered my look.

"I didn't even know John was coming," my brother said. "Michael sent out the invitations; I didn't have anything to do with them."

I might have believed my brother if he hadn't invited Gotti to his own wedding five years earlier. I looked at him again, amazed at how easily lying came to him. And now, even if he was telling the truth, who could believe him, since he lied so fluently in the past? I shook my head, got up from the table, and walked away.

My disgust with my brother's stupidity and anger at John Gotti strengthened my determination to become consumed with work for Mario Cuomo. He was the counterpoint to them; working with Cuomo was running toward sunlight; a positive step for my son to see that Italian-American men could be educated, literate, respect the law, and be dedicated to the public good. And now, *especially* after Gotti and his goons endangered the lives of everyone I loved by their very presence at my nephew's wedding, I did not want to do anything else *but* boost Mario Cuomo.

Shortly after I returned to run the Governor's New York City Press Office, a 16-year-old black man named Yusef Hawkins was chased by a mob of thirty white men, many wielding baseball bats, and then shot to death in Bensonhurst, Brooklyn, a heavily Italian-American enclave. Hawkins was responding to a newspaper ad to purchase a used car.

Like many New Yorkers, I was sickened by the murder, and outraged at the young, Italian tough-guys, Gotti-wannabes, who rushed to tell news reporters that the "nigger" had no place in their neighborhood. I kept the Governor informed by phone all day of the rapidly unfolding events following Hawkins' death. My voice was shaking and Cuomo could hear how the killing affected me. He planned to attend Yusef Hawkins' funeral in East New York on August 30, 1989. He asked me to draft a statement about the murder, and to attend the funeral with him.

The Hawkins murder by violent Italian-American punks haunted me. I *knew these people*; I left them all behind to fester in their own ignorance. No matter how pristine my life now, I knew these people. I tried to push them away, out of my memory and my experience, but what good did all of that do when a 16-year old Black boy was dead? I detested these wise guys who swaggered around their neighborhoods, swimming in their own smugness; despised them for what they made people think of us, and how little they made us think of ourselves. I blamed myself for Yusef Hawkins' death because, somehow, in my haste to get out, I lost sight of how I might have changed some other life like mine; shown another young Italian-American kid struggling with his identity and his place in the world that there were avenues of understanding and education to escape from all of our personal Bensonhursts. Yusef Hawkins was my child, a son of the whole city, and no matter how hard I scrubbed. I could not get his blood off my hands.

The next day, I attended Hawkins' funeral with Mario Cuomo. We were among a small smattering of white faces in the crowd jamming the streets of East New York, not far from where I was born. I stood there, amidst a group of mostly white reporters covering the funeral, and found an uneasy comfort in the presence of Louis Farakkhan's bow-tied Muslim soldiers, who lined the streets in front of the church to keep some semblance of peace.

Mayor Ed Koch, locked in a brutal primary election battle with David Dinkins, emerged from his car and was pelted with a barrage of boos and screams so intense, I expected Koch's presence to ignite a riot. Racial tensions in the City had been exacerbated during the twelve years Koch was Mayor. In the 1988 Democratic Presidential Primary, Koch heaped criticism and scorn upon the Reverend Jesse Jackson, locked in a close battle with Massachusetts Governor Michael Dukakis. The Mayor declared that any Jew in New York would be "crazy" to vote for Jackson because of his "Hymietown" comments about NYC four years earlier. Dislike for Koch was visceral in East New York's Black neighborhoods, but even Mario Cuomo, with his history of warm relations with the African-American community across the City and State, was heckled as he entered the church for the funeral service. Cuomo had been sharply criticized the day before by movie director Spike Lee, whose film about racism in New York, *Do The Right Thing,* came out earlier that summer. Lee chastised Cuomo for not visiting Bensonhurst, and "talking some sense out there to the Italians." The street taunts toward Cuomo reflected this sentiment.

Only Dinkins was greeted respectfully, foreshadowing his primary victory over Koch two weeks later. The Manhattan Borough President ran as a "healer" for the City's racial tensions, easily defeating Koch by a nine-point margin. Ninety percent of African American voters supported Dinkins, who carried the heavily populated Boroughs of Manhattan, Brooklyn and the Bronx. David Dinkins went on to win in November, being elected New York's first African-American Mayor in the City's 325-year history, beating Rudy Giuliani, 51%-48%. Giuliani carried Bensonhurst by a 10-1 margin.

Days after David Dinkins' inauguration, my elation over his election evaporated. Throughout January and February 1990, the year Mario Cuomo would seek his third term as Governor, John Gotti was a front-page fixture in New York's tabloids. Gotti was on trial for conspiracy and assault in the murder of Manhattan Carpenters' Union leader John F. O'Conner. Yet, New York's media was enamored with his $2,000 suits, brightly colored ties and matching pocket hankies, his silver gray hair and his swagger. It was a Gotham-sized tabloid war, and the newcomer on the block, *New York Newsday,* struggling to carve out its own niche between the *New York Daily News* and the *New York Post,* ran a full-color photo of John Gotti on the front page of its January 25, 1990 issue, with the headline, "GOTTI: 'God's Gift to the Underworld.'"

The quote about Gotti was his own, recorded on tape by federal prosecutors, who introduced it at the Mob boss' trial. The *New York*

Post ran the same photo in black and white on its front page, the same day, with a one-word headline: "GABFATHER."

Television reporters swooned over Gotti each day in court, with WNBC-TV's blond, telegenic crime reporter John Miller sucking up to Gotti and his entourage. Gotti, and access to him, became a marketing tool in the highly competitive New York City media market. WNBC decided to promote it's own crime-coverage star Miller with a tape showing him and Gotti. In the promo, Miller is chasing Gotti on the street, walking one step behind the Gambino Family boss, when Gotti gruffly asks the reporter: "You behavin' yourself?" Miller responds with a sly smile, "I'm behavin' myself, I'm behavin' myself." It was as if NBC's crime reporter was telling the most powerful organized crime figure in the nation that he was being a good boy. Everything had been turned upside down.

NBC's promo was shameless; its message was clear: Miller knows Gotti and Gotti knows Miller. The Gotti trial held in late January and early February was a media carnival, with real movie stars like Tony LoBianco and Ray Sharkey traipsing back and forth to Gotti's side, sharing the spotlight and elevating the street hood's seedy status to movie-star proportions.

On February 9, 1990, John Gotti was acquitted on four separate charges of assault and two charges of conspiracy in connection with the O'Conner shooting. Gotti, surround by his lawyers and body-guards, was rushed from the State Supreme Court Building in Lower Manhattan to the Ravenite Social Club on Mulberry Street. When the Gambino Crime family boss' maroon-colored Cadillac pulled up in front of the Ravenite, crowds of New Yorkers cheered him as he stepped out in the street.

The sight of this made me physically ill. These were the same Italian-Americans who chanted "Nigger go home," at Yusef Hawkins and were gleeful over his murder. They were the same crowd that voted overwhelmingly against David Dinkins because of his race, and the same ignorant group who criticized Mario Cuomo for being "soft" because he opposed the death penalty. I wanted nothing to do with them, or my brother. The tabloid coverage of Gotti's going free made matters worse. *Newsday's* front page called Gotti "UNTOUCHABLE." The *New York Post* ran a picture of the Mob boss, stepping toward his waiting Cadillac with the headline: "DANCING DON." A small measure of solace came in Jimmy Breslin's Sunday, February 11, *Newsday* column:

...television news on Friday night was pornographic, the newspapers on Saturday, mainly sickening...The City celebrates its first celebrity of the '90's: a gangster from 101st Avenue in Ozone Park. Marvelous.

There are no displays for persons with Italian names who get up in the morning in this City and go to work on time, feed families and get children through college. But now as they leave for work, they have the legend of John Gotti walking with them.

Breslin expressed the fury and flagrant unfairness of the entire New York media orgy better than any Italian-American writer did. The day before, the *New York Daily News* reported on "several extremely well-dressed young men with extremely colorful neckties waiting to congratulate their role model in private," at the Ravenite Social Club—the same place where my brother welcomed John Gotti to power on Christmas Eve, five years earlier. I re-read the phrase "role-model" in disbelief. Dress like Gotti; be like Gotti; act like Gotti.

The glorification of Gotti drove me into despair. My brother Michael, "of no significance in organized crime," as Judge Mishler said at his sentencing, was a Mob minion who had taken a fall for this goon, ripping our family apart and disrupting our lives. Now the bum he bowed down to, and went to jail for, was being treated like a celebrity. I clung to Mario Cuomo like a life raft in a raging sea, my strongest hope for survival, obsessed with advancing the Governor as a counterweight to the cult growing around Gotti. Italian-American kids in Bensonhurst or Ozone Park or Babylon or Buffalo needed to see there was a far better role model to imitate. My mission went beyond getting Mario Cuomo re-elected; it was to use the Governor's fine example to wrestle my life, and the lives of other young Italian-Americans like my son, and other sons, from the grip of Gotti, and my brother's friends.

That grip would not be loosened easily. Two months later, the *New York Daily News* (April 8, 1990) ran a story by its premier organized crime reporter Jerry Capeci, prominently featuring photos of my brother Michael entering the Ravenite, and detailed his business relationship with MCA Universal's Gene Giaquinto. Capeci's story quoted extensively from the FBI's files that described my brother's acting as Gotti's go-between with Giaquinto, his imprisonment on income tax evasion charges, and Gotti's attendance at my nephew's wedding—when the Mob boss sat right behind my family. The story strengthened my resolve to resign without hesitation if my brother's connection to Gotti became an issue in the Governor's re-election. Mario Cuomo's life and work were far too important to the lives of all Italian-Americans to be derailed by the family of one.

My work for the Governor was my elixir, raising my spirits and restoring hope. Each time he spoke, it mattered more to me than ever before that he simply be the best; that he demonstrate his intelligence and humanity as only he could, and speak to audiences only he was capable of reaching.

Race relations in New York City were still simmering five months after David Dinkins became Mayor, with wounds from the killing of Yusef Hawkins still raw. In a bold move to get in front of the issue, the Mayor scheduled a major event on race-relations at the Cathedral of St. John the Divine, on the Upper West Side of Manhattan. Mario Cuomo was invited to speak, but it was clearly understood to be the Mayor's opportunity to begin to heal, and bring a badly divided City together. All major New York City television networks would be carrying the event live, during local prime-time. The Governor was aware of the delicate role he was being asked to play. He could not upstage the City's first African-American Mayor, yet there were people—like those in Bensonhurst—he needed to reach.

He was not comfortable with the remarks prepared for him by his speechwriters in Albany, who failed to capture the depth of racial tension in New York. An hour before we were scheduled to leave the World Trade Center for the trip uptown to the Cathedral, Mario Cuomo called on his inter-office phone.

"Steve, I'm not satisfied with the speech for tonight's rally," the Governor said. "Would you take a look at it?"

"Sure, Governor," I said, looking nervously at my watch.

I ran down the hall to his office, picked up a draft of the speech and read it quickly. The speech was flat, unemotional, and would make Mario Cuomo look out of touch with what was happening in the City. I sat down at my computer and pounded out a few suggestions for him to personalize the speech much more. Earlier that week, a news story broke about high school drop-out rates among Italian-American youth being as high as 21%—the third highest in NYC— behind Hispanics and Blacks. Stunned by the statistic, I stitched it into some suggested comments for the Governor:

With a 21% drop-out rate for Italian-American young people in the City—second only to Hispanics and Blacks—the enemy is not each other, but ignorance, poverty, joblessness, hopelessness, low aspirations, fear of others and demagogues who prey on those fears. Why are we fighting among ourselves when we must save our strength for the real battles—and for fighting the closed minded people: the skinheads, the anti-Semites, the racists, the anti-Italian bigots—who denigrate all of us and rejoice in our division.

My heart was pounding. I wanted Mario Cuomo to make people cry with his words. Maybe, I thought, just maybe, if one 14-year-old Italian kid in Bensonhurst walked past the television at home and heard Cuomo's speech, that would be one less kid lost to John Gotti, and one who could choose to follow Mario Cuomo's eloquent example. The Cathedral was packed with several thousand people when we arrived. They were primed for David Dinkins, who did not disappoint them, delivering the most stirring and passionate speech of his career. Then it was Mario Cuomo's turn.

He began graciously, acknowledging the special place the Mayor held in the hearts of New Yorkers:

I commend the Mayor for what has already been an immense performance. Mayor Dinkins has swiftly proven to the people of this City and this State and this nation that he is a man for all seasons, especially now; especially now, he is the man for this season of our troubles.

Then, Mario Cuomo found his cadence, and the huge crowd seated in pews and standing in aisles throughout the cavernous Cathedral began to rock with him:

There is hostility, and I don't like it. It makes me cringe. I've seen a lot of it in my time….but we need to refocus our hostility away from one another and onto the government policies that neglect people in need…You can be angry, justly angry, about the policies that leave a whole generation of children threatened by a terrible plague of drugs and violence, and more homeless than at any time since the Great Depression…The Mayor teaches us again, the absurdity of African-American, Italian-Americans, Korean-Americans, struggling over the same scraps of bread…

The Governor's voice rose, and began to crackle with emotion:

Think of it: with a 21% drop-out rate among my Italian-American young people—my Italian Americans—we are second only to Hispanics and African Americans. For Italian-American youth, the enemy is not Hispanics or African-Americans, or any of the bright new immigrants sweating to make a place alongside us. The enemies are hopelessness, and illiteracy, ignorance and fear…

Cuomo's voice, quaking with feeling, rang out throughout the massive Cathedral, as if he were Job, calling out to God:

Tell me, for God's sake, why are we fighting among ourselves? We must save our strength for the real battles; for fighting the closed-minded people, the skin-heads, the anti-Semites, the racists, the gay-haters…We must save our strength for all the small-minded, shrunken-souled, big-mouthed demagogues who seek to tear us apart.

223

I stood off to the side from where the Governor was speaking, electrified by his performance, and in tears. Mario Cuomo finished his speech and the crowd went wild, filling the catacombs of the Cathedral with thunderous applause. He had walked a rhetorical tightrope before thousands of people—and millions more watching live on their televisions at home—delivering a powerfully emotional speech that both bested and boosted the first African-American Mayor in New York City's long history, and elevated everyone who watched it.

The response stunned Cuomo. He stepped down from the pulpit, and when I met him, seemed dazed by what he had done and the emotional reaction it precipitated. He made his way through a crowd of people, faces streaked with tears, and slipped out the back door of the church. We got back into the black Chevy Impala and he sat in the front seat in silence, unable to put his large hands around what had just happened. A few more seconds of silence passed before he asked me what I thought. I cleared my throat to compose myself, feeling as overwhelmed by what I witnessed, as Cuomo did by what he had accomplished.

"Governor," I said. "Considering what you were up against here, this may have been the greatest speech you've ever delivered—even better than the keynote."

Mario Cuomo thanked me, and was quiet for the entire ride back down from the Cathedral of St. John the Divine to our offices at Two World Trade Center.

Writing in the *New York Post* two days later, (May 24, 1990), Pete Hamill perfectly captured what happened:

Cuomo's voice shook with emotion. For he spoke with the personal authority of a man who had triumphed over stereotypes, over bigotry, over ignorance. Growing up Italian-American he never surrendered to the morons who scorned him for his ethnicity; he conquered them, through language and passion and intelligence. Not guns. Not swinishness. Not by descending to their level in the gutter...

And, it was possible to hear parents and uncles and school-teachers and principals saying to those young Italian-Americans: Don't drop out; don't give in to the stereotypes; don't let yourself be defined by a handful of idiots. Read books. Read history. Be proud and not vain; be generous and tolerant and invincibly human. Be like Cuomo. He did it, so can you.

I wanted to kiss Pete Hamill, right then and there.

Mario Cuomo coasted to re-election, winning his third term as Governor of New York State on Tuesday, November 6, 1990. His votes tallied a little less than two million, or 54% over two challengers: Pierre Rinfret, the Republican, and Herbert London, the Conservative. Within hours of his victory, speculation began anew about whether he would enter the 1992 Democratic presidential primaries.

Exhausted from the campaign and constant worries about my brother and John Gotti, I needed a rest. With a three-day Veterans Day weekend approaching, Carol and I, and our son who was just turning 15, headed out to Montauk Manor on the eastern most point of Long Island's South Fork. I wanted to get as far away as I could during this short respite and simply walk along a deserted beach. That Sunday morning, I bundled up against the chilly ocean breeze, and walked to the Montauk general store where I knew I could buy a copy of Sunday's *Newsday*. My friend and *Newsday* writer Larry Levy tipped me off that the paper was running a powerful editorial in the main Sunday edition urging Cuomo to run for President. I paid for the paper and turned immediately to the editorial page, where a headline of "C'MON MARIO, GO FOR IT," jumped out at me, accompanied by a full page picture of Cuomo with his hands raised, as if holding something back.

"Hamlet on the Hudson," read the subhead: "To be president or not to be, that is the question." I shuddered when I read that line, closed up the paper and tucked it under my arm, planning to read it when I got back to the hotel.

The editorial, written by *Newsday*'s Editorial Page Editor, Jim Klurfeld, was a laudatory, cheerleading piece about Cuomo, calling him: *One of the Democrats most articulate, most intelligent candidates... with the bigness, the stature, the charisma that make people sit up and take notice....Cuomo's time has come. He might be the one figure who is capable of articulating a new Democratic agenda for the party, of defining what Democrats stand for in the last decade of the 20th Century.*

The November 11th editorial included nine recommended steps for the Governor to take to get on the Democratic ticket for 1992: make up your mind now, get the State's fiscal house in order, form a team of advisors, establish a credible economic plan, learn more about foreign policy. Then, I got to Step # 8, and read it slowly: "Cuomo must deal with the Mob issue early and directly." I read it over and over again. I knew my brief vacation had just ended. I dialed the Governor's number at the Executive Mansion in Albany and he took my call immediately. I informed him about the *Newsday* editorial and he asked me to read it to him. I read each word carefully, hesitating when I came to Step # 8.

"Step Number Eight," I said, pausing for a moment, and began to read:

Cuomo must deal with the Mob issue early and directly. Just as John Kennedy confronted the issue of his Catholicism, Cuomo must puncture the charge that somehow he or his family is tied in with the Mob. It is an issue that lurks just below the surface, especially outside the Northeast, and wherever anti-Italian bias still lingers. 'There's something there, isn't there? That's why he won't run,' is a common refrain. It is not fair, and it is not true. He has been investigated by newspapers and political opponents for years and there is not a thing on him. Cuomo will not willingly answer such innuendos. But that is the only way to neutralize the poison.

The Governor interrupted my reading.

"*Sons-of-bitches*," he said. "Sons-of-bitches!"

I had never heard Mario Cuomo so angry.

"Those sons-of-bitches at *Newsday* spent a million and a half dollars investigating me and my family and they found nothing," the Governor said. "Now, they want me to answer a 'When did you stop beating your wife question?' I don't have to make a statement against the mob—*my whole life has been a statement against that crap.*"

I tried to calm Mario Cuomo down by telling him that Larry Levy told me a few days earlier that the editorial was meant to be constructive, to offer supporting suggestions for him to run for president.

"You call Levy," the Governor ordered me. "Tell him I told you not to go near him or his family. Ask him to explain how *Newsday* spent more than $1.5 million and never found *anything*. Of all the people—call him, tell him what I said."

I left the phone number of the Montauk Manor where the Governor could reach me, hung up the phone and searched for Levy's number. Before I could dial it, the telephone rang in our room. It was Andrew Cuomo. He was calm, controlled.

"Stephen. Andrew. The Governor just told me about *Newsday's* editorial. Could you read it to me, please?" Andrew Cuomo asked.

I read the editorial in its' entirety to Andrew, waiting for him to unload on me the way his father had minutes earlier.

"It's not so bad," Andrew said. "You know, sometimes I think Sam Roberts of the *New York Times* is right; that we pick out one line or one part of a piece and criticize it without looking at the whole piece."

Andrew's analysis and demeanor was a relief. After he hung up, I dialed Levy's number. I told Larry what the Governor said and that in all my years of working with Mario Cuomo, I had never heard him so furious.

"I can't believe this guy," Levy said, "because what the editorial amounts to is an endorsement of Mario Cuomo for the Democratic nomination."

"I know that, Larry," I said, "but that paragraph on the Mob—he just won't do it."

"Look, Steve, we want him to run," Levy said. "We want to tell him as advisors what's out there. If he doesn't want to listen that's really too bad. He could be so eloquent on this. He could talk about rooting out all vestiges of unfairness that forces Italian-Americans to defend themselves, that stereotypes Blacks and Jews. He could turn it around because he has been the victim of it; he can say that as a fundamental issue of fairness, this will no longer be tolerated."

Levy said what I wanted to say to the Governor, but could not. My self-interest in using him to make such a statement was palpable. I needed Mario Cuomo to give a Houston Minister's-like speech about organized crime far more than Mario Cuomo needed to deliver one. From the Governor's perspective, *there was no air to clear.* Kennedy *was* a Catholic; Cuomo *had no Mob connections.* Consequently, as Mario Cuomo saw it, and he was technically correct in his analysis: *there was no comparison, and no need for him to give "the speech."*

Plus, there was one more big difference between him and JFK: Cuomo knew he was not running for President.

That was the unique combination that was incomprehensible to *Newsday* and many others: Mario Cuomo was *not* connected to organized crime in any way—*Newsday's* own Special Investigative Unit concluded that—and he did not want to run for President. Cuomo's clear competence, intelligence, integrity and eloquence towered over every other national political figure of the time, making those two separate thoughts inconceivable to most people. How could *he* not want to run for President when *we* wanted him to? *Newsday* knew there were no "skeletons in Cuomo's closet." With the possible exception of Nick Pileggi, they had vetted him more thoroughly than anyone else. The fact was, Mario Cuomo had nothing to prove to anyone.

Fortunately, the same could not be said about John Gotti. One month later, shortly before the Christmastime release of the third movie in the *Godfather* trilogy, NYPD Detectives and FBI agents raided the Ravenite in lower Manhattan, arresting Gotti, and two other leaders of the Gambino Crime Family, Sammy "The Bull" Gravano, and Frank Locasio. All three were indicted on racketeering charges and for five murders, including the killing of Paul Castellano five years earlier.

Gotti and his associates were immediately jailed and denied bail by U.S. District Court Judge I. Leo Glasser, who would preside over Gotti's trial in a few months. Gotti's star kept sinking rapidly throughout 1992, especially when his top Capo, Gravano, agreed to testify against his boss.

There was thick irony to Gotti, Gravano, and Locasio being busted days before *The Godfather III* hit movie theatres across the country, and not simply because the movie chronicled the collapse of the Corleones. Mobsters, like members of the Gambino crew, found validation for "The Life", as John Gotti, Jr. called the organized crime culture, in Coppola's *Godfather* series. Eight years after Gravano's testimony helped federal prosecutors put John Gotti away for life, he told Jeffrey Goldberg, in a *New York Times Magazine* article ("The Lives They Lived: Mario Puzo, b. 1920; Sammy the Bull Explains How the Mob Got Made," January 2, 2000) about the influence *The Godfather* had on him and his fellow gangsters:

"... it didn't hurt our image," Gravano says. "It made our life, I don't know, it made our life seem honorable..."

Mario Cuomo detested the way *The Godfather* movies demonized and demeaned all Italian-Americans, and did not believe the portrayals of mobsters brought honor to anyone. Research reinforced Cuomo's instincts: a 1990 poll conducted by the Response Analysis Corporation of Princeton, New Jersey, found that 74 percent of Americans associated Italian-Americans with organized crime, and, even more shockingly, so did 78 percent of Italian-Americans.

Despite the depth of that existing ethnic bias, and his own protestations of having "no plans to run for President," calls for Mario Cuomo to enter the 1992 Democratic presidential primaries intensified from Democratic Party officials around the country, members of the press, and citizens.

As the political calendar pushed into summer, just six months before the early 1992 Democratic primaries would begin in New Hampshire, speculation about a Cuomo candidacy increased. At an appearance before the New York State Broadcasters Association in July, a reporter asked Cuomo "the question:" whether being Italian-American would work against his candidacy for President, if he decided to run. Cuomo gave the kind of measured response *Newsday*'s editorial writers were recommending he give back in November, when he angrily dismissed the mere suggestion of the question:

I think distinct ethnics are always threatening to somebody. There are still people out there who, if you tell them your are an Italian-American and you are a politician and your are doing well, some of them will think, 'Well, this person is in the Mafia.

The response to the Governor's impromptu remarks was immediate and widespread, with calls coming in from reporters around the world. To extinguish the media fire he ignited, we issued a written statement on Cuomo's behalf:

I have been asked, in effect: Do you believe Italians, Jews or Blacks could not succeed as candidates in the presidential race? ...It's a fact that some prejudices persist in our society. That's what the Willy Horton controversy is about. And quotas. That's what the "Mafia" syndrome which I mentioned this morning at an appearance of the New York State Broadcasters Association is about.

It is true that more and more women, Blacks, Hispanics and other distinctly ethnic Americans are being elected to major offices by the American people...surely, no one should be discouraged from trying because they are ethnic or members of minority groups. I have said all of this many times before. I repeat it now, at the outset of the new Presidential campaign.

The Governor's clever clarification of his Broadcasters' Association remarks allowed me to exhale, and take one short breath. Then he requested some ideas on other ways he could handle the "presidency" question, knowing that his standard "no plans" response was growing stale. The comments ranged from FDR to Adlai Stevenson, and JFK to Walter Mondale. Cuomo loved Stevenson's remarks, made in 1952, when, after saying he had no desire for the office, he was asked, "What happens if we nominate you anyway?"

"I guess I'd have to shoot myself," Stevenson said. As it turned out, the Democrats did nominate Stevenson that year, and he lied about what he would do if they did.

The closest parallel was to FDR, who, during his tenure as New York State Governor, in 1932, unequivocally disavowed having any interest in running:

I am giving no consideration or thought or time to anything except the duties of the governorship and to be clearly understood you can add that this applies to any candidacy national or otherwise in 1932.

"He lied, too!" Cuomo said to me, after reading the quote, and we both laughed.

Lying, and reneging on his constitutional obligation to the people of New York State to serve, were two things Mario Cuomo did not want to do. His sense of duty—of doing the job he was elected to do—was extraordinarily powerful. Yet, the cat-and-mouse game between Cuomo and the media continued because it served a useful purpose for both sides. For Mario Cuomo, the more his name was mentioned in conjunction with the presidency, the more he could leverage the perception of his growing political power on behalf of the people of New York State.

For the media, chasing Cuomo was far more interesting—and resulted in better ratings or readership—than covering lesser known Democrats, like the Governor of Arkansas, Bill Clinton, who had lulled the nation to sleep at the 1988 Democratic National Convention with a boring, hour-long keynote speech. Cuomo was anything but boring, and besides: Reporters *and* Cuomo were enjoying the tantalizing Kabuki dance, with the choreography of the final scene still unknown.

Suddenly, it appeared that a revealing veil had been lifted at a private breakfast for wealthy Cuomo supporters held in the Regency Hotel on Park Avenue and 60th Street in early October. The Governor told the crowd of his most ardent backers that he would "think" about a possible candidacy for President of the United States. Time froze. Everyone's breathing seemed to stop when Mario Cuomo matter-of-factly said, "All right; I'll think about it," in response to a question from a member of the audience. A low murmuring began at each table and built into a buzz of incredulity. Had he really said "it?" Would he actually consider running?

A few people from the breakfast bolted out of the room, making a bee-line for a bank of telephones in the hotel's lobby. As the Governor slowly worked his way through the room, greeting individuals in the crowd whom he had known for many years, I dashed upstairs, identified myself as a member of the Governor's staff to the concierge, and asked for the use of a private phone, since all the public telephones were being used by breakfast attendees rushing to call friends in the media about the breaking story. I called WNBC-TV's Gabe Pressman, with whom the Governor was scheduled to tape NBC's local Sunday morning public affairs program *News Forum, New York*, after we finished at the Regency, told him what just happened, and to check wire service news reports before we arrived.

Pressman thanked me and responded: "Not bad timing for my show, eh?"

Mario Cuomo finished working his way through the small group of loyal supporters, walked outside into a sparkling October morning in Manhattan, and slipped into the front passenger seat of the State Police's unmarked car. I climbed into the back seat, and once the car door was closed, the Governor turned toward me.

"What do you think, Steve?" he asked, without the slightest hint of a smile creeping into the large, deep creases framing his face.

"What do I think, Governor?" I said. "I think you've just made front page news all over the country."

"Why should it be front page news?" he said, without turning around again. "I didn't say anything different than I've been saying before."

"Yes, it *was* substantially different, Governor," I said. "You've ratcheted things up a notch. You've gone beyond 'no plans,' and everyone knows it. There was a stampede for the phones when you were done. I'm sure AP has the story already."

I braced myself for his response, but it never came, frightening me even more than the intense counter arguments I was expecting from him. Something had changed, and I began to think of my exit strategy away from Mario Cuomo once again.

Gabe Pressman met us at the door the NBC studios in Rockefeller Center, already having read a few early Associated Press paragraphs from the Friends of Mario Cuomo breakfast at the Regency. His reporter's instincts coupled with the good fortune of having a previously scheduled taping with the Governor, made the first question inevitable:

Pressman: Good morning, Governor. Before we get down to the meat and potatoes of certain issues facing the State and the City, I understand that on Friday morning you told a group of supporters at a private fund-raiser that you'll take a look at the possibility of seeking the Democratic nomination for President. What do you mean by that? Is it true, first of all?

Cuomo: No. No, not in those words. I don't really think this is worth a lot of our time. Since 1984, I've said the same thing, and that is that I have no plans, no plans to make plans. That has not changed, Gabe, and I wouldn't want to give any other impression... What I did say to supporters, in essence, a lot of them said: 'Governor, we supported you for a lot of years and people are suggesting you should run for President." And I said, "Well, that's very flattering"; and they said, "You should think about it." And I said, "Ok, I'll think about it." But that's all it was. There is nothing new.

Pressman: Except that you're thinking about it...

Cuomo: It would have been hard not to have the subject course through your mind at least, when every time you do an interview somebody brings it up...What I was saying is I will be respectful about the question, and I will try to deal with it intelligently as I always have...but I wouldn't want to give the impression that I said anything to my supporters that was new, exciting or worth anybody's attention…

Pressman: So until you walk up to a microphone and say no, no, no, a thousand times no… there will be a large group of people who will believe you are going to run. Are you ready to do that? Are you ready to raise your right hand and give a Sherman oath?….

Cuomo: …You know something, Gabe? Nobody ever made the Sherman statement but Sherman, and Sherman wasn't even a politician…

We left the taping of Pressman's show and went directly to the only public event on the Governor's schedule that day: an appearance with the actor Bill Cosby promoting the benefits of volunteerism and community service. The event was being held at the McGraw Hill building on the Avenue of the Americas, only a few minutes away from Rockefeller Center. Arriving early, Cuomo immediately went into a private room to meet with Cosby and several top ranking McGraw Hill officials. Stepping outside, I picked up string of messages, including one from Andrew Cuomo. I reached Andrew at his office of HELP, the homeless housing non-profit organization he founded.

"Tell the Governor *this thing is out of control,*" the Governor's oldest son said. "The story is all over the place. It's going to be front page news all over the country tomorrow. He's got to do something to contain this."

I agreed with Andrew and got off the phone. I tried to corner the Governor before he went on stage, but he and Cosby had already taken their seats. I went out into the auditorium to see which reporters already arrived. Every New York City newspaper, radio and television political reporter was there, along with national political reporters from CNN, the *LA Times*, and the national newsweekly magazines. Photographers from each photo agency in the City were perched, like parrots on a clothesline, behind the last row of auditorium seats. A few reporters spotted me sizing up the crowd.

Art Athens of WCBS Radio asked: "Will he stop and talk with us about what he said this morning, Steve?"

"I think so, Art," I said, "but I can never be sure."

"Welcome to the beginning of the national campaign," joked WABC-TV's Pat Dawson, who covered the 1988 Presidential Campaign for CNN. "He's going to talk to us afterwards, isn't he?"

"I'm working on it, Pat."

Mario Cuomo did talk with reporters after his appearance with Cosby, but he sparred with them the way he parried Pressman's questions a few hours earlier. The press was in a frenzy for Cuomo to announce he was running. Everything he said, or did, was scrutinized against that backdrop. The following week, we had a routine editorial session scheduled with the Editorial Board of the *New York Daily News*. Cuomo intensified the drama:

"I'll do whatever I can to help the Democratic Party," he said in response to a question about what his plans were for 1992.

Cuomo went on for a few minutes about the fundamental policy differences between the Reagan/Bush Republicans and the Democrats, and then, without prompting, dropped his bombshell: he had instructed New York State Democratic Party Chairman John Marino to give him a list of all the presidential primaries, dates and states where they were being held.

"If you want to go to Iowa, to New Hampshire, when do you have to sign the paper?" the Governor said. "That much I need to know."

Eyes opened wide around the big table in the *Daily News* first-floor conference room. Joel Benenson, the *News* Albany Bureau Chief, stopped writing, his head snapping to attention. Frank Lombardi, the paper's political editor looked stunned. Mario Cuomo had given them smoking-gun evidence that he was preparing to run for President.

From the reactions his comments received, Cuomo realized he needed to rapidly reel his words back. He tried to explain away what he said; he was the Governor of New York, after all, and he needed to know these things to better help the Democratic Party. Nobody in the room believed him, not even me. Lombardi asked him if being Italian-American and battling the Mafia stereotype would hurt him as a presidential candidate. The room was silent all around. I could hear my heart beating faster. Cuomo quickly pulled his rhetorical "ju-jitsu" maneuver and turned the question around:

"I don't think there's an anti-Catholic vote," he said, "or an anti-Italian-American vote. In fact, there are a lot of Italian-Americans who are very conservative who would vote for me just because I'm Italian-American. I'm not even sure it wouldn't be a plus, to be honest with you. All I have to do is get up and say, 'they say I can't win because I'm Italian-American'. You'd get votes just for saying that. It's that perverse instinct in the American people to say: 'Wait a minute; that's not right! Let's show them!'"

Lombardi then raised the issue of negative attacks by the White House upon him, citing as an example how Bush's people had savaged Anita Hill during the Clarence Thomas hearings just the week before. Cuomo's reply to the question was swift:

"I can shout pretty hard," he said, looking around the table.

And, of course, everyone in the room knew he could, compounding the confusion. We left the *Daily News* offices at 200 East 42nd Street—just up the block from the Pershing Square Building where my father ran the steam boilers for 35 years—and climbed into the Governor's waiting car.

"We didn't get into any trouble in there, did we Steve?" he asked.

"Well…" I said, hesitating to complete my sentence. Mario Cuomo stared at me.

"It depends on what you call trouble, Governor," I said. "A few things could be big headlines tomorrow." I began reading from my notes, going over his quotes line-by-line to buttress my case.

Cuomo listened quietly as I read his own words back to him; then he insisted he had said nothing new. But he had, and he knew it.

The next morning, October 23, 1991, Joel Benenson's double-page lead story in the *Daily News*, accompanied by a tabloid-sized front page headline which screamed "CUOMO: HOW I'D BASH BUSH," referred to the Governor's comments as giving us "the clearest indication to date of how far he has moved beyond merely flirting with the concept of seeking the Presidency."

Andrew Cuomo was correct; *the thing was out of control.* The Governor's appearance at the Radio and Television News Directors Association annual meeting at the Sheraton Hotel, New York, two days later did not help contain the clamor for his candidacy. We arrived at the hotel ahead of Mario Cuomo's scheduled speech, and held a courtesy meeting with a group of visiting dignitaries from Taiwan who wanted to do business in New York. When the Taiwanese leaders left, Cuomo sat and chatted for a few minutes with Vincent Tese, his Commissioner of Economic Development, long-time confidant Tonio Burgos, and me. He was taking a breather, shifting gears to think about what he was about to say to hundreds of radio and television news people from across the country.

"So what do these people downstairs want to know, Steve?" Mario Cuomo asked.

"Governor, there's only one thing on the mind of every reporter and news director in town today: *Are you going to run for President?*" I said.

"How disappointed will they be if I say no?" Mario Cuomo asked.

Tonio Burgos, listening closely, interrupted. "It'll be no more than a one-day story, Governor," Burgos said.

I looked at Tonio, a savvy Cuomo loyalist for many years, shook my head, then turned toward the Governor.

"No way, Governor," I said. "It'll be the story for the rest of the year; maybe for the rest of your career."

There was silence in the room for several seconds. Then we all stood up and went downstairs to one of the big ballrooms at the Sheraton, where Mario Cuomo began tantalizing the press into imagining what a Cuomo candidacy would be like. Midway through the Governor's speech, Pat Dawson came over to me and whispered: "Where is he *going* with this?"

I shrugged. "I have no idea, Pat."

"Well, if he takes it any further along the lines of where it sounds like he's going, you'd better get out of the way, because a ballroom full of reporters will run right over you to get to the phones," Dawson said.

But Cuomo did not give Dawson or his colleagues what they were looking for. At the precise moment when it appeared to everyone in the room, including Walter Cronkite, that there was no place else for Cuomo to go but headlong into the race for President, his crescendo slid softly into pianissimo tones, leaving the audience as puzzled as they were when he began.

The following day, Kevin Sack of the *New York Times* called. He was working on the "Reporter's Notebook" column for the Sunday *Times*, focusing on how Mario Cuomo's aides were handling the anxiety of not knowing whether or not Cuomo would run for President.

"I get to the point when he goes into one of these speeches that I say, 'Is this it?'" I told Sack. "You try to be ready for whatever happens. It's agita. It's like if you could swallow the word 'oy.'"

12 ▫ Ground

One year after Gambino Crime Family boss John Gotti was
arrested and charged with the murders of Paul Castellano and three
others, Mario M. Cuomo was scheduled to give a speech about immigration at the United Nations. Cuomo was particularly eloquent
on the subject; as a child of Italian immigrants chided for their "difference," he felt the sting of discrimination acutely.

I met him and New York's First Lady, Matilda Cuomo, that frigid
December night in 1991, at the East 34th Street Heliport where they
would land on a flight from Albany. A black, unmarked State Police
car shuttled me and the governor's friend and counsel, Fabian Palomino, from our offices at the World Trade Center.

Fabian and I waited in the warm sedan for the governor's
helicopter to arrive. There was a tap at the back window. A young,
dark haired, well-dressed man stood outside the car, grasping a plain
clasped envelope and shivering against the cold. I recognized him
as Gene Ingoglia, from State Democratic Headquarters, a campaign
worker who graduated from Northport High School, the same
school my son attended. I opened the car's back door and let him
in to get warm. I motioned to the large envelope he was carrying.

"Are those the candidate authorization forms for the governor to
enter the New Hampshire primary?" I asked. Ingoglia, eyes opening
wide, nodded "yes." The deadline for candidates to file for appearing
on the ballot in the 1992 Democratic Presidential New Hampshire
primary was the end of the next day, December 20.

I smiled at him. "Well, Gene, two Italian kids from Northport
might be witnessing history today," I said. He smiled back, afraid to

utter a word.

When the chopper landed, Ingoglia and I got out to greet the Cuomos. Fabian and Mrs. Cuomo took our places in the car's back seat. The Governor removed his hat and coat, and slid into the front passenger seat. Ingoglia handed him the candidate filing forms, and stood next to me, in the bitter early evening air, outside of the open car door. We stood there and witnessed Mario Cuomo write his signature on several copies of the forms.

"What are those, Mario?" Mrs. Cuomo asked.

The governor turned his head toward the back seat.

"This is just in case we get things worked out with the budget, Matilda," he said, wanting to end any further discussion. He placed the signed forms back into the envelope, handed it to Ingoglia, and shut the front passenger door.

From that moment, all that remained for Mario Cuomo to be a candidate for President of the United States in 1992 was for his campaign organization to file those signed documents in New Hampshire within 24 hours. Earlier that week, State Party Chair John Marino asked me to put together a framework for a national media campaign. Cuomo loyalists, fellow young, progressive Italian-American professionals who looked to the governor as a strong, positive role model, became intoxicated with the thought of traveling around the country to end twelve years of Reagan/Bush policies. A few months earlier, during the U.S. Senate's Supreme Court confirmation hearings for Clarence Thomas, Cuomo called to ask me why I, unlike many of my colleagues, wasn't pushing him hard to run for President.

"So what about the presidency, Steve," he asked. "Aren't you thinking about it?"

"Governor," I said, pausing. "I think about it all the time," I quoted himself back to him. "Do I think you'd make a great candidate? Absolutely. Do I think the country needs you now? No question. Those things aren't at issue. I have many of the concerns you've articulated, and one you haven't."

"What's that?" he asked.

"Like you, I watched what the Bush White House did to Anita Hill this weekend," I said. "They used innuendo, everything they could to smear this one woman, who threatened one nominee, for one position. If you ran against them, a candidate who would threaten all of their jobs and beliefs, they would stop at nothing. They would make what happened to Anita Hill look like kindergarten finger-painting. Knowing how they would try to destroy you and your family, I can't in good conscience say you should run. That's a decision you have to make yourself."

Mario Cuomo listened, and thanked me.

What I didn't share with the Governor then, nor at the moment he signed the New Hampshire Democratic Presidential Primary forms, was that I had already made my decision about the 1992 Election. The closer he moved to a presidential candidacy, the closer I moved to resigning from his administration. If he was in, I was out. I worried that the pull to stay, the euphoria of a national election, and the outside possibility of serving in the White House might overpower me as it grew more real each day. Strangely, as the governor's car pulled away from the heliport, I felt free and at peace. I had prepared for this moment for six years. Now, my only worry as I headed home to Long Island that night for my son's holiday concert, was how to support my family when I left the administration.

The following day, the last day to enter the 1992 New Hampshire Democratic Presidential Primary, Mario Cuomo relieved my agita, but generated a whole new wave of indigestion for a lot of other people. The whole world was waiting, watching and listening, when Cuomo stepped up to the large, dark wooden podium with the plastic seal of the State of New York affixed to its front. He looked out at the rows of 170 reporters jammed into the ornate Court of Appeals Room in the State Capitol Building in Albany. It was 3:30 in the afternoon, Friday, December 20, 1991. Some 200 miles to the south, more than 30 colleagues on the Governor's staff were packed into my office on the 57th Floor of the Two World Trade Center, overlooking Battery Park City, the Hudson River and New Jersey, waiting to find out what our futures might hold.

I already knew. John Marino, then State Democratic Party Chair, called me a few minutes before 3:00 pm, fatigue filling his voice.

"Villano," Marino said. "He just called me. He's not doing it."

"For real?" I said.

"For real," Marino said. "Only don't tell anybody."

I hung up the phone and, for a full half-hour, pretended to a room full of co-workers that I did not know what Marino told me. Then, Mario M. Cuomo began to speak about New York State's unresolved budget problems, ninety minutes before the filing deadline for the 1992 New Hampshire Democratic Presidential Primary:

It's my responsibility as Governor to deal with this extraordinarily severe problem. Were it not, I would travel to New Hampshire today and file my name as a candidate in its Presidential primary. That was my hope and I prepared for it, but it seems to me I cannot turn my attention to New Hampshire while this threat hangs over the head of the New Yorkers that I've sworn to put first. I asked for and won that responsibility to deal with their vital interests in the Governor's race of 1990. The commitment I made then to do all that I could do to protect New Yorkers from the kind of problem we now face was not a commitment of convenience to be set aside if and when I was offered another grander opportunity for public service.

Faces of friends and fellow staff members surrounding me went blank; some began to softly sob; others closed their eyes. Cuomo continued speaking from the prepared comments he wrote:

Finally, I wish to express my gratitude to all of those who worked so hard in recent days to prepare for a possible candidacy…and I want to extend my thanks to the many, many hundreds—even thousands—who indicated that they were prepared to support me. Thank you very much.

Some of my colleagues stared out over the Hudson River as if in a trance; a few, just kept shaking their heads, mumbling words of disbelief. I felt guilty being so relieved by Cuomo's decision and asked everyone in my office to quiet down to better hear the Governor's responses to the questions reporters were shouting at him. One Q & A in particular cut through all the clutter:

Q: Governor, does it pain you that you may have missed a moment in history for yourself, for the country?

Cuomo: I will work toward that level of egoism. I haven't arrived at it yet, though.

It was a brilliant and succinct response, perfectly encapsulating Mario Cuomo's utter groundedness as well as his passionate indifference to what may appear, to some, to be obvious. His deep humility and spirituality would not allow such self-aggrandizement, choosing instead to continue to dutifully deal with the challenges of human endeavor, paraphrasing Teilhard in *The Divine Milieu*.

I listened to Cuomo's answer, remembering how many times I heard him express precisely the same thoughts under far less stressful circumstances: pooh-poohing the news that our college interns viewed him as an inspirational figure the way my generation viewed Martin Luther King, Jr., and Robert F. Kennedy; or, dismissing the astute political observations by Democratic leader Jack English that he could unite black and white, working people and intellectuals, the way RFK did, and was the best hope for the country. Then, as now, Mario Cuomo "had not arrived at that level of egoism," to encourage others, or himself, to think that way.

Thirty minutes after the Governor's press conference ended and my stunned colleagues slipped back to their offices, Mario Cuomo called. He sounded exhausted, his voice subdued.

"Hi, Steve," he said.

"Hello, Governor."

I tried to be just upbeat enough to lift his spirits, guarding against allowing my great sense of relief to creep into my tone. Nuance was often everything in our conversations, since we could read each other's moods.

"I just wanted to tell you that I hope you're not too disappointed,"

Cuomo said, sounding as if he believed he let the nation down.

"Governor, you could never disappoint me," I said.

I thought back to the day my brother was sentenced to jail for income tax evasion, when I called the Governor to inform him.

"*I don't see how it should affect you,*" Mario Cuomo told me that day. "*I certainly feel for you, but I don't see how it affects you. You are a superb public official and I don't think it should have any effect on you.*"

I knew I owed him much more than one line of comfort.

"You've given me so many terrific opportunities since I've been working with you, Governor. You could never disappoint me," I said.

"Thanks for your kind words, Steve," he said, and hung up.

I was grateful to have the chance to point us ever so gently toward the light, as he had done for me many times before, and knew we would have the common ground of our work to help us forge ahead.

Only five weeks after Mario Cuomo announced he would not seek the presidency in 1992, he was the subject of a widely publicized, tape-recorded conversation between Democratic Presidential candidate Bill Clinton and Gennifer Flowers, a cabaret singer from Arkansas who claimed to be one of Clinton's mistresses. The transcript of the Bill Clinton/Gennifer Flowers exchange was faxed to Fabian Palomino from Jimmy Breslin on January 27, 1992, the day Flowers held a press conference in New York City. Conversations between the two of them were taped before Cuomo withdrew his name as a potential candidate in the Democratic Party's New Hampshire Presidential primary:

Clinton: Well, no…Most people think, you know, that except for Cuomo, I'm doing the best right now, and uh…we're leading in the polls in Florida, without Cuomo in there, but Cuomo's at 87% name recognition, and I have 54%, so, I mean, I 'm at a terrible disadvantage in name recognition still, but, we're coming up, and well…so I…we're moving pretty well; I'm really pleased about it…"
Flowers: I don't particularly care for Cuomo's, uh, demeanor…
Clinton: Boy, he is so aggressive.
Flowers: Well, he seems like he could get real mean (laughs).
Clinton: (garbled)

Flowers: Yeah…I wouldn't be surprised if he didn't have some Mafioso major connections.

Clinton: Well, he acts like one (laughs).

Flowers: Yeah.

The Bill Clinton/Gennifer Flowers' "Love Tapes," exploded on the front pages of newspapers around the nation and topped all major television network newscasts.

I flew into a rage when I heard the Governor's name and the word "Mafioso" spoken in the same sentence. Cuomo went ballistic, as was accurately reported, and immediately phoned reporters at the *New York Post*, *New York Daily News*, *New York Newsday*, and the *New York Times*. Clinton's attempt at an apology, as Cuomo described to Mike McAlary, of the *New York Post*, was "worse than the original insult." Clinton's apology read:

> *If the remarks on the tape left anyone with the impression that I was disrespectful to either Governor Cuomo or Italian-Americans, then I deeply regret it. At the time the conversation was held, there had been some political give-and-take between myself and the Governor and I meant simply to imply that Governor Cuomo is a tough and worthy competitor.*

New York's tabloids feasted on the clash of the two Democratic titans. The *New York Post* stacked photos of Cuomo and Clinton on its front page with the bold headline: "CUOMO SAYS CLINTON TALKS LIKE BIGOT." The *New York Daily News* ran a photo of Cuomo dominating the front page, with the banner headline: "CUOMO TO CLINTON: SHAME ON YOU." The *News* Frank Lombardi's story ("Cuomo Scalds Clinton," January 29, 1992), pulled no punches, reflecting Cuomo's anger:

"A fuming Gov. Cuomo yesterday slammed Bill Clinton as insensitive to ethnic stereotyping for saying Cuomo 'acts like' a Mafioso.

"If you say it this casually about Italian-Americans," Cuomo bristled, "what do you say about blacks, what do you say about Jews, what do you say about women, what do you say about poor people, what do you say about all the other groups who traditionally become the scapegoats?...

"Cuomo was clearly seething, particularly when first told that Clinton expressed regrets "if the remarks left anyone with the impression that I was disrespectful to either Governor Cuomo or Italian-Americans.""

"What do you mean IF?" Cuomo snapped to reporters in Albany. "If you're not capable of understanding what was said, than don't try to apologize."

Still furious over Clinton's comments, I poured out an Op-Ed piece for either the *New York Times* or *Newsday*, emboldened to submit under my own name, as a member of Cuomo's staff:

Bill Clinton simply doesn't get it. His flippant comparison of Mario Cuomo to a 'Mafioso' demonstrates that he understands neither what the most prominent Italian-American politician in the nation's history means to us, nor how his acceptance of the word 'Mafioso' in connection with Cuomo's name is like a dagger thrust into our chest.

I faxed the essay to the Governor, and within the hour he sent it back with his comments written across the top in dark, felt-tip marker: "Steve—I am concerned people will think this is something I influenced because of our relationship. What do you think? M—".

Of course, Mario Cuomo was correct. I re-tooled my tirade and sent it over to one of the Italian American civic organizations for them to use anyway they wanted to express maximum outrage on behalf of the entire community. Still, I wanted to scream from the stoops and rooftops of New York, telling the press I grew up with 'Mafioso' and that Cuomo was as far from them as anyone could be, but accepted the Governor's limitations on my lividness. In the few months between the Clinton/Flowers 'Mafioso' flap and the April 7, New York State Democratic Presidential Primary, it was that other Italian-American from Queens who dominated the headlines, as John Gotti's murder and racketeering trial moved into high gear.

Gotti, and the chief prosecution witness against him, Sammy 'The

Bull' Gravano, became media darlings, made into competing folk figures by New York's insatiable television, radio and newspaper outlets. "TODAY'S GOTTI GARB," became a daily fashion feature in *New York Newsday*, complete with colorful artist's renderings of the clothing either Gotti, his wise guy friends, or one of their attorneys wore in court. One particular issue of *New York Newsday,* on March 31, 1992, focused on the "Feds Threads" of the United States Attorney Andrew Maloney who was leading the prosecution case against Gotti. The story accompanying the sketch of Maloney in his Brooks Brothers suit was insulting to Italian-Americans: "In this outfit, he could go unnoticed almost anywhere outside of Little Italy…especially the University Club."

Incensed by the implications of the drawings and the sentiment, I called Dan Forst, Managing Editor of *New York Newsday,* expressing my outrage at his paper's stereotyping Italian-Americans as too ignorant to wear Brooks Brothers suits, or be admitted to any University Clubs. Forst made light of my complaint and bragged that the feature helped *Newsday* sell papers in Howard Beach, Queens, where many Gotti supporters lived. Four days later, Gotti was convicted on all 13 counts in the federal murder/conspiracy/racketeering case against him, making it just a little less acceptable for New York's tabloids to lionize a convicted murderer.

Before the week was out, Gotti receded from the headlines and Bill Clinton won the New York State Democratic Presidential Primary with 41% of the vote, beating Massachusetts Senator Paul Tsongas (29%) and California's Jerry Brown (26%). Only 27% of New York's registered Democrats bothered to vote in the Primary, and one-third of those who did, said they would have preferred to vote for Mario Cuomo. It was no consolation at all for the Governor, who called me the morning after the primary to discuss Bill Clinton's victory. Cuomo knew I was still furious at Clinton for using the "Mafioso" slur against him. I told the Governor I cast my vote for Jerry Brown, and did not know if I could ever forgive Clinton, even if he became the Democratic nominee.

"A superficial candidate for a superficial age," Mario Cuomo said to me about Clinton. Struck by the power of the Governor's condemnation, I wrote it down.

This comment made it all the more remarkable that Cuomo, three short months later, was able to constrain his feelings and accept the responsibility of nominating Bill Clinton at the Democratic National Convention in New York in mid-July. The issues at stake in the national election mattered more to Mario Cuomo than the insults made at his expense months earlier.

I accompanied the Governor to Madison Square Garden on the morning of July 15, 1992, one month after his sixtieth birthday. Cuomo was scheduled to deliver a practice presentation of his nominating speech before a room full of members of Clinton's top campaign team, including Gene Sperling, who previously worked for Cuomo, and Robert Boorstin, the nephew of historian Daniel Boorstin. Mario Cuomo was relaxed, dressed casually, with a sport jacket over a dark, open-neck sport shirt. He was in good spirits, teaching all of us by example how to overlook personal slights to achieve a larger purpose.

We entered the small practice room at the Garden and Luciano Siracusano, one of the Governor's speechwriters, handed a copy of Cuomo's draft speech to Clinton's staff for insertion into the teleprompter. Cuomo made it clear to Boorstin, who was in charge of the practice session, he did not want to see any of the speech released ahead of time. It was simply the way Mario Cuomo operated with his speeches, since he often improvised as he went along. Boorstin agreed to the Governor's request.

Cuomo mounted a makeshift platform which simulated the platform out on the main stage of Madison Square Garden, and read through the speech using the practice teleprompters available and stopping occasionally, when he thought changes needed to be made. Following the first run-through, a handful of Cuomo and Clinton staff members, retreated into a small room to review the speech, making suggestions for changes. Cuomo agreed to include a few more explicit references to Bill Clinton and to draw a stronger analogy between growing up poor in New York, and growing up in poverty in Arkansas.

We left the Garden and went back to the Sheraton Hotel on West 53rd Street and 7th Avenue, where the New York State Delegation was staying. Mario Cuomo's nominating speech for Bill Clinton would be reworked there. Less than an hour after arriving at the Sheraton, I received a message from the *New York Post's* Fred Dicker: Cuomo's nominating speech for Clinton was already on the newswires. Not trusting Dicker or the *Post* to tell us the truth, I reached out to *Newsday's* Albany Bureau Chief Nick Goldberg who was supervising my son as a high school intern covering the convention for Long Island *Newsday's* "Student Briefing Page." Goldberg confirmed that the speech—Cuomo's first draft which we specifically told Clinton's people *not* to release—was already out on the convention wire.

Mario Cuomo let his displeasure be known the moment we walked into the Madison Square Garden practice room for a final 4:00 pm rehearsal, before the main event that evening. We invited *Daily News* sportswriter Mike Lupica to join us for the speech rehearsal. Both of us watched Cuomo mount the makeshift podium and pointed straight at Clinton's staff member, Boorstin.

"You broke your word to me on the speech," Cuomo said, glowering at him.

Boorstin began to stammer in response, but Cuomo ignored him, going right to the speech, reading it straight through without a pause and abruptly exiting the room the moment he was finished. Mario Cuomo had put up with the last indignity he would tolerate from Clinton and his people, and wanted them to be nervous about what he might say when he spoke before millions of Americans that night, placing Bill Clinton's name into nomination for President of the United States, something, Lupica later wrote, someone should have been doing for Cuomo.

Despite the insults from Clinton and his team during the "Mafioso" incident earlier in the year, and their behavior throughout the preparation for the nominating speech, Mario Cuomo was brilliant that evening, as I knew he would be. His voice rang out with emotion when he spoke about the "quiet catastrophes that every day oppress the lives of thousands," and how some children were "more familiar with the sound of gunfire before they've even heard an orchestra." His passionate indictment of the Reagan and Bush Administrations and their war against working people and the poor, rallied Progressives, and the country, behind Bill Clinton, making the unsung story of the 1992 Democratic Convention how he buried his personal and political differences with the Democratic nominee for the good of the country.

Cuomo had every justification, both personal and political, to treat Clinton with disdain, the way Teddy Kennedy did to Jimmy Carter at another Democratic National Convention held 12 years earlier at Madison Square Garden, when Carter—an incumbent President— chased Kennedy around the stage to get a half-hearted handshake of support. While not a rival candidate commanding the commitment of 35% of the convention delegates as Kennedy did, Cuomo captured the hearts and imagination of a far greater number of Democrats around the nation. Had he given a less than enthusiastic endorsement to Bill Clinton, it could have tipped the election to the Republicans. It was one of Mario Cuomo's finest moments in a public life punctuated by many, marking a graceful end to six-years of unrelenting pressure for him to seek the Presidency, and six years of untempered tension for me being torn between Mario Cuomo and my family.

The month before Cuomo's nomination of Clinton my two worlds came into sharp relief, with events underscoring the parallel universes. In mid-June, Mario Cuomo delivered an address on immigration before New York University's Urban Research Center describing how immigrants were the essence of America:

Having to defend immigration—as an American—and especially as a New Yorker—is a little like having to convince people that breathing is good for them...In Abraham Lincoln's day, the Nativists wrapped themselves in the flag and called themselves "The American Party." But, leaders like Lincoln saw them for what they were and called them something else: "Know-Nothings." Support for exclusion, Lincoln said, was nothing less than "degeneracy."

Less than two weeks after Mario Cuomo's soaring speech on the contributions of immigrants to America, with scarcely any media attention paid to his arguments since he was no longer a prospective presidential candidate, the Nativists' nightmare dominated the national news. Gambino Crime family boss John Gotti, and his associate Frank Locasio were sentenced to life-in-prison without parole for racketeering and murder. In his final statement before Judge I. Leo Glasser at the Federal Courthouse in Downtown Brooklyn, Locasio addressed the court, while Gotti remained silent:

"First, I would like to say emphatically that I am innocent," Mr. Locascio declared in a loud, firm voice, denying each charge against him. "I am guilty though," he added, "I am guilty of being a good friend of John Gotti. And if there were more men like John Gotti on this earth, we would have a better country." (*New York Times*, June 24, 1992, "Gotti Sentenced to Life in Prison Without the Possibility of Parole" by Arnold H. Lubasch.)

Locasio, who delivered his full-throated endorsement of Gotti, and the low-level hoods who packed the Brooklyn courthouse and the plaza outside to express their support for the Mob boss, lived in a world light years away from Mario Cuomo's. I read the *Times* story in the Governor's World Trade Center office, incredulous over who my brother's friends held up as heroes, and how hard I struggled to remove myself from their reality:

"Mr. Gotti's trial lawyer, Albert J. Krieger, said Mr. Gotti patted Mr. Locascio on the shoulder after the sentencing and told him, "We have just begun to fight." Mr. Krieger described Mr. Gotti's mood as "dignified, strong, resolute" and "confident of winning on appeal."

I re-read the words "dignified, strong, resolute;" words I associated with Mario Cuomo, never with John Gotti or any of my brother Michael's friends. Cuomo's entire comportment underscored the meaning of dignity, moral strength and resoluteness in his powerful defense of immigrants, as well as his rousing nominating speech of Bill Clinton. Yet, within 22 days and a subway ride of each other—and for far, far different reasons—Mario Cuomo and John Gotti simultaneously moved off center-stage in the country's conscious-ness, in New York, and in my life. On the ground once again, and not straddling the chasm that existed between my life and my broth-er's, and the lives of Mario Cuomo and John Gotti, everyone and everything became much more life-sized, smaller. My fear of falling disappeared.

Travelling to Italy with Mario Cuomo on an economic devel-opment trip one week after Bill Clinton was elected President, was an instruction in Cuomo's humanity and fallibility. The Governor changed his mind several times about making the trip, loathe to trav-el long distances to begin with, coupled with concern about how the Italian media would greet him so soon after Clinton's victory, and how he would be welcomed by his Italian relatives. He arrived in Rome jet-lagged and ill-tempered, snapping at staff members during his six-day visit, especially when Italian reporters asked him why he did not run for President.

I was the first member in my American-born family to ever visit Italy. Despite Mario Cuomo's misgivings about going, I embraced the trip to find out a bit more about who I was, or, perhaps, what clues I could uncover about the source of what pulled me toward my brother. I wanted to visit the place where my father's father was born to learn something, *anything*, about what invisible force bound me to my family. On Saturday, when we had a break from our business meetings, the Governor wanted to travel to Tramonti, Italy, outside of Naples, to visit the place where his mother was born. It was a small mountain town, just up the hill from the birthplace of my father's parents, Nocere Inferiore. I spotted the road sign to "Nocere Inferiore" as we sped past it, wanting to stop and get out, and touch the place whose name I had seen only in the halting handwriting on Par Avion, onion-skin envelopes addressed to my fathers' sisters in Brooklyn. But we did not. We were on a mission for Mario Cuomo, not for me.

In Tramonti, as we stepped out of the dark, unmarked police car, Mario Cuomo was mobbed by hundreds of squat-looking townspeople, hardship hewn into their full faces, cheering and crying at the sight of this Italian-American hero who came to their small town. We worked our way through the exuberant crowd with little police protection. The Governor climbed atop the high first-step of the Giordano's house, where his mother was born. He looked out over the sea of smiling faces, arms outstretched and shouted for all to hear: "*Mi se figlio de Tramonti*—I am a son of Tramonti!" The townspeople went wild.

I shed tears of joy for Mario Cuomo, and of remorse for myself. He knew who he was, where he came from; he had made a pilgrimage to see his mother's birthplace while she was still living. I was overwhelmed by the Governor's completion of a circle of connection, and how it visibly moved him—and found myself craving that same epiphany much more powerfully than I had ever experienced.

Following a warm, welcoming service in a tiny, overcrowded parish church, we turned and headed down the hill, this time slowly passing through Nocere Inferiore. I was surprised at how developed and modern-looking the little city was, expecting it to be a peasant, mountain town like Tramonti, or Nocere Superiore, further up the hill, where Cuomo's father was born. The name of the place "Inferiore" always bothered me—"inferior"—until I discovered the name was derived from its geographic location at the bottom of the hill, not from its place in Italy's social pecking order, or any trait of its inhabitants.

As we drove toward Naples, I looked out at Mt. Vesuvius, the volcano that destroyed Pompeii, and watched the sun setting behind it. I thought of my father's father, the first Michael Villano, looking up at the same sight a century earlier, feeling as insignificant as I did; small, helpless in a world where volcanoes or earthquakes or poverty could control your life; external forces governing who you are, what you fear, or how you act. Maybe that's why my grandfather left Nocera, Inferiore, at age 32, ten years younger than I was; maybe he could no longer take the uncertainty of Vesuvius or of no work or food for his family. My mind tripped across snapshots of my brother's desperation counting his money, and I, reaching for mine, just as the sun's rays back-lighted Vesuvius, enchanting me. Maybe my grandfather could not take it any more; could no longer wait for the mountain to explode, or, himself, could no longer stand waiting for something to happen to *him*, but was finally forced to act *for himself* and his family. I looked out at the long, purple shadow cast by Vesuvius over Nocera Inferiore, in the late afternoon, and understood, at last, that seeing this sacred ground completed a circle for me while my father was still living.

Italy eased my acceptance of my father, and my brother, helping me gain a few more insights into their motivation, and mine. I no longer feared slipping into patterns of their lives. Our relationships entered a comfortable rhythm for a few months. In mid-May, 1993, my father called me from California to bet on the Preakness for him through New York's Off-Track-Betting Corporation.

"Stevens and McCarron," he said. "Gary Stevens and Chris McCarron."

He was speaking in choppy, half-breaths, having difficulty breathing, but minimized how badly he was feeling. My father had a habit of slurring his words, but now it sounded as if he had invented a new, more economical language.

"You want me to bet the horses that Stevens and McCarron are riding in the Preakness, tomorrow, Dad?" I asked him.

"That's it. The Preakness," he said, happy that I understood. "Stevens & McCarron."

Gary Stevens was riding a horse named Personal Hope, and Mc-

Carron was atop Koluctoo Jimmy Al—perfect horses for my father, who lived in hopes of hitting it big, and loved the whimsical names of horses whose names sung of chance. My father's "ship" did not come in that Preakness, and the next day my sister called to tell me he was hospitalized with pneumonia. I grabbed the first plane I could to the West Coast.

Arriving at the hospital in Orange County, California, at 2:00 am, I found my father alert, his eyes wide. Temporarily free from his oxygen mask, he asked if my brother Michael had called to find out how he was.

"Little Michael called," I said, referring to my nephew. "Michael is in Puerto Rico on business. He said he'll fly out as soon as he can."

My father rolled his eyes. I imagined him thinking of my brother's Sundays with "Uncle Charlie," but did not want to open on old wound while a new one was endangering his life.

Each morning for the next week, I carried the daily newspapers into the intensive care unit and read him the sports pages, telling him how the Yankees did, recounting specific games we saw together at the Stadium and describing the greedy plan by George Steinbrenner to move the Yankees out of the Bronx, so the Yankee owner could make more money. My father shook his head in disgust. At least once a year, every August since I was ten years old, my father was given use of the field box owned by the Pershing Square Building Corporation, his employer. The seats were situated a few rows directly behind the Yankee dugout.

My father knew I loved watching double-headers, and that none of the corporate executives who had first dibs on the tickets wanted to sit in the sweltering sun on an August Sunday to watch two baseball games. For me, six solid hours of baseball was a double treat. The world consisted of nothing but baseball all day, and I didn't have to share my father with anyone.

Perhaps it was seeing, only six months earlier, the place in Italy where my father's father was born, and from which he fled to start a new life; or maybe, it was finally understanding how much baseball was our common language of love, but watching my father's death-bed response to the news of the old ballpark in the Bronx facing its own death filled me with rage, and a blind determination to save the Stadium's life, even if I could not save my father's. *Especially* since I could not save my father's.

When I had left New York to be by my father's bedside in California, I knew that talks were underway within the Cuomo Administration to offer the Yankees a range of options to stay in New York—not move to New Jersey, as Steinbrenner was threatening—including a move to the West Side of Manhattan, on the site of the West Side rail yards. I heard the discussions in the distance but was too dazed by the sudden decline of my father's health to pay much attention to them. I trusted that Mario Cuomo, baseball traditionalist that he was, as well as a former Major League prospect, would never allow the Yankees to leave the old Yankee Stadium. But I underestimated the pressures pulling at Cuomo to make sure he wasn't a spectator while the Yankees followed the football Giants and Jets out of New York. I failed to fathom the powerful, irrational pull the Stadium would have over me, following my father's death.

Two weeks after my father died, just before Father's Day, my friend Jim Morgo, asked me to attend a Yankee/Red Sox game with him. Morgo's seats were a few rows behind where my father and I sat, year after year, inning after inning. My father's death was still so raw for me that I imagined I spotted him everywhere I looked around the Stadium. There he was, getting a beer, or mopping the sweat off his brow with a clean, white handkerchief. Each time I got a glimpse an old guy with a beer belly, I thought of my father hauling his paunch up and down those flattened Stadium steps to "hit the 'head'," as he would have said. Maybe coming to Yankee Stadium so soon after my father's death was not such a good idea, despite my friend's gracious gesture to pull me out of my melancholy.

I sat there drinking in the Stadium's atmosphere, memories swirling around me like one of those tiny dust tornadoes that swept across the infield every so often. I looked at the majestic white facades towering over right field and realized what a place of peace this always was for us from our otherwise chaotic life. To remain silent while the old Stadium's future was being decided would have been to commit a sacrilege against the memory of my father. Somehow, I had to find a way to stop this from happening.

That "way" came within days of my first fatherless Father's Day visit to Yankee Stadium. I uncovered a copy of a scheduled secret meeting between the Governor, Steinbrenner, Rupert Murdoch (looking to build a massive Fox media center on the new site) and Vincent Tese, Cuomo's Commissioner of Economic Development. The subject line of the meeting was two words: "Yankee Stadium." I knew I had to act quickly to create a public outcry to have any hope of prolonging the life of the old ballpark. With the forces of money and political power in New York aligned against the original House that Ruth Built, I took the only route open to me: I leaked the information about the "secret" Yankee Stadium meeting to *New York Times* sportswriter, Richard Sandomir.

The following day, June 30, 1993, a front page story by the *Times'* Ian Fisher carried a headline announcing: "Fearing Move by Yankees, Cuomo Explores Idea for a New Stadium." When the story hit, the Governor was furious, but never suspected—or ever knew—the identity of the "source close to the Governor" quoted by the *Times*. He immediately assumed it was former Administration official, Sandy Frucher, who was working for the real estate developer Olympia York, who had a financial interest in the West Side rail yards. The uproar caused by the *Times* story embarrassed Mario Cuomo as I knew it would, and stopped the proposed move of Yankee Stadium to Manhattan, literally, in its West Side tracks, giving the old ballpark a reprieve of another fifteen years, keeping the Bronx Bombers in the Bronx for good, and prolonging the life of that sacred ground, still fertile with sweet memories of my father.

On the Sunday before my father died, I sat in the hospital waiting room. The attending physician came in to tell me that my father had no more than twenty-four to forty-eight hours to live, and we should consider taking my father off the respirator and letting him die peacefully. Just then, the doctor's beeper sounded and he dashed out, leaving me alone.

I grabbed a piece of paper and tried to write, but tears flowed faster than ink and I struggled to compose myself. I did not want anyone to see me that way, yet wanted someone to be there with me to share the burden of deciding when and how my father should die. Suddenly, my brother Michael, who flew in the day before and was staying at the hotel across the street from the hospital, walked into the waiting room. I wiped my tears on the back of my hand, but could not control my sobbing.

"What happened? What's the matter?" Michael asked, taking the chair opposite me, clearly shaken to see me that way.

"The doctor was just here and told me we should consider taking Daddy off the respirator," I said. "He doesn't give him much time; the prostate cancer has advanced rapidly to his spine."

I stared at the television in the visitor's lounge, which was tuned to the Sunday morning public affairs shows. My brother was silent. I did not want to look at him, but somehow, someway, I wanted him to comfort me; to get up from his seat and hold me, to tell me that he was there, my older brother, and that together, we would find a way through the dark.

But Michael didn't do that; there was no way he could have known what I wanted. As far as he knew, I was still repulsed by the life he led, for all the time he spent with John Gotti and "Uncle Charlie," for his jail time, and all the slights, large and small, he had made against our father.

I pulled myself together, recognizing that responsibility was mugging me again. Years of distancing myself from my family, forced me to become skilled at comforting myself. Someone needed to take control, and I was the only one in the room willing to do it. I told my brother we needed to get my mother to the hospital that night to see my father, for what might be the last time, and that I wanted to drive out to see the military cemetery in Riverside, California, where our father, a World War II Veteran, would be buried.

At first Michael was reluctant, holding to a superstition of not visiting the gravesite before death. But I was unyielding and said I would go alone. I needed to see where our father would be buried, before I could participate in any decision to end his life. We entered into his room to see him for an hour, until he dozed off. Then, Michael and I headed out to the cemetery in the car he was renting. We stopped at a local supermarket along the way, buying some bread and cheese and fruit and bottled water for the hour-long ride into the mountains.

We spoke little, but I was glad to have his company. I felt like his kid brother again, out for a ride, simply because Michael liked to drive.

"This is far," I said. "Daddy should be buried in Brooklyn, where his mother and father are buried."

"His life's out here now," Michael said. "He wouldn't be buried in Brooklyn anyway, even if he was back east. That Veterans' cemetery is full. They would take him out to Calverton, which is an hour from where his parents are buried."

My brother was right, and hearing him say it, hearing him reason it out and advance the notion that my father's home was now in California, gave me great comfort. We arrived at the cemetery, which was just across the road from a stretch of orange groves.

"It's odd that Daddy should end up here," I said to Michael. "This is the first part of California he saw fifty years ago, and fell in love with, before being shipped off to the Philippines."

"It's nice country out here," my brother said.

We went inside the cemetery's visitors' center, received information about the gravesite, and drove around to find its' location. The plot was too close to a roadway which bounded Riverside, but the grounds were neatly kept, "like a park," my brother said. We drove around the entire cemetery, so I could get a feel for the place where Al Villano would be buried. I was calmed by the fact that there was no mountain casting a long, dark shadow over his grave, no volcano threatening to erupt, and that my brother Michael and I made the trip together.

When we arrived back at the hospital, my father was awake, and looking around at the machines that kept him alive. He pointed to the respirator—the ever-wheezing respirator next to him—and turned his palms upward as if to say "What's the use?"

He kept eyeing the machines that were giving him nourishment, oxygen, medicine, and blood, with the look of a wild animal wanting to rip the invasive tubes out of his body. I grabbed one of his hands and stroked it to calm him, and my brother held the other. It was a strange sight, the three of us connected for the first time since I was a child, all holding hands. Of all the exactas or trifectas my had father played in his years of gambling on the horses, this one went right down to the wire.

Acknowledgments

Nurturing and writing *Tightrope: Balancing A Life Between Mario Cuomo and My Brother* has been a journey that has occupied nearly half of my lifetime. Over those three decades, there are many people whose help, inspiration and encouragement made this book possible.

My work for New York State Governor Mario M. Cuomo, and my brother Michael's connection to Gambino Crime family boss John Gotti, made for an improbable and unpredictable collision-by-proxy of two very real and dramatically different worlds: Mario Cuomo's and John Gotti's, each at their pinnacle of power and public imagination at precisely the same time. Their only link, unbeknownst to either, was someone named Villano.

I began writing this story during the summer of 1988, after witnessing my brother being sentenced to prison for income tax evasion. Over the next three years, I wrote more than 1,000 pages of a fictionalized version of the events, in two different drafts of two separate books. In 1992, the great writer Gay Talese asked Mario Cuomo to write a book jacket blurb for his newest work, *Unto The Sons*, an autobiography. The Governor, in the midst of finalizing New York State's multi-billion-dollar budget, asked me to read Talese's book and write the book endorsement for him. It was a fortuitous request.

After completing Talese's book, and the endorsement, I met Gay for lunch at one of his favorite restaurants on the East Side of Manhattan, just around the corner from his townhouse. We talked for a while about his family and the book, and about the difficulty, in general, that Italian-American writers experienced in revealing family secrets. Talese, a journalist's journalist who knows how to probe, asked me about my family secrets. He was the first person, outside of my family and my therapists, with whom I shared my story.

When I informed Gay that I had written two fictionalized versions of the saga, he told me that it was a powerful story that begged to be told in non-fiction form, a format he favored. He challenged me to do a 10-page outline of a non-fiction book, and then get back to him with it. I got a little carried away. My 10-page outline grew into a 154-page annotated outline, complete with verbatim quotes and contemporaneous notes. Talese took one look at it and told me, "you've got the book right here."

"There's only one problem with it, Gay," I said. "I won't publish this story in non-fiction form while my mother is alive. It would kill her. And, she'd never forgive me for 'airing the family's dirty laundry in public.'"

My father died in 1993, shortly after Gay Talese and I had spoken for the last time about my book. My mother's increasing frailty over the next decade made it impossible for me to even think of the story as a non-fiction one. During that time, I tried reworking *Tightrope* in several other forms that would mask the identities of our family members and of Mario Cuomo. I took a playwriting course at the New School with Susan Charlotte, who struggled to pull the story out of me, while I drafted a one-act stage play. I studied screen-writing under Loren Paul Caplin of NYU/Columbia, and the New School, who recognized the power and immediacy of the story, and whose brilliant teaching and guidance helped me work-shop and complete a full-length, 120 page screenplay entitled *Sweet Blood* by the end of 1999.

Life again intervened with the all-consuming responsibilities of leading a national non-profit organization that promoted HIV/AIDS awareness, and produced and distributed documentaries and 30-second television spots on AIDS education. My mother died, in December 2007, just after her ninety-second birthday, while I was visiting her.

It took two years following her death for me to even look at my 154 page-annotated chronology of the non-fiction version of *Tight-rope*, which I had packed away in a box at the bottom of my clothes closet. When I read back through the story, I felt more compelled than ever to tell it correctly. But first, I needed to talk with my brother Michael about it.

On my brother's seventieth birthday in 2010, during lunch in a restaurant overlooking Long Island Sound, I told him I had been nurturing our story for years, that I believed it was an important one to share, and that I was the only one who could tell it. To my surprise, he was supportive.

"Just don't rat anybody out," my brother said.

"That would be kind of hard, Michael, since everyone is dead," I said, smiling.

Still more time passed. Carol, my partner, and I moved to Northern California to be near our son, shortly after our first granddaughter was born. We carted boxes full of memos and contemporaneous notes from my years of working with Mario Cuomo, along with my four different formats of *Tightrope*. Not once in our many moves in and around New York, or while schlepping my files of notes and rewrites across country did Carol ever say, "Are you ever going to write this book?" Her patience and belief in my passion to tell the story was extraordinary.

So was my son Matt Villano's, a superb writer, who grew up during my years of turmoil and tension, and too often witnessed my anger over circumstances beyond my control. Yet, right through the final edits on this book, Matt encouraged me to keep writing. He reminded me that, as long as he could remember, I had expressed a burning desire to complete the book.

In Spring 2015, I learned that my brother was battling pancreatic cancer. I no longer had an unlimited amount of time, nor did he. I knew I needed to connect with an agent and publisher who intuitively "got" my work and understood my urgency to tell the story. I attended the Writers' Digest Annual conference in NYC in late July and early August, 2015, to do just that. I signed up for a workshop which addressed the decades-long genre-hopping phases my work went through. This workshop featured, among others, Naomi Rosenblatt, Publisher of Heliotrope Books and a terrific editor.

Rosenblatt's advice was clear, concise and encouraging, and I liked her directness, vision, and knowledge of New York. When I gave her a brief synopsis of my book, she saw the story immediately. I went back to the West Coast, rewrote my first three chapters in non-fiction form, and sent them off to her.

The following month, my brother lost his nine-month struggle with pancreatic cancer. My manuscript now had the chance to give new life and meaning to the memories of my brother, complicated as they were, and to our relationship. Within 60 days of my brother's death, Mario Cuomo died. Everyone now really was dead. I had run out of excuses for not finishing my book, and had two powerful new reasons—two fresh, raw recollections of men I loved—to get it done.

On an odyssey such as this one, there are many people to tip my hat to for their help, inspiration and encouragement for completing the journey. Some, like Carol, my son Matt Villano, Gay Talese, Naomi Rosenblatt and Loren Paul Caplin, have already been acknowledged.

To others, like my former Cuomo Administration colleagues Peter Quinn and Stephen Schlesinger, I am grateful for their constant cheerleading and support. Taped on my desk during my entire last year of writing was one single word of advice which Peter Quinn, a wonderful writer and human being, gave to me: "PERSIST!" On days when it would have been so easy to just stop writing and get out among people, I would look at Peter's word "PERSIST," and carry on.

I was fortunate to find light and hope in the works and words of many others during the course of writing this book, including the actor/writer/director Stanley Tucci whose pioneering movie *Big Night* inspired me to realize that one person could help redefine how an entire ethnic group was perceived through art, as well as in everyday actions, as Mario Cuomo had. The writings of Professor Richard Gambino, Ken Auletta, Arthur Miller, Mario Puzo in *The Fortunate Pilgrim*, Jimmy Breslin and Pete Hamill, as well as Lisa Belkin, Miriam Pawel, and Viet Thanh Nguyen served as further elixirs. I regret that Breslin died before this book went to press, since I wanted to personally deliver a copy of it to him. Others like the great TV journalist Gabe Pressman, of WNBC New York, and Chiara Coletti, who worked with Murray Kempton and many great writers at *Newsday*, have endorsed my efforts every step of the way.

Several other individuals had no idea of how they enabled me to "persist," as Peter Quinn advised, and tell this story from the very earliest days. My sister, Vera Lofaro, stood by me through the height of the storm from my youth until the weekend when I thought my world had ended, following our brother Michael's sentencing. Her unconditional love and protection has always been a beacon during dark times. Her husband, Carlo Lofaro, played the same role for my mother, extending her life with his gentleness, without knowing that she had once saved his with her ferocity. Additionally, I appreciate some of the colorful family play-by-play offered by my surviving brother, Vincent Villano.

I am grateful to Governor Andrew M. Cuomo of New York, who, as a 27-year-old unpaid adviser, originally hired me to work in his father's Administration, on the same day that Mario Cuomo's first Lt. Governor, Alfred DelBello, quit. I suggested to Andrew that I'd take the DelBello spot, but he wisely recommended me for a lower level position. Throughout my eight years of working in the Administration of the first Governor Cuomo, Andrew was one of my biggest boosters, welcoming me with warmth and grace, especially when I returned to the Administration after my own self-imposed exile.

Finally, I must acknowledge the support of two people central to this book, without whom there could be no story. First, my brother Michael, who, as I write in *Tightrope*, was my first hero and whose kindness and love for me never wavered, up until the very end. Secondly, Mario Cuomo, who gave me more opportunities for public service than I ever imagined, and whose integrity, basic human decency and respect for individuals regardless of difference or family background, drove me to be better than I was, and become part of something far bigger than myself.

About the Author

Steve Villano, a native of Brooklyn, New York, is the former head of Governor Mario M. Cuomo's New York City Press Office, with decades of experience in public service, public education, public health, and as CEO of several national, non-profit organizations. As a key member of Cuomo's staff during two presidential boomlets, Villano wrote op-ed pieces and worked on speeches that ranged from the First Amendment, to immigration, race relations, affordable housing, higher education, nuclear power, the environment, and ethnic stereotyping.

His writing has appeared in mass-circulation newspapers and magazines such as the *New York Times, Newsday,* the *Albany Times Union, The Rochester Democrat and Chronicle, the Suffolk Sun,* the *Napa Valley* (CA) *Register Newspaper Group,* the *North Shore* (Long Island) *Newspaper Group, Working Mother Magazine, Multichannel News, Cable Fax Daily, The Jewish World, Associations Now Magazine,* and *Today's Education.* Villano has published professional articles in the *Federal Communications Law Journal, Free Speech* (the Commission of Freedom of Speech, Speech Communication Association of America), and in *Contexts: A Forum for the Medical Humanities* (Institute for Medicine in Contemporary Society). His essays have been published online in WritersDigest.com, www.thenationalmemo.com, with a subscription circulation of 300,000; on Medium.com., and on his blog, Radical Correspondence, (www.socialvisionproductions.com).

Villano has authored major pieces on ethnic stereotyping in *Ambassador Magazine,* (the National Italian American Foundation's 100,000 circulation magazine) about actors Stanley Tucci, John Turturro, and the HBO series *The Sopranos.*

A labor journalist for the National Education Association for a decade, Villano has written about censorship, the rise of the Far Right in America and about sweatshop conditions at cap-and-gown factories in New York. He developed a national Holocaust curriculum for classroom use while with the NEA, and a curriculum on

Ethics in the Workplace for Cornell University's ILR School's Labor Studies Program. His writing has received numerous awards from the Educational Press Association of America, the Long Island Press Club and the New York State Press Association, and a leadership award from the Arthur Ashe Institute for Urban Health.

Additionally, Villano's digital poetry book, *We, Haiku,* an interactive e-book of Haiku, received a QED (Quality, Excellence and Design Award) from the Digital Book Publishers of America in 2014, and is available on Amazon and Barnes & Noble.

He holds a Bachelors Degree in Political Science from the State University of New York at Albany, a Masters Degree in Communications, and a Juris Doctorate (JD) from Hofstra University Law School. Villano presently lives in Northern California.

CPSIA information can be obtained
at www.ICGtesting.com
Printed in the USA
BVOW03s1324040817
491191BV00001B/3/P